fine Cooking

Soups & Stews

No-Fail Recipes for Every Season

Editors of *Fine Cooking*

The Taunton Press

The Taunton Press
Inspiration for hands-on living®

The Taunton Press, Inc.
63 South Main Street
PO Box 5506
Newtown, CT 06470-5506
e-mail: tp@taunton.com

Editor: Carolyn Mandarano
Copy editor: Li Agen
Indexer: Heidi Blough
Jacket/Cover design: Alison Wilkes
Cover photographer: Scott Phillips, © The Taunton Press, Inc.
Cover food stylist: Mariana Velasquez
Interior design: Kimberly Adis
Layout: Kimberly Shake
Photographers: Photos by Scott Phillips except the following: Mark Ferri (p. 119), Ben Fink (p. 175), Leo Gong (p. 146), Martha Holmberg (p. 131), Steve Hunter (p. 114), Sarah Jay (p. 4 and p. 11), Paul Johnson (p. 86 and p. 132), Pernille Pedersen (p. 85), Mark Thomas (p. 129)

Fine Cooking® is a trademark of The Taunton Press, Inc., registered in the U.S. Patent and Trademark Office.

The following names/manufacturers appearing in *Fine Cooking Soups & Stews* are trademarks: Anchor Steam® Liberty Ale®, Bob's Red Mill®, Pyrex®, Shiner Bock®

Library of Congress Cataloging-in-Publication Data

Fine cooking soups & stews : no-fail recipes for every season / editors of Fine cooking.
    pages cm
 Includes index.
 ISBN 978-1-62113-795-5
1. Soups. 2. Stews. I. Taunton's fine cooking. II. Title: Soups & stews. III. Title: Fine cooking soups and stews.
 TX757.F55 2013
 641.81'3--dc23
                    2013026914

Printed in the United States of America
10 9 8 7 6 5 4 3 2 1

contents

carrot-ginger soup
(recipe on p. 55)

puréed soups

puréed summer squash soup with raita

SERVES 4; MAKES ½ CUP RAITA

FOR THE RAITA

- ½ cup whole-milk yogurt

  Kosher salt

- 1 tsp. vegetable oil

- ½ tsp. brown mustard seeds

- ¼ tsp. cumin seeds

- ½ tsp. onion seeds (optional)

FOR THE SOUP

- 12 sprigs fresh cilantro with roots, if possible (1 packed cup); more leaves for garnish

- 1 small head garlic, cut across the equator; plus 1 Tbs. minced garlic

- 3 Tbs. unsalted butter

- 1 large onion, sliced (to yield 1½ cups)

- 2 Tbs. minced jalapeño

- 1 Tbs. minced fresh ginger

  Kosher salt

- ½ tsp. cumin seeds

- ½ tsp. coriander seeds

- ⅛ tsp. cardamom seeds or 1 green cardamom pod (optional)

- 1 lb. zucchini or other summer squash (unpeeled), sliced ½ inch thick

- ¼ tsp. fresh lime juice

This soup is a great way to use a bumper crop of squash from your backyard garden or farmer's market.

MAKE THE RAITA

In a bowl, combine the yogurt and ¼ tsp. salt. Heat the oil in a small pan over medium heat until it shimmers. Add the mustard seeds, cumin seeds, and onion seeds, if using. When they start to pop, add the oil and seeds to the yogurt. Stir, taste, and add salt, if needed. Refrigerate until needed.

MAKE THE SOUP

1. Put the cilantro, both halves of the garlic head, and 5 cups water in a large saucepan or a stockpot. Bring to a boil, reduce to a simmer, and cook uncovered for 15 minutes. Strain the broth.

2. Melt the butter in a large, heavy saucepan over medium heat. Add the onion, jalapeño, ginger, 2 tsp. salt, cumin seeds, coriander seeds, and cardamom, if using. Cover and cook, stirring occasionally, until the onion is translucent, about 10 minutes; don't let it brown. Stir in the 1 Tbs. minced garlic and the zucchini, cover, and cook, stirring occasionally, until the squash is softened, about 5 minutes. Add 4 cups of the broth, bring to a simmer, and cook until the zucchini is tender, about another 3 minutes.

3. Purée the mixture in a blender and strain it (see the sidebar at right).

4. Add the lime juice; taste and add salt if needed. Serve warm, garnished with 1 to 2 Tbs. raita and the cilantro leaves. *—Eve Felder*

PER SERVING: 165 CALORIES | 5G PROTEIN | 15G CARB | 11G TOTAL FAT | 6G SAT FAT | 3G MONO FAT | 1G POLY FAT | 25MG CHOL | 1,120MG SODIUM | 3G FIBER

how to purée a vegetable soup

A blender, rather than a food processor, creates the smoothest texture.

Ladle about 1 cup of vegetables and about half as much broth into a blender. Cover the blender, but remove the center cap or keep the lid slightly cracked with the opening away from you. Cover the lid with a folded dishtowel. Purée in batches, blending in pulses or on low speed at first and then continuously until you have a completely smooth purée, adding more broth only if needed. With the blender on, carefully ladle in more vegetables and broth through the feeder hole, keeping the ratio about the same, until the blender is half full.

Strain the purée through a fine-mesh sieve set over a bowl, pressing it through with a rubber spatula. Purée and strain the remaining vegetables, including any spices. Thin the soup, if necessary, so it has the consistency of heavy cream (you may not use all the broth). Continue as the recipe directs.

white bean soup with wild mushrooms and chive mascarpone

MAKES 8 CUPS; SERVES 6 TO 8

- 1 Tbs. fennel seeds
- ½ cup plus 2 Tbs. extra-virgin olive oil
- 1 small sprig rosemary (leaves only)
- 1 chile d'árbol (or other small, hot dried chile), stemmed and crumbled
- 1 cup chopped yellow onion
- ½ cup chopped fresh fennel
- 1 Tbs. plus 1 tsp. fresh thyme leaves
- 2 cups dried cannellini beans, picked through and rinsed

  Kosher salt
- ½ cup mascarpone cheese
- 1 Tbs. minced shallots
- 1 Tbs. minced fresh chives

  Freshly ground black pepper
- 1 Tbs. unsalted butter
- ½ lb. fresh wild mushrooms, stems trimmed, caps thinly sliced (such as shiitake, oyster mushrooms, or chanterelles)
- 1 Tbs. chopped fresh flat-leaf parsley

This elegant soup is just a simple purée of white beans, but when topped with earthy sautéed wild mushrooms and a dollop of herbed mascarpone cheese, it becomes a refined first course. The trick to getting a smooth, silky texture is to purée the beans and vegetables with only a small amount of the cooking liquid first and then to slowly pour in more liquid until you get a nice, creamy consistency.

1. Toast the fennel seeds in a small dry skillet over medium heat until they release their aroma and are golden brown, 2 to 3 minutes. Pound them coarsely in a mortar or grind them coarsely in a spice grinder.

2. Heat a 6- to 8-quart heavy pot over high heat for 2 minutes. Pour in ½ cup olive oil and add the rosemary leaves and crumbled chile. Let them sizzle in the oil for about 1 minute. Add the onion, fennel, fennel seeds, and 1 Tbs. of the thyme and cook until the onion is softened, 3 to 4 minutes.

3. Add the beans to the pot and cook for a few more minutes, stirring to coat well. Add 3 quarts water and bring to a boil over high heat. Turn the heat to low and place a round of parchment over the beans to keep them underwater. Simmer, stirring occasionally. After 30 minutes, add 1½ Tbs. salt to the beans and continue cooking at a low simmer until the beans are tender, another 1 to 1½ hours.

4. While the soup is cooking, stir the mascarpone, shallots, and chives in a small bowl. Season to taste with salt and pepper, cover with plastic wrap, and refrigerate.

5. Separate the bean mixture from the liquid by straining the soup over a bowl. Put half the bean mixture in a blender with ½ cup of the liquid (you'll need to purée the soup in batches). Process on the lowest speed until the mixture is puréed. With the blender running at medium speed, slowly pour in more of the liquid until the soup is the consistency of heavy cream. Turn the speed up to high and blend until completely smooth, about 1 minute. Set aside and repeat with the second batch. Taste and adjust the seasonings with salt and pepper. Keep the soup warm in a pot on the stove. If making ahead, let cool completely before refrigerating.

6. Sauté the mushrooms: Turn on the exhaust fan. Heat a 12-inch skillet over high heat for 1 minute. Swirl in the remaining 2 Tbs. olive oil and the butter. When the butter melts, scatter the mushrooms into the pan. Season with ¼ tsp. salt and a pinch of pepper. Cook the mushrooms, stirring occasionally, until they're tender, browned, and a little crisp, about 5 minutes. Stir in the parsley and the remaining 1 tsp. thyme and remove from the heat.

7. Ladle the hot soup into warm bowls. Scatter the warm mushrooms over the top and add a dollop of the mascarpone.　*—Suzanne Goin*

PER SERVING: 490 CALORIES | 15G PROTEIN | 40G CARB | 32G TOTAL FAT | 10G SAT FAT | 16G MONO FAT | 2.5G POLY FAT | 40MG CHOL | 700MG SODIUM | 9G FIBER

Make Ahead

The soup and chive mascarpone can be made up to 1 day in advance and refrigerated. The mushrooms can be sautéed a few hours ahead. Reheat the soup and mushrooms just before serving.

If making the soup ahead, save the leftover cooking liquid. The soup will thicken as it sits and may need to be thinned with more of the liquid before serving. If necessary, adjust the seasonings as well.

southwest tomato and roasted pepper soup

MAKES ABOUT 5¾ CUPS; SERVES 6

- 1 large red bell pepper
- 3 Tbs. plus ½ tsp. extra-virgin olive oil
- 1 large yellow onion, finely chopped
- 1 tsp. chili powder
- 1 tsp. ground cumin
- ¼ tsp. ground coriander
- 3 cups homemade or lower-salt chicken broth
- 1 28-oz. can whole peeled plum tomatoes, drained (reserve the liquid) and coarsely chopped
- 1 cup small-diced zucchini
- ½ cup sour cream
- 1 Tbs. fresh lime juice
- ½ tsp. finely grated lime zest
  Kosher salt and freshly ground black pepper
- 2 Tbs. loosely packed fresh cilantro leaves

For Your Safety

When puréeing soup in a blender or food processor, fill the jar no more than half full and be sure to vent the lid and hold a folded dishtowel over the top to prevent splashes.

A little heat and spice kicks up the flavor of classic tomato soup. It will keep for a few days refrigerated and tastes even better the second day. Or freeze it for up to 3 months.

1. Coat the bell pepper with ½ tsp. of the oil. Roast directly on the grate of a gas burner over high heat or under a broiler, turning the pepper occasionally until charred all over. Put the pepper in a bowl while still hot and cover the bowl with plastic wrap. Let rest until cool enough to handle. Core, seed, and peel the pepper, using a table knife to scrape away the charred skin. Coarsely chop the pepper and set aside.

2. In a 5- to 6-quart Dutch oven, heat the remaining 3 Tbs. oil over medium-low heat. Add the onion and cook, stirring occasionally, until just soft, 8 to 10 minutes. Stir in the chili powder, cumin, and coriander. Add the chopped roasted pepper and cook for another 1 minute. Add the broth and tomatoes and bring to a simmer over medium-high heat. Reduce the heat to low, cover, and simmer for 40 minutes.

3. Let cool briefly and then purée the soup in two or three batches in a blender or food processor. Rinse the pot and return the soup to the pot. If it is too thick, add some of the reserved tomato liquid. Add the zucchini and cook for another 10 minutes over low heat.

4. Meanwhile, combine the sour cream, lime juice, and lime zest in a small bowl.

5. Season the soup to taste with salt and black pepper. Serve garnished with the lime sour cream and the cilantro leaves. —*Perla Meyers*

PER SERVING: 170 CALORIES | 5G PROTEIN | 11G CARB | 12G TOTAL FAT | 4G SAT FAT | 7G MONO FAT | 1G POLY FAT | 10MG CHOL | 220MG SODIUM | 3G FIBER

Tips for Freezing Soups

• Chill soup thoroughly before freezing; this allows it to freeze faster. The ice crystals that form will be smaller, so your soup will have better texture and flavor.

• Freeze soup in plastic containers, leaving about ½ inch at the top to allow for expansion. Or fill plastic freezer bags about three-quarters full and squeeze out as much air as possible.

• Freeze soups in large amounts or in smaller, portion-size containers that are ready to heat and serve. The smaller the container, the quicker it will freeze and defrost.

• Before freezing, cover, label, and date your soup. As a general rule, stocks and broths can be frozen for up to 6 months; vegetable soups, about 4 months; meat, fish, or chicken soups, about 3 months; and soups with egg and cream, about 2 months.

• Keep a thermometer in the freezer to make sure the temperature remains constant at 0°F. If you're freezing a large quantity at once, turn the thermostat to its coldest setting until the soup freezes.

• Leave the soup in its container and thaw in the refrigerator, microwave oven, or under cold running water. You can also remove it from the container and reheat the frozen soup in a saucepan over low heat. A microwave oven is better for small amounts of soup.

• Serve soup as soon as possible after thawing.

• Don't be alarmed if puréed soup separates after thawing. To fix it, just whisk it back together. Be aware that soups containing cream, wine, or lemon juice (or those thickened with eggs or flour) don't always freeze well. When reheating, simmer gently and whisk constantly to prevent curdling. Or better yet, add these ingredients after reheating.

puréed eggplant soup with tomato relish

SERVES 4;
MAKES ¾ CUP RELISH

This soup has no thickener and no cream, making it light-bodied yet intensely flavorful.

FOR THE SOUP

- ¼ cup olive oil
- 1 lb. eggplant (1 medium eggplant), sliced in half lengthwise

  Kosher salt and freshly ground black pepper
- 5 cups homemade or lower-salt chicken broth
- 8 large sprigs fresh basil
- 12 stems fresh flat-leaf parsley
- 2 sprigs fresh thyme
- 1 large onion, sliced (to yield 1½ cups)
- 1½ Tbs. minced fresh garlic

FOR THE RELISH

- 2 tsp. extra-virgin olive oil; more for garnish
- 2 tsp. minced fresh garlic

  Kosher salt
- 1 medium-size ripe tomato, peeled, seeded, and cut into small dice
- ½ tsp. sherry vinegar
- ¼ tsp. freshly ground black pepper
- 2 Tbs. chopped fresh flat-leaf parsley

MAKE THE SOUP

1. Heat the oven to 375°F. Spread 2 Tbs. of the oil on a rimmed baking sheet. Season the cut side of the eggplant with salt and pepper and put the halves face down on the pan. Roast until tender, about 40 minutes; a knife will enter the flesh easily. When the eggplant is cool enough to handle, scrape out the flesh with a spoon. Discard the skin.

2. Meanwhile, put the chicken broth, basil, parsley stems, and thyme in a large saucepan or a stockpot. Bring to a boil, reduce the heat, and simmer uncovered for 15 minutes. Strain the broth.

3. Heat the remaining 2 Tbs. olive oil in a large, heavy saucepan over medium heat. Add the onion and cook, stirring frequently, until golden and caramelized, about 20 minutes. Stir in ¾ tsp. salt and the garlic. Add 4 cups of the broth, bring to a boil, add the eggplant flesh, reduce to a simmer, and cook for 5 minutes.

4. Ladle about 1 cup of the vegetables and about half as much broth into a blender. Cover, but remove the center cap or keep the lid slightly cracked with the opening away from you. Cover the lid with a folded dishtowel. Blend in pulses or on low speed at first, and then continuously until you have a completely smooth purée, adding more broth only if needed. With the blender on, carefully ladle in more vegetables and broth through the feeder hold, keeping the ratio about the same, until the blender is half full.

5. Strain the purée through a fine-mesh sieve set over a bowl, pressing it through with a rubber spatula. Purée and strain the remaining soup. Thin the soup with some of the remaining broth, if necessary, so it has the consistency of heavy cream.

MAKE THE RELISH

In a small pan, combine the oil, garlic, and ¼ tsp. salt. Heat over low until the garlic is tender but not colored, 3 to 4 minutes. Add the tomato and cook just until warm, about 2 minutes. Stir in the sherry vinegar, pepper, and parsley. Remove from the heat and serve within a few hours.

FINISH THE SOUP

Taste the soup and add salt if needed. Serve warm, garnished with the relish and a drizzle of extra-virgin olive oil. —*Eve Felder*

PER SERVING: 230 CALORIES | 5G PROTEIN | 15G CARB | 18G TOTAL FAT | 160G SAT FAT | 12G MONO FAT | 2G POLY FAT | 0MG CHOL | 420MG SODIUM | 4G FIBER

velvety carrot soup

MAKES ABOUT 8½ CUPS;
SERVES 8

FOR THE BROTH

- ¼ **cup medium-diced peeled carrots**
- ½ **cup medium-diced dark green leek tops (from 1 to 2 leeks; rinse thoroughly after dicing; save the white and pale green parts for the soup)**
- ½ **medium onion, cut into medium dice (about ¾ cup)**
- ¼ **fennel bulb, cut into medium dice (about ½ cup)**
- ¼ **celery rib, cut into medium dice (about 2 Tbs.)**
- 1 **small clove garlic, smashed and peeled**
- 1 **small bay leaf**
- 1 **sprig fresh thyme**
- 1 **sprig fresh parsley**

This recipe looks long, but half of the ingredients are for making a quick vegetable broth. Look for carrot juice in the produce section of your supermarket.

MAKE THE BROTH

Put the carrots, leek tops, onion, fennel, celery, garlic, bay leaf, thyme, and parsley in a 4-quart (or larger) saucepan. Add 10 cups cold water and bring to a simmer over medium-high heat. Reduce the heat to medium low and simmer for 1 hour. Strain the broth into a heatproof bowl and discard the solids. Measure out 5 cups of broth for use in the soup; save the remaining broth for another use. Rinse and dry the saucepan and return it to the stove.

MAKE THE SOUP

1. In the saucepan, heat the olive oil over medium-low heat. Add the shallots, leeks, garlic, and a generous pinch of salt. Cook, stirring occasionally, until the vegetables are softened but not browned, about 5 minutes. Stir in the carrots and sugar. Cover, reduce the heat to low, and cook, stirring occasionally, until the carrots are soft, 15 to 20 minutes. Add the 5 cups broth and the carrot juice. Bring to a simmer, uncovered, over medium-high heat. Reduce the heat to low and simmer gently for 10 minutes.

FOR THE SOUP

- 3 Tbs. extra-virgin olive oil
- 5 medium shallots, thinly sliced (about 1 cup)
- ¾ cup thinly sliced leeks, white and pale green parts only (from 1 to 2 leeks; rinse thoroughly after slicing)
- 2 small cloves garlic, smashed and peeled
- Kosher or sea salt
- 3¾ cups medium-diced peeled carrots (about 1½ lb.)
- 2 Tbs. granulated sugar
- 2 cups carrot juice, either homemade or store-bought
- 1 Tbs. peeled finely grated fresh ginger
- Freshly ground black pepper
- 3 to 4 tsp. fresh lemon juice
- 1 small Fuji apple

2. Wrap the ginger in a small square of cheesecloth and use the cloth to squeeze the ginger juice into the soup (discard the squeezed-dry ginger). Remove the pan from the heat.

3. Working in batches, purée the soup in a blender until smooth (fill the jar no more than half full). Pour each batch of the puréed soup into a medium-mesh sieve set over a clean heatproof container. Use a rubber spatula to help the soup pass through, but don't press on the solids yet. Once the last batch has drained through the sieve, press lightly on the solids (but don't mash them through the sieve) to extract the remaining liquid. Discard the solids. Season to taste with salt, pepper, and 1 to 2 tsp. of the lemon juice.

4. When ready to serve, peel and core the apple and cut it into medium dice. In a small bowl, toss the apple with 2 tsp. of the remaining lemon juice. Reheat the soup, if necessary, and ladle it into individual serving bowls or cups. Serve immediately, garnishing each bowl with a small spoonful of the diced apple. —*Dan Barber*

PER SERVING: 130 CALORIES | 2G PROTEIN | 19G CARB, 5G TOTAL FAT | 0.5G SAT FAT | 3.5G MONO FAT | 0.5G POLY FAT | 0MG CHOL | 200MG SODIUM | 3G FIBER

Buying and Storing Carrots

At the market, look for firm carrots with smooth skin. And if possible, taste before you buy. If you're shopping at a farmstand, you might have several varieties to choose from. Nelson, Napoli, and Mokum all have slender orange roots and terrific flavor. Vibrant orange Chantenay carrots are a bit stouter but just as snappy, juicy, and sweet.

Once you've purchased your carrots, use them soon, as they lose flavor and nutrients over time. True baby carrots—not those whittled-down stumps sold in plastic bags—should be used within 5 days, while more mature carrots should last about 2 weeks. Store carrots in the coldest part of the refrigerator (usually that's the back of the bottom shelf). They will stay crisp longer in a plastic bag.

creamy asparagus soup

MAKES 7 TO 8 CUPS; SERVES 8

- 2 **lb. asparagus**
- 3½ **Tbs. unsalted butter**
- 2 **small ribs celery, coarsely chopped (about 1 cup)**
- 1 **large yellow onion, coarsely chopped (about 2 cups)**
- 1 **large leek, trimmed, halved lengthwise, thoroughly rinsed, and thinly sliced crosswise (keep dark green parts separate from light green and white parts)**
- 8 **whole peppercorns**
- 5 **sprigs fresh flat-leaf parsley**
- 2 **sprigs fresh thyme**
  Kosher salt
- 2 **medium cloves garlic, chopped**
- 1 **large or 3 small red potatoes (about ½ lb.), peeled and cut into ½-inch dice (1 heaping cup)**
- ¼ **cup heavy cream**
  Freshly ground white pepper

You can use either thick or thin asparagus spears. This soup is also delicious served cold.

1. Snap off the tough ends of the asparagus, but don't discard them. Cut about 1½ inches of the tips off the asparagus spears and cut the spears crosswise in thirds; set the spears and tips aside separately.

2. Melt 1½ Tbs. of the butter in a 3-quart saucepan over medium-low heat. Add the tough asparagus ends, about half of the celery, the onion, and the dark green parts of the leek. Cook uncovered, stirring occasionally, until the vegetables look very soft, about 30 minutes (if the vegetables show any sign of browning, reduce the heat to low). Add 6 cups cold water and the peppercorns, parsley, thyme, and ½ tsp. salt. Bring to a boil over high heat, reduce the heat to medium low, cover, and simmer for 30 minutes to make a flavorful vegetable stock.

3. Meanwhile, bring a 2-quart pot of salted water to a boil over high heat. Add the asparagus tips and cook until just tender, 2 to 3 minutes. Drain in a colander, shower with cold water to stop the cooking, and drain again. Set aside.

4. In another 3-quart (or larger) saucepan, melt the remaining 2 Tbs. butter over medium-low heat. Add the white and light green sliced leeks and the remaining celery and season with a generous pinch of salt. Cook, stirring occasionally, until the leeks look soft but not browned, 3 to 4 minutes. Add the garlic and cook for 1 minute more. Add the asparagus spears and the potato.

asparagus 101

Asparagus is commonly sold in bundles of about a pound standing upright in a tray of water. Choose fresh-looking, firm spears with tight tips. Smell them first to make sure they don't give off an unpleasant odor (if they do, they're old). Check the cut ends of the stalks; they should be moist, not dried out. If dried ends are all that's available, cut about half an inch off the bottom. To make sure they stay fresh, stand asparagus bundles in about an inch of water in a jar or a shallow tray and keep them in the refrigerator. Cook the spears within 2 or 3 days.

5. Set a wire-mesh sieve over the pot and pour in the stock from the other pot; discard the solids. Stir well and bring to a boil over high heat. Reduce the heat to medium low, cover, and cook at a lively simmer until the potatoes and asparagus are very tender, about 20 minutes. Turn off the heat and let cool slightly.

6. Purée the soup in a blender in batches. Return the puréed soup to the soup pot, add the cream, and stir well. Reheat the soup gently over medium-low heat. Season to taste with more salt and a large pinch of white pepper. Ladle the soup into bowls or soup plates and scatter in the asparagus tips, distributing them evenly among the servings.
—Ruth Lively

PER SERVING: 120 CALORIES | 2G PROTEIN | 11G CARB | 8G TOTAL FAT | 5G SAT FAT | 2G MONO FAT | 1G POLY FAT | 25MG CHOL | 230MG SODIUM | 2G FIBER

peppery pink lentil soup

MAKES 10 TO 11 CUPS;
SERVES 10

FOR THE SOUP

- ½ Tbs. coriander seeds
- ¾ tsp. whole black peppercorns
- 1½ cups pink lentils (also known as red lentils or masoor dal), picked over and rinsed
- 1 medium white onion, cut into ½-inch dice (about 2 cups)
- 2 ribs celery, cut into ½-inch dice (about 1 cup)
- 1 medium carrot, peeled and cut into ½-inch dice (about ½ cup)
- 3 cloves garlic, thinly sliced
- 1 1-inch piece fresh ginger, peeled and coarsely chopped
- ½ fresh serrano chile, thinly sliced (don't remove seeds)
- 15 sprigs fresh cilantro, left whole and tied in a cheese-cloth pouch

  Kosher or sea salt
- 1 cup plain yogurt, whisked until smooth, for garnish
- 2 Tbs. sliced fresh chives, for garnish

FOR THE TARKA

- 2 Tbs. canola oil
- 1 tsp. mustard seeds
- 1 tsp. cumin seeds

Warm toasted spices and a flavor-packed tarka–small, whole edible spices bloomed in hot oil and added to a dish at the end of cooking–come together in this velvety soup.

MAKE THE SOUP

1. Heat a small, dry sauté pan over medium-high heat. When the pan is hot, add the coriander seeds and toast them—stir constantly (or shake the pan gently) to keep the seeds from burning—until they darken slightly and become very fragrant, 1 to 2 minutes. Immediately transfer them to a dish and set aside. Return the sauté pan to the heat; add the peppercorns and toast, shaking the pan, for about 2 minutes. Pour onto the plate with the coriander seeds. Put the toasted coriander and peppercorns in a spice grinder or mortar and pestle and grind to a fine powder.

2. In a large (at least 4-quart) saucepan, combine the lentils, onion, celery, carrot, garlic, ginger, chile, cheesecloth-wrapped cilantro sprigs, and 2 tsp. salt with 2½ quarts water. Bring to a boil over medium-high heat. Reduce the heat to medium low and simmer for 30 minutes. Remove the cilantro sprigs. Add the ground coriander and pepper to the soup and simmer for another 10 minutes. Purée the soup using a hand blender or a regular blender until the soup is very smooth. Strain the purée through a medium-mesh sieve into a large serving bowl. (The soup can be made to this point 1 day ahead; reheat it gently before continuing.)

MAKE THE TARKA AND GARNISH THE SOUP

Set a small deep saucepan over medium heat and add the canola oil. When the oil is shimmering, add the mustard seeds and cook, uncovered, until they pop, 30 to 60 seconds. Add the cumin seeds and cook for another 1 minute. Quickly but carefully, pour the hot tarka over the soup and mix well. Season with salt to taste. Ladle the soup into individual bowls and garnish with a dollop of yogurt and a sprinkling of the chives. *—Floyd Cardoz*

PER SERVING: 140 CALORIES | 8G PROTEIN, 20G CARB | 4G TOTAL FAT | 0.5G SAT FAT | 16G MONO FAT | 1G POLY FAT | 5MG CHOL | 500MG SODIUM | 5G FIBER

tomato-fennel soup with orange

SERVES 8 AS A FIRST COURSE

- 2 Tbs. extra-virgin olive oil
- ⅓ cup medium-diced onion
- ¼ cup thinly sliced celery (halved lengthwise then sliced crosswise)
- ⅓ cup thinly sliced carrots (peeled, halved or quartered lengthwise, then sliced crosswise)
- ⅓ cup finely chopped shallots
- 2 tsp. minced garlic
- Kosher salt
- 1 tsp. crushed fennel seeds
- 2 28-oz. cans whole tomatoes, drained and coarsely chopped
- 5 cups vegetable broth, preferably homemade
- 3 Tbs. orange juice
- ¼ cup heavy cream
- ½ tsp. rice vinegar; more as needed
- Freshly ground black pepper
- 1 cup homemade croutons

A touch of crushed fennel seeds and orange juice brightens typical tomato soup.

1. In a 4- to 5-quart saucepan or Dutch oven, heat the olive oil over medium-low heat. When hot, add the onion, celery, carrots, shallots, garlic, and a pinch of salt. Stir well, cover, reduce the heat to low, and cook, stirring occasionally, until the vegetables are softened, 8 to 10 minutes. Stir in 1 tsp. salt and the crushed fennel seeds. Add the tomatoes, vegetable broth, and orange juice, stir well, and bring to a simmer over medium heat. Cook, uncovered, stirring occasionally, until the vegetables are very tender and the soup is full-flavored, 7 to 20 minutes. Take the pan off the heat and let the soup cool for 5 minutes.

2. Working in batches, pureé the soup in a blender (fill the jar no more than half full). Wipe the pan clean and put the soup back into the pan. Add the cream and the vinegar. Season the soup with salt and pepper. Taste and adjust the seasonings with more salt, pepper, or vinegar as needed.

3. Ladle into 8 soup bowls and garnish each serving with 1 to 2 Tbs. of the croutons. —*Susie Middleton*

PER SERVING: 110 CALORIES | 15G PROTEIN | 13G CARB | 6G TOTAL FAT | 3G SAT FAT | 2.5G MONO FAT | 0G POLY FAT | 15MG CHOL | 540MG SODIUM | 2G FIBER

More about Fennel

The general name "fennel" applies to two varieties of the plant: Florence fennel and common fennel. Florence fennel has a bulbous base, long celery-like stalks, and bright green fronds. The bulb is crunchy with a sweet aniseed flavor and can be eaten raw or cooked. The stalks and fronds can also be used in cooking. Common fennel is the variety from which fennel seeds are harvested. It doesn't have a bulb, but its stalks and fronds can be used like those of Florence fennel.

Buying
Choose firm bulbs with no browning. Any attached greens should look fresh and bright green.

Storing
Refrigerate fennel for up to 5 days.

Using
Florence fennel is unwieldy to work until you cut off the stalks (slice them close to the bulb). Peel the stringy fibers off the outer layer of the bulb with a vegetable peeler or a sharp paring knife. Then cut the bulb into wedges or slices.

summer corn soup with crisp prosciutto

**MAKES ABOUT 8 CUPS;
SERVES 4 AS A MAIN COURSE
OR 8 AS A FIRST COURSE**

- 3 **very thin slices prosciutto**
- 3 **to 4 large ears fresh
  sweet corn**
- 4 **Tbs. unsalted butter**
- 1 **medium yellow onion,
  chopped (about 1½ cups)**

  Kosher salt
- 2 **cups homemade or lower-
  salt chicken broth**
- 1½ **cups medium-diced peeled
  red potatoes (2 to 3 medium)**

  Freshly ground black pepper
- 2 **Tbs. coarsely chopped
  fresh basil**

*This silky soup is the perfect way
to use up a bumper crop of fresh
corn. The cobs themselves lend
great corn flavor to the broth, so be
sure to save them.*

1. Position an oven rack about 4 inches below the broiler and heat the broiler on high. Arrange the prosciutto in a single layer on a small baking sheet and broil until it begins to curl, 1 to 2 minutes. Flip the prosciutto and broil until it appears dry-crisp and has curled a bit more, about 1 minute. Let cool, then finely chop or crumble by hand; set aside.

2. Slice the kernels off the corn cobs for a total of 3 cups corn. Reserve the cobs.

3. In a medium Dutch oven over medium heat, melt the butter. Add the onion and cook until softened and slightly golden, 5 to 7 minutes. Season with a generous pinch of salt. Add 4 cups water, the broth, potatoes, 1½ cups of the corn, the cobs, and 2 tsp. salt. Bring to a boil. Reduce the heat to medium low and simmer until the potatoes are tender, 10 to 15 minutes. Remove from the heat and discard the cobs.

4. Working in batches, carefully purée the soup in a blender. Transfer each batch to a large heatproof bowl or large liquid measuring cup. Pour the puréed soup back into the pot. Add the remaining 1½ cups corn and bring to a boil over medium-high heat. Reduce the heat to medium low and simmer, stirring occasionally, until the corn kernels are tender, 3 to 5 minutes. Season to taste with salt and pepper.

5. Ladle into bowls and garnish each serving with the crisped prosciutto and basil. *—Maryellen Driscoll*

PER SERVING: 170 CALORIES | 5G PROTEIN | 24G CARB | 7G TOTAL FAT | 4G SAT FAT | 2G MONO FAT | 0.5G POLY FAT | 20MG CHOL | 440MG SODIUM | 3G FIBER

roasted red bell pepper soup with star anise

MAKES 9 CUPS

¼ cup olive oil

4 large onions (about 24 oz. total), chopped

4 cloves garlic, chopped

1 1-inch piece fresh ginger (about ½ oz.), peeled and chopped

2 medium carrots, peeled and chopped (about 4 oz. chopped)

2 quarts homemade or lower-salt chicken broth

7 red bell peppers, roasted, peeled, and seeded (see Step 1 on p. 9); liquid reserved

2 whole star anise (or 1½ tsp. broken pieces)

Kosher salt and freshly ground black pepper

Pinch of cayenne

12 leaves fresh basil

Extra-virgin olive oil and sherry vinegar, for garnish (optional)

Serve this soup with a drizzle of extra-virgin olive oil and a splash of really flavorful vinegar on each serving. It's also delicious served cold, and it can be garnished with a few cooked shrimp, a mound of crabmeat, or a bit of goat cheese.

1. Heat the olive oil in a 6-quart soup pot over medium heat. Add the onion, garlic, ginger, and carrots and sauté until very soft but not browned, 20 to 25 minutes.

2. Add the broth and turn the heat to high. Add the roasted bell peppers and any reserved liquid, as well as the star anise, 1 tsp. salt, ½ tsp. black pepper, and the cayenne. As soon as the mixture comes to a boil, reduce the heat and simmer, uncovered, for 30 minutes. Stir occasionally.

3. Purée the soup 2 cups at a time in a blender, with all the basil leaves going in the blender along with the first 2 cups of soup. Purée each batch of soup in the blender for at least 1 minute. Combine all the puréed soup in one container, taste, and add more salt and black pepper to bring all the flavors into balance. (For a thinner soup, strain through a wide-mesh sieve.) Serve with a drizzle of extra-virgin olive oil and a splash of sherry vinegar, if you like. —*Brian Patterson*

PER SERVING: 200 CALORIES I 6G PROTEIN I 21G CARB I 11G TOTAL FAT I 2G SAT FAT I 7G MONO FAT I 1G POLY FAT I 0MG CHOL I 590MG SODIUM I 4G FIBER

More about Star Anise

This star-shaped spice is the dried fruit of a small Asian evergreen tree (a member of the magnolia family). Harvested when it's still green and unripe, it's dried in the sun, where it develops its red-brown color and a sweet warm flavor that's reminiscent of licorice, clove, fennel seed, and aniseed (although it's botanically unrelated to any of these spices). Ground star anise is a dominant ingredient in Chinese five-spice powder.

Many supermarkets carry whole or ground star anise, but your best bets for the freshest spice are Asian markets, natural food stores, and mail-order spice houses. If you need ground star anise, you can grind the whole stars (both seed and pod) in a spice grinder or mortar and pestle.

Like all spices, star anise should be stored in an airtight container away from heat and light. Whole stars will stay fresh for about 2 years; ground star anise lasts for about 1 year. To check the freshness of a whole star, break off a point and squeeze it until the seed pops. If you don't immediately smell the distinctive aroma, it's past its prime.

roasted carrot soup

**MAKES ABOUT 1 QUART;
SERVES 4**

1 lb. carrots, peeled and cut
  into 3-inch lengths

1 Tbs. olive oil

1 Tbs. unsalted butter

½ medium onion, chopped
  (to yield about ¾ cup)

1 large rib celery, cut into
  medium dice (to yield about
  ½ cup)

1 Tbs. minced fresh ginger
  (from about ½-inch piece,
  peeled)

2 cups homemade or lower-
  salt chicken broth

  Kosher salt

⅛ tsp. ground white pepper

  Chopped fresh chives or
  chervil, for garnish
  (optional)

A tablespoon of ginger gives nice heat to this soup, which tastes even better the day after it's made.

1. Heat the oven to 375°F. Put the carrots in a medium baking dish (11x7 inches is a good size, or any dish that will hold the carrots in a single layer without touching) and drizzle them with the olive oil. Toss them to coat well and roast, stirring once halfway through, until they're tender, blistered, and lightly browned in a few places, about 1 hour.

2. Melt the butter in a medium (at least 3-quart) heavy saucepan set over medium heat. Add the onion and cook until it's translucent and fragrant, 2 to 3 minutes. Stir in the celery and ginger and cook until the celery softens a bit and the onion starts to brown, 4 to 5 minutes. Add the roasted carrots, chicken broth, 1 tsp. salt, the pepper, and 2 cups water. Bring to a boil, reduce the heat to medium low, and cover. Cook at a lively simmer until the carrots are very tender, about 45 minutes. Turn off the heat and let the liquid cool somewhat (or completely).

3. Purée the soup in a blender in batches. If serving immediately, return the soup to the pot and reheat; garnish with the chives or chervil if you like. Otherwise, refrigerate for up to 5 days; reheat gently and taste for salt before serving. *—Ruth Lively*

PER SERVING: 140 CALORIES | 4G PROTEIN | 15G CARB | 8G TOTAL FAT | 3G SAT FAT | 4G MONO FAT | 1G POLY FAT | 10MG CHOL | 720MG SODIUM | 4G FIBER

sweet potato and celery root soup

MAKES ABOUT 3 QUARTS;
SERVES 12

- 2 lb. sweet potatoes, peeled and diced (about 5½ cups)
- 1 lb. celery root, peeled and diced (about 3½ cups)
- ¾ lb. purple-top white turnips, peeled and diced (about 2 cups)

  Sea salt
- 3 Tbs. extra-virgin olive oil; more for drizzling
- 2 medium yellow onions, chopped
- 1 Tbs. chopped fresh thyme
- 2 Tbs. sweet sherry or Marsala
- 4½ to 5 cups homemade or store-bought vegetable or chicken broth (or water)
- ½ tsp. freshly grated nutmeg
- ⅛ tsp. ground allspice
- ⅛ tsp. cayenne; more as needed

Make Ahead

The soup may be made up to 3 days ahead and refrigerated; reheat it gently before serving. You can also freeze the soup for up to 1 month.

The secret to the not-too-sweet flavor of this velvety soup is celery root, or celeriac. Its light celery-parsley notes balance the sweetness of the potatoes and the peppery bite of the turnips.

1. Put the sweet potatoes, celery root, and turnips in a 6-quart pot. Add 4½ cups water and 1 tsp. salt. Bring to a boil over medium-high heat; then lower the heat to maintain a simmer and cook until completely tender, about 40 minutes.

2. Meanwhile, heat 2 Tbs. of the olive oil in a 12-inch nonstick skillet over medium-high heat. Add the onion and ¼ tsp. salt; cook, stirring often, until just beginning to color, about 5 minutes. Stir in the thyme, reduce the heat to low, and cover. Cook, stirring occasionally, until the onion is very soft and amber in color, about 20 minutes. Stir in the sherry or Marsala and simmer until the liquid is absorbed, 1 to 2 minutes.

3. Add the onion mixture, 4½ cups of the broth, the nutmeg, allspice, and cayenne to the pot. Simmer for 5 minutes and then add the remaining 1 Tbs. olive oil. Let cool slightly.

4. Working in batches, purée the soup in a blender. Season to taste with salt and cayenne. If the soup seems too thick, add the remaining broth.

5. Reheat the soup if necessary. Ladle into bowls and drizzle some olive oil over each serving. —*Anna Thomas*

Storing and Grinding Spices for Freshest Flavor

How to Store

When possible, buy whole spices and grind only what you need for a recipe because spices begin to deteriorate the instant they're ground. The most fragrant spices come from stores with a high rate of turnover. Many grocery stores have a good selection of spices, and if you live near an Indian or Middle Eastern market, check out its spice section, which may have more variety. You can also order by mail. Air, light, and heat are the enemies of spices, so keep them in airtight containers in a drawer or cupboard, but never over the stove.

How to Grind

Grinding releases a spice's flavorful aromatic oils. A coarser grind adds textural interest and a mosaic of flavors to a dish. (But not all spices should be left coarse: Cinnamon, clove, mace, nutmeg, and green and black cardamom are so strongly flavored that biting into a big piece is not pleasant.) Finer grinds tend to be more subtle, with the flavors more evenly blended. A small electric coffee grinder lets you grind a few tablespoons of spice at a time. If you use a mortar and pestle, grind in a circular motion and hold a piece of plastic wrap over the bowl while you grind to keep the spices from sneaking out.

purée of sweet potato and ginger soup with apple-mint raita

SERVES 6

FOR THE SOUP

- 2 Tbs. unsalted butter
- 1 medium yellow onion, roughly chopped
- 2 cloves garlic, minced
- 1 ½-inch chunk (1 oz.) fresh ginger, peeled and thinly sliced
- ¼ tsp. ground cardamom
- ½ fresh jalapeño, seeds and ribs removed, and left whole
- 2 lb. sweet potatoes (about 4 medium), peeled and cut into 1-inch cubes
- 5½ cups homemade or lower-salt chicken broth

  Kosher salt
- ½ cup heavy cream (optional)
- 1 Tbs. fresh lime juice
- 1 Tbs. light brown sugar

  Freshly ground white pepper

FOR THE RAITA

- ½ cup plain nonfat or low-fat yogurt
- ½ firm, sweet apple, such as Gala or Pink Lady, peeled, cored, and finely diced
- ¼ cup chopped fresh mint
- ½ tsp. finely minced fresh jalapeño; more as needed

  Kosher salt and freshly ground black pepper

Slices of fresh ginger are simmered with the soup base to gently infuse it with warmth and mellow sweetness. The raita is the perfect cooling counterpart. If you like heat, leave the ribs attached to the jalapeño half.

MAKE THE SOUP

1. Melt the butter in a soup pot over low heat. Cook the onion in the butter, stirring occasionally, until very soft but not browned, 10 to 13 minutes. Add the garlic, ginger, and cardamom and cook for another 1 minute. Increase the heat to high and add the jalapeño, sweet potatoes, 4 cups of the broth, and 1 tsp. salt. Bring to a boil, reduce the heat to medium low, cover, and simmer until the potatoes are very soft, 15 to 20 minutes.

2. In a blender, purée the soup in batches until very smooth. Rinse and dry the pot and return the puréed soup to it. Add the remaining 1½ cups broth and the cream, if using, and bring to a simmer over medium-low heat. Add the lime juice and brown sugar, and season with salt and white pepper to taste.

MAKE THE RAITA

While the soup is simmering, combine the yogurt, apple, mint, and jalapeño in a small bowl. Season with salt and pepper to taste. Refrigerate until ready to serve.

TO SERVE

Ladle the soup into individual bowls and add a dollop of the raita.
—Eva Katz

PER SERVING: 250 CALORIES | 7G PROTEIN | 46G CARB | 5G TOTAL FAT | 3G SAT FAT | 1G MONO FAT | 1G POLY FAT | 10MG CHOL | 480MG SODIUM | 6G FIBER

how to cut ginger

Ginger can be sliced into planks or matchsticks, chopped, grated, puréed, or minced, depending on its final destination. Use minced, chopped, or thin matchsticks of ginger when you want a textural component as well as flavor. Planks or slices are perfect for infusing flavor into a broth, as in the soup at left. When it's just the flavor and essence of the ginger that you want to capture, grate it. Try grated ginger in salad dressings and dipping sauces, or whenever the ginger should have a smooth, nonfibrous consistency to readily blend with other ingredients.

PLANKS Diagonally slice the ginger across the fibers to cut it into planks and use to infuse flavor into liquid. Cutting planks is also the first step to making matchsticks or a mince.

MATCHSTICKS To cut ginger into julienne-style matchsticks, stack the ginger planks and slice them into thin strips.

MINCED To take the ginger to the chopped or minced stage, turn the stack of matchstick pieces 90 degrees and chop to the consistency you want.

GRATED Use a Microplane to grate ginger. It does an amazing job of grating even the most fibrous knob of ginger into a juicy, paste-like consistency.

pumpkin soup with sage and gruyère croutons

SERVES 4 AS A MAIN COURSE, OR 6 AS A FIRST COURSE

2 Tbs. unsalted butter

1 medium yellow onion, sliced

6 cups 1-inch-diced peeled and seeded pumpkin; for varieties, see p. 28

2 medium cloves garlic, sliced

½ cup dry white wine

8 medium fresh sage leaves

4 to 6 cups homemade or lower-salt chicken broth

2¼ cups packed grated Gruyère

Kosher salt and freshly ground black pepper

6 slices rustic bread (each about 6x2 inches and ½ inch thick)

1 tsp. minced fresh sage

Large sage-laced Gruyère croutons offer a crunchy contrast to the silky, creamy soup.

1. Melt the butter in a heavy 4- to 5-quart pot over medium heat. Add the onion and cook, stirring occasionally, until tender, 6 to 8 minutes. Stir in the pumpkin and garlic and cook, stirring, for 1 minute more. Add the wine and sage leaves and cook, stirring, until the wine evaporates, about 5 minutes. Stir in 4 cups of the broth, cover, and simmer, adjusting the heat as needed, until the pumpkin is very tender, about 25 minutes.

2. Add ¼ cup of the Gruyère and, using a hand-held or standard blender, purée the soup (in batches, if necessary). Season to taste with salt and pepper.

3. Return to a gentle simmer, stirring constantly and adding more broth as necessary to achieve a thin soup with the consistency of heavy cream. (The soup can be prepared up to 3 days ahead. Cool, cover, and refrigerate. Reheat gently to serve.)

4. Position a rack about 6 inches from the broiler and heat the broiler on high. Arrange the bread on a baking sheet. Toast under the broiler, 1 to 2 minutes per side. Sprinkle the croutons with the remaining 2 cups cheese and the minced sage and season with pepper. Broil until the cheese melts and is bubbly, about 2 minutes. Ladle the soup into warm bowls and serve with the croutons. *—Jeanne Kelley*

PER SERVING: 350 CALORIES | 19G PROTEIN | 25G CARB | 18G TOTAL FAT | 10G SAT FAT | 6G MONO FAT | 1G POLY FAT | 55MG CHOL | 480MG SODIUM | 1G FIBER

continued on p. 28

More about Pumpkins

Save the hefty, perfectly shaped jack-o'-lantern varieties like Connecticut Field and Spirit for Halloween; their flesh is thin and stringy, with little flavor. Instead, look for heirloom varieties, which are great for cooking. Local pumpkins will vary by region, but here are three relatively common types that make delicious eating.

Sugar Pie (and the similar Baby Pam and New England Pie)
These small, volleyball-size, thin-skinned, burnt-orange pumpkins are probably the most commonly found baking pumpkins. They have sweet, smooth flesh that tends to be firm and dry, so they're especially good for pie. If you find one with stringy flesh, don't bake or cook with it, because it will spoil the texture of the finished dish.

Casper
Casper pumpkins are white on the outside and dark orange inside. They resemble the traditional jack-o'-lantern pumpkin in shape and tend to be heavy, at 10 to 20 lb.

Marina DiChioggia (aka Chioggia Sea Pumpkin)
This Italian heirloom pumpkin originally comes from Chioggia, near Venice. It's a large (about 10-lb.), blue-green, bumpy, ridged pumpkin, with dense, meaty, yellow-orange flesh.

Buying
Look for pumpkins that are free of cracks and soft spots. Be sure to inspect both the stem and bottom ends. If you're at a farmers' market or pumpkin patch, ask the farmer if the pumpkins have been exposed to frost. If they have, they will spoil quickly.

Storing
Most pumpkins can be stored, or cellared, in a cool, dark place for 2 to 6 months, depending on the variety. Arrange them in a single layer on top of a breathable surface such as cardboard or wood. Check on them every 2 weeks and use immediately (or discard) any that are starting to soften.

curried carrot soup with cilantro

SERVES 4 TO 6

- 2 Tbs. vegetable oil
- 1½ lb. carrots, cut into 1-inch chunks (about 4 cups)
- 1 large yellow onion, cut into 1-inch chunks
- 3 large cloves garlic, thinly sliced
- 1 tsp. curry powder
- 3 cups homemade or lower-salt chicken broth

    Kosher salt

- 1½ cups carrot juice; more as needed
- ¼ cup packed fresh cilantro leaves

    Freshly ground black pepper

    Chopped peanuts, for garnish (optional)

This carrot soup, infused with curry, has a beguiling aroma. Peanuts are an unusual garnish but add welcome texture.

1. Heat the oil in a 10- or 11-inch straight-sided sauté pan over medium-high heat until hot. Add the carrots and then the onion. Cook, stirring very little at first and more frequently toward the end, until the vegetables are golden brown, 6 to 8 minutes.

2. Add the garlic and curry powder and cook, stirring, for about 30 seconds. Add the broth and ½ tsp. salt and bring to a simmer over medium-high heat. Reduce the heat to low, cover, and simmer until the vegetables are very tender, 10 to 15 minutes. Add the carrot juice and cilantro.

3. Purée the soup in a blender, working in two batches.

4. Return the soup to the pan, heat through, and season to taste with salt and pepper. If necessary, add more carrot juice to thin to your liking. Ladle into bowls and serve, sprinkled with the peanuts, if using.
—*Pamela Anderson*

PER SERVING: 140 CALORIES | 4G PROTEIN | 21G CARB | 6G TOTAL FAT | 1G SAT FAT | 2.5G MONO FAT | 2.5G POLY FAT | 0MG CHOL | 230MG SODIUM | 4G FIBER

roasted hubbard squash soup with hazelnuts and chives

MAKES ABOUT 10 CUPS;
SERVES 8 TO 10

- **3** Tbs. extra-virgin olive oil
- **3** large cloves garlic
- **1** Tbs. coriander seeds
- **1½** tsp. fennel seeds
- **1½** tsp. dried sage
- **1** small (5½- to 6-lb.) Hubbard squash, halved lengthwise and seeded
- **2** Tbs. unsalted butter
- **1** large leek (white and light green parts only), halved lengthwise and thinly sliced crosswise
- **2** medium carrots, peeled and cut into small dice

  Kosher salt
- **5** cups homemade or lower-salt chicken or vegetable broth

If you can't find Espelette pepper, use just a pinch of cayenne instead. The soup keeps for 3 days in the refrigerator or 2 months in the freezer.

1. Position a rack in the center of the oven and heat the oven to 400°F. Line a heavy-duty rimmed baking sheet with parchment. In a mortar and pestle, pound the oil, garlic, coriander seeds, fennel seeds, and sage until they resemble a coarse paste. Rub the spice mixture on the flesh of the squash halves. Set them cut side down on the prepared pan and roast until tender when pierced with a fork, about 1 hour. Let cool, cut side up. When cool enough to handle, scrape the flesh away from the skin—you'll need about 5 cups.

2. Melt the butter in a 5- to 6-quart Dutch oven over medium heat. Add the leek, carrots, and a big pinch of salt and cook, stirring occasionally, until the leek is softened, 8 to 10 minutes. Add the squash, broth, bay leaf, and 1 tsp. salt and bring to a boil over high heat. Reduce the heat to a low simmer, cover, and cook for 30 minutes to develop the soup's flavor.

1   **bay leaf**

2   **tsp. fresh lemon juice**

    Freshly ground black pepper

½   **cup hazelnuts, toasted, skinned, and chopped**

2   **Tbs. thinly sliced fresh chives**

    Several small pinches of Espelette pepper or cayenne

3. Remove the bay leaf and allow the soup to cool slightly. Purée the soup in batches in a blender. Return the soup to the pot and add the lemon juice. Season to taste with salt and pepper. Garnish with the chopped hazelnuts, chives, and Espelette pepper or cayenne.
—*Ivy Manning*

PER SERVING: 240 CALORIES | 9G PROTEIN | 29G CARB | 13G TOTAL FAT | 3G SAT FAT | 7G MONO FAT | 2G POLY FAT | 5MG CHOL | 180MG SODIUM | 7G FIBER

how to handle big squash

Probably the largest squash you'll find at the market, the teardrop-shaped Hubbards are often sold in manageable chunks, so you can buy only what you need. Don't be afraid to buy a whole squash, however. If you prick the squash several times with a fork and microwave it for 3 minutes, it will soften slightly, making it easier to cut open. Or bake the whole squash directly on the rack in a 350°F oven until slightly softened and the skin begins to change color, about 10 minutes. Follow these steps to cut open any large squash.

Set the squash on a towel on a cutting board to prevent it from slipping, and push the tip of a sharp chef's knife into the squash near the stem. Carefully push the knife through the squash to the cutting board to cut off the stem.

Cut lengthwise through half of the squash, starting with the tip of your knife in the center of the squash. If the knife sticks, don't try to pull it out; this is dangerous, since it may come out suddenly. Instead, tap the handle with a rubber mallet or meat tenderizer until the knife cuts through the squash.

Rotate the squash and cut through the other side the same way.

Push the halves apart with your hands. With a soupspoon, scrape the seeds and stringy bits away from the flesh and discard.

pea and spinach soup with coconut milk

MAKES 5½ CUPS SOUP; SERVES 6

- **2** large leeks (white and light green parts), quartered and sliced to yield 2 cups (or 2 cups chopped scallions or 2 cups thinly sliced white onion)
- **1** Tbs. unsalted butter
- **2** Tbs. white basmati rice

  Kosher salt
- **2** tsp. curry powder
- **4** sprigs fresh cilantro, plus leaves for garnish
- **4** cups Vegetable Stock (recipe on p. 226) or home-made or lower-salt chicken broth
- **1½** to 2 lb. peas, shucked (to yield 1½ to 2 cups)
- **4** cups lightly packed, coarsely chopped spinach leaves, any thick stems removed
- **7** oz. coconut milk (½ a can, or about 1 cup)

  Freshly ground white pepper

Peas are just as good with curry spices, cilantro, and coconut milk as they are with fresh herbs. Make this soup, which includes spinach, when it's hard to gather enough peas for a pure pea soup. The pea flavor still comes through nicely.

1. Soak the leeks in a bowl of cold water to remove any grit. Meanwhile, in a soup pot over medium heat, melt the butter and stir in the rice. Scoop the leeks from the water, shaking off excess water, and add the leeks to the pot along with 1 tsp. salt, curry powder, cilantro, and 1 cup of the stock. Cook over medium-low heat at a vigorous simmer for about 12 minutes, so the rice is almost done. Add the remaining 3 cups stock, the peas, and the spinach and bring to a boil. Boil for about 3 minutes. Turn off the heat and stir in the coconut milk.

2. In a blender or a food processor, purée the soup in batches until smooth. Taste for salt, season with white pepper, and serve, garnished with fresh cilantro leaves. (If you prefer a soup with more texture, purée just 1 cup and return it to the pot, season, garnish, and serve.)
—*Deborah Madison*

PER SERVING: 170 CALORIES | 4G PROTEIN | 16G CARB | 10G TOTAL FAT | 8G SAT FAT | 1G MONO FAT | 0G POLY FAT | 5MG CHOL | 840MG SODIUM | 3G FIBER

asparagus and spinach soup with roasted garlic custards

SERVES 6

FOR THE GARLIC CUSTARDS

1 large head garlic

3 large eggs

Kosher salt and freshly ground black pepper

¾ cup light cream or half-and-half

¾ cup homemade or lower-salt chicken broth

Softened unsalted butter or oil, for the ramekins

FOR THE SOUP

2 Tbs. unsalted butter

¼ cup chopped shallot or onion

½ tsp. whole fennel seeds

Pinch of crushed red pepper flakes

Kosher salt

1½ lb. thick asparagus, tough ends trimmed, spears chopped, and tips reserved

1 cup peeled and diced Yukon Gold potatoes

1 quart homemade or lower-salt chicken broth

2 cups lightly packed spinach leaves

½ cup crème fraîche

Make Ahead

The custards can be made up to 1 day ahead; cover and refrigerate. Return to room temperature before serving.

This elegant soup is a perfect spring first course. Creamy garlic-imbued custards lend rich flavor and texture.

MAKE THE GARLIC CUSTARDS

1. Heat the oven to 350°F. Cut about ¼ inch from the top of the garlic head to expose the cloves. Wrap the head in foil and bake until the garlic is very soft, about 45 minutes. When cool enough to handle, separate the cloves and squeeze the garlic from the skins into a blender or food processor. Add the eggs, 1 tsp. salt, and ½ tsp. pepper to the roasted garlic and pulse until completely smooth. Pulse in the cream and broth.

2. Generously butter or oil six 4-oz. ovenproof ramekins and put them in a deep roasting pan. Portion the custard mixture among the ramekins and fill the roasting pan with enough boiling water to come three-quarters of the way up the sides of the ramekins. Bake the custards until the centers are just set and the tops are very lightly browned, 35 to 40 minutes. Remove the ramekins from the water bath and let cool on a rack to room temperature before unmolding.

MAKE THE SOUP

1. In a 4-quart saucepan, melt the butter over medium heat. Add the shallot or onion, fennel seeds, red pepper flakes, and a big pinch of salt. Cook, stirring occasionally, until the shallot is tender but not brown, about 2 minutes. Add the chopped asparagus spears and the potatoes; cook for 1 minute. Stir in the broth and bring to a boil. Reduce the heat to medium low and simmer until the vegetables are tender, about 10 minutes.

2. Meanwhile, have ready a bowl of ice water. Bring a small pot of well-salted water to a boil over high heat. Add the asparagus tips and cook until tender but still bright green, about 2 minutes. Drain and then transfer the tips to the ice water to cool. Drain again and set aside.

3. Remove the soup from the heat, add the spinach, and stir until wilted. Working in batches, purée the soup in a blender. Return the soup to the stove. Stir in the crème fraîche and heat through. Season to taste with salt.

TO SERVE

Run a knife around the edge of each custard, tap the sides of the ramekins with your hand to loosen the custards, and invert them onto a cutting board. Set out wide-rimmed shallow soup bowls and carefully place one custard, top side up, in the center of each. Ladle the soup around the custards, garnish with the asparagus tips, and serve. —*John Ash*

pea and mint soup with lemon cream

SERVES 4 TO 6

- **2 Tbs. unsalted butter**
- **½ cup coarsely chopped shallots**
- **1 tsp. minced garlic**
- **4 cups fresh shelled peas (3½ to 4 lb. unshelled) or frozen peas**
- **2 cups homemade or lower-salt chicken broth**
- **½ cup chopped fresh mint**
- **Kosher salt and freshly ground black pepper**
- **Pinch of granulated sugar (optional)**
- **½ cup heavy cream**
- **Finely grated zest of ½ medium lemon**

You can serve this soup hot or cold. Its flavor is brighter if you use very fresh, young peas. The starchiness of mature peas can give the soup a split-pea flavor, so if you can find only older peas, use frozen instead.

1. Melt the butter in a 3- to 4-quart saucepan over medium heat. Add the shallots and garlic and cook, stirring frequently, until both are very soft, 6 to 8 minutes. They shouldn't brown. If they're cooking too fast, reduce the heat to medium low.

2. Add the peas, broth, half of the mint, and 2 cups water. Season generously with salt and pepper. Bring to a boil, reduce the heat to medium low, and simmer vigorously until the peas are very tender, 8 to 10 minutes. In batches, purée the soup in a blender until smooth. Season to taste with salt and pepper. If the peas aren't very sweet, stir in the sugar.

3. Pour the cream into a medium bowl and whip it to soft peaks with a whisk. Fold in the lemon zest and season to taste with salt and pepper.

4. Ladle the soup into serving bowls and top with a generous spoon-ful of the lemon cream. Scatter the remaining chopped mint over the soup and serve. If you choose to serve the soup cold, chill it in the refrigerator, but take it out 15 minutes before you serve. Adjust the seasonings if necessary before serving. *—Annie Wayte*

PER SERVING: 200 CALORIES | 7G PROTEIN | 17G CARB | 12G TOTAL FAT | 7G SAT FAT | 3.5G MONO FAT | 0.5G POLY FAT | 35MG CHOL | 240MG SODIUM | 5G FIBER

Buying and Storing Peas

Choosing

For best flavor, choose small peas, which are younger, sweeter, and more tender than large ones, and make sure they're as fresh as possible. Once picked, peas' high sugar content changes, causing them to lose their sweetness and become starchy and dull. You know peas are fresh when their pods are firm and green, so avoid any that are yellowing or wilting. Go for medium pods rather than large, thick-skinned ones, which are more mature and contain larger, tougher peas. Break open a pod and check the peas. They should be small, bright green, and firm; they should taste tender and sweet.

Storing

Peas don't have much of a shelf life, so don't store them—in their pods or shelled—for very long. Store pods in a plastic bag in the crisper drawer of the refrigerator and use them within a couple of days. Once they're shelled, the best way to store peas is to freeze them. First blanch them for a minute or two in boiling salted water and then shock them in an ice-water bath until cool, to help maintain their bright color. Drain and freeze them in zip-top bags. They will keep for 5 to 6 months.

asparagus soup with leeks and mustard seeds

SERVES 8 AS A FIRST COURSE

- **2 Tbs. unsalted butter**
- **1¼ cups thinly sliced leeks (white and light green parts), rinsed well**
- **2 tsp. minced garlic**
- **Kosher salt**
- **2 tsp. mustard seeds**
- **2¼ lb. asparagus, tough ends trimmed, spears cut into ½-inch pieces**
- **2½ cups homemade or lower-salt chicken broth**
- **3 Tbs. dry white wine**
- **¼ cup heavy cream**
- **½ tsp. fresh lemon juice; more as needed**
- **Freshly ground black pepper**
- **⅓ cup chopped fresh flat-leaf parsley**

Mustard seeds add a little bite to this creamy, mellow soup, a perfect starter for Easter or any spring supper.

1. In a 4- to 5-quart saucepan or Dutch oven, heat the butter over medium-low heat. When hot, add the leeks, garlic, and a pinch of salt. Stir well, cover, reduce the heat to low, and cook, stirring occasionally, until the aromatics are softened, 8 to 10 minutes. Stir in 1 tsp. salt and the mustard seeds.

2. Add the asparagus, chicken broth, and wine, plus 2½ cups water. Stir well and bring to a simmer over medium heat. Cook uncovered, stirring occasionally, until the vegetables are very tender and the soup is full-flavored, 7 to 20 minutes. Take the pan off the heat and let the soup cool for 5 minutes.

3. Working in batches, pureé the soup in a blender (fill the jar no more than half full and vent the lid, topping it with a folded kitchen towel to prevent hot splashes). Wipe the pan clean and put the soup back into the pan.

4. Add the cream and ½ tsp. lemon juice. Season the soup with salt and pepper. Taste the soup and adjust the seasonings with more salt, pepper, or lemon juice as needed.

5. Ladle into soup bowls and garnish each serving with 1 to 2 tsp. chopped parsley. —*Susie Middleton*

PER SERVING: 100 CALORIES | 4G PROTEIN | 8G CARB | 7G TOTAL FAT | 3G SAT FAT | 2.5G MONO FAT | 0.5G POLY FAT | 15MG CHOL | 200MG SODIUM | 2G FIBER

parsnip and parmesan soup

**MAKES 5½ TO 6 CUPS;
SERVES 5 OR 6**

- ¼ cup unsalted butter
- 1½ lb. parsnips, peeled, cored, and cut into ½-inch dice (to yield a scant 4 cups)
- 6 oz. shallots, cut into ¼-inch dice (to yield about 1¼ cups)
- 8 cloves garlic, minced
- 1 Tbs. finely chopped fresh oregano; plus tiny sprigs for garnish
   Kosher salt and freshly ground black pepper
- 4½ cups homemade or lower-salt chicken or vegetable broth
- 1½ oz. (½ cup) freshly grated Parmigiano-Reggiano
- 2 tsp. soy sauce
- 2 tsp. fresh lemon juice

Salty and savory Parmigiano-Reggiano marries well with sweet parsnips, and fresh oregano pulls it all together.

1. Melt the butter in a 5-quart or larger stockpot set over medium heat. While the butter is still foaming, add the parsnips and cook until lightly browned, 7 to 10 minutes (resist the urge to stir too often or they won't brown). Stir in the shallot, garlic, chopped oregano, 1½ tsp. salt, and ½ tsp. pepper and cook until the shallots are very limp and the entire mixture is beginning to brown, 8 to 10 minutes. Add the broth, using a wooden spoon to scrape up any browned bits in the pot. Bring to a boil, reduce the heat to maintain a low simmer, and cook until the parsnips are very soft, 6 to 8 minutes. Remove from the heat and let cool somewhat.

2. Purée the soup using a stand or immersion blender (you'll need to work in batches if using a stand blender; be sure to vent the lid and hold a folded dishtowel over the top to prevent splashes). Return the soup to the pot and stir in the Parmigiano, soy sauce, and lemon juice. Taste and add more salt and pepper if needed. Reheat the soup and garnish each serving with an oregano sprig, if you like. *—Jill Silverman Hough*

PER SERVING: 230 CALORIES | 9G PROTEIN | 26G CARB | 11G TOTAL FAT | 6G SAT FAT | 3G MONO FAT | 0.5G POLY FAT | 25MG CHOL | 600MG SODIUM | 5G FIBER

Coring Parsnips

Running down the center of a parsnip is a tough woody core that should be removed before cooking. Before doing this, trim the ends and peel the parsnip, then quarter it lengthwise. Hold a sharp paring knife parallel to the cutting board and slowly run the knife between the core and the tender outer part of the parsnip. The core curves with the shape of the parsnip, so you won't be able to get it all, but that's fine—just remove as much as you can without sacrificing too much of the tender part.

parsnip and leek soup with cumin and mustard seeds

This soup gets a delicious kick from whole cumin and mustard seeds toasted in hot oil with garlic and stirred in just before serving. This traditional Indian seasoning technique is called tarka.

FOR THE SOUP

- 2 Tbs. unsalted butter
- 1 large yellow onion, cut into medium dice (2 cups)

  Kosher salt and freshly ground black pepper
- 6 cups homemade or lower-salt chicken broth; more as needed
- 2 medium leeks (white and light green parts only), trimmed, washed, and sliced crosswise about ½ inch thick (2 ½ cups)
- 1 lb. medium parsnips, peeled, cored, and cut into medium dice (about 2 cups)
- 1 lb. yellow potatoes (like Yukon Gold), peeled and cut into medium dice (2¾ cups)
- 2 tsp. ground turmeric
- ½ tsp. cayenne, more as needed

FOR THE TARKA

- 2 Tbs. extra-virgin olive oil
- 4 medium cloves garlic, roughly chopped
- 2 tsp. cumin seeds
- 2 tsp. black mustard seeds

MAKE THE SOUP

1. Melt the butter in a heavy 6- to 8-quart pot over medium heat. Add the onion, ½ tsp. salt, and a couple of grinds of pepper and cook, stirring occasionally, until the onion is soft and lightly browned, 8 to 10 minutes. Add the broth, leeks, parsnips, and potatoes and raise the heat to medium high. Simmer briskly for 5 minutes and then reduce the heat to low. Add the turmeric and cayenne, stirring well, and simmer slowly until the vegetables are very soft, about 20 minutes.

2. Working in batches, purée the soup in a blender (vent the lid and hold a folded dishtowel over the top to prevent splashes) and then strain it through a medium-mesh sieve. The soup should be about as thick as a thin milk shake; add more broth if it's not thin enough. Return the soup to the pot and season to taste with salt. (The soup can be made up to this point 1 day ahead and refrigerated. Reheat before proceeding.)

MAKE THE TARKA

Shortly before serving, heat the olive oil in a small skillet over medium-high heat. When the oil is hot, add the garlic, cumin seeds, and mustard seeds. Stir with a wooden spoon until the seeds begin to pop and the garlic is lightly browned, 30 to 60 seconds. Carefully stir the hot oil and spices into the soup (it may spatter). Season to taste with more salt, pepper, or cayenne. —*David Tanis*

PER SERVING: 200 CALORIES | 6G PROTEIN | 29G CARB | 8G TOTAL FAT | 2.5G SAT FAT | 4G MONO FAT | 1G POLY FAT | 10MG CHOL | 140MG SODIUM | 5G FIBER

creamy tomato soup with zucchini

**SERVES 4 AS A LIGHT
MAIN COURSE**

- **6 Tbs. unsalted butter**
- **3 medium zucchini (about 1½ lb.), cut into medium dice**
- **Kosher salt**
- **2 cloves garlic, minced**
- **1 cup chopped yellow onion**
- **3 15-oz. cans whole peeled tomatoes, drained**
- **1½ cups homemade or lower-salt chicken broth**
- **½ cup dry white wine**
- **1 cup heavy cream**
- **½ cup fresh basil leaves, chopped, for garnish**

This soup is delicious served with toasted baguette slices smeared with goat cheese.

1. Melt 4 Tbs. of the butter in a large stockpot over medium-high heat. Add the zucchini and 1 tsp. salt and cook, stirring occasionally, until the zucchini is crisp-tender but not browned, about 5 minutes. Add the garlic and cook for 1 minute. Using a slotted spoon, transfer the zucchini mixture to a medium bowl.

2. Melt the remaining 2 Tbs. butter in the stockpot over medium-high heat. Add the onion and cook, stirring, until it becomes translucent, about 3 minutes. Increase the heat to high, add the tomatoes and 1 tsp. salt to the pot, and cook, stirring constantly, for 1 minute. Add the chicken broth and the wine and bring to a boil. Reduce the heat and simmer, stirring occasionally, until the liquid has reduced by half, about 20 minutes.

3. Remove the stockpot from the heat and let the tomato mixture cool slightly. Purée the soup in the pot with a hand blender or in batches in a stand blender (be sure to vent the stand blender's top and hold a folded dishtowel over the top to prevent splashes). If you used a regular blender, return the soup to the pot. Add the cream. Bring to a boil and cook until heated through, about 2 minutes. Stir in the zucchini. Garnish each serving with some of the chopped fresh basil. *—Julie Grimes Bottcher*

PER SERVING: 530 CALORIES | 9G PROTEIN | 33G CARB | 40G TOTAL FAT | 25G SAT FAT | 11G MONO FAT | 1.5G POLY FAT | 130MG CHOL | 1,460MG SODIUM | 8G FIBER

Tips for the Best Puréed Soups

- Cut your vegetables small for faster cooking. A ½-inch dice needs no more than 10 minutes of simmering before it's soft enough to purée.

- Don't stir the vegetables too often during the sauté; once every 2 minutes is good. This helps them brown, and that, in turn, will flavor your soup, giving it nuance.

- Use a blender to get the smoothest soup. If you use a stand blender, be sure to let the liquid cool slightly, work in batches, and hold a towel over the lid to avoid overflowing. An immersion blender works well, too, and is even more convenient.

- Don't be afraid of salt—it can make all the difference. Taste your soup before serving and add salt to taste. The flavors will get brighter and more pronounced.

- An attractive garnish can really give soup pizzazz. Use a sprig of an herb that's in your soup, a drizzle of a flavored oil, or a sprinkle of shredded cheese. A dollop of sour cream or crème fraîche can also enhance a simple puréed soup.

creamy roasted garlic soup with sautéed cauliflower and fresh herbs

SERVES 4

FOR THE SOUP

- **4** heads garlic, loose, papery skins removed and ¼ inch of the tops cut off to expose the cloves
- **3** Tbs. extra-virgin olive oil

  Kosher salt
- **½** cup chopped onion
- **1** leek (white and light green parts only), chopped and well rinsed
- **2** large boiling potatoes, peeled and chopped
- **1** Tbs. fresh thyme, chopped
- **½** cup dry white wine
- **4** cups homemade or lower-salt chicken or vegetable broth

  Freshly ground black pepper
- **¼** cup chopped fresh sorrel leaves or chives, or a combination

Serve this thick and intense soup with a swirl of herb butter along with the fresh herb garnish. To make this, mix equal parts softened butter and chopped sorrel leaves, a small amount of finely chopped chives, and salt to taste. It brings a fresh note to the soup.

MAKE THE SOUP

1. Heat the oven to 375°F. Put the garlic heads in a small baking pan. Drizzle on 2 Tbs. of the olive oil and sprinkle on the salt. Add 2 Tbs. water to the pan, cover with foil, and roast until a squeezed clove yields a soft purée, 30 to 45 minutes. When cool, squeeze the pulp from each clove.

2. In a soup pot over low heat, sweat the onion and leek in 1 Tbs. of the olive oil until very soft but not brown, about 10 minutes. Add the potatoes and thyme and cook for another 1 minute. Turn the heat to medium high, add the wine, and let it reduce to just a few teaspoons, about 4 minutes. Add the broth; bring to a boil. Reduce the heat and simmer for 10 minutes. Add the garlic pulp and simmer until the potatoes are very soft, another 15 to 20 minutes.

3. Strain the soup, reserving both the liquid and solids. In a blender or food processor, purée the solids in batches, using some liquid to help it blend, and pour the puréed solids back into the pot. When all the solids are puréed, add as much of the remaining liquid as necessary to get a consistency like heavy cream. Season to taste with salt and pepper.

FOR THE CAULIFLOWER

2   **Tbs. extra-virgin olive oil**

1   **small head cauliflower
    (2 lb.), cut into small florets
    (about ½ inch at the widest
    point)**

    **Kosher salt and freshly
    ground black pepper**

SAUTÉ THE CAULIFLOWER

Heat 2 Tbs. oil in a large sauté pan over medium heat. Add the cauliflower florets and sauté. Once they begin to soften, after about 5 minutes, season with salt and pepper. Continue to sauté until the cauliflower is deep golden brown and tender but still firm, another 7 to 10 minutes.

TO SERVE

Reheat the soup if necessary. Ladle it into individual bowls, add the cauliflower, and garnish with the sorrel or chives. —*Peter Hoffman*

PER SERVING: 440 CALORIES | 12G PROTEIN | 43G CARB | 25G TOTAL FAT | 4G SAT FAT | 18G MONO FAT | 3G POLY FAT | 0MG CHOL | 360MG SODIUM | 9G FIBER

Choosing and Using Garlic

Choosing

Buy firm, plump heads with tight, unbroken papery skins. The heavier the garlic, the fresher, juicier, and better tasting it is. Avoid bulbs that are dried out or have soft spots or mold. Green shoots in a bulb are a sign of internal growth in the clove, an indication of old garlic.

Varieties vary in size, and many people find that a smaller bulb has more flavor than a larger one. Resist the convenience of prechopped garlic. It doesn't taste nearly as good as fresh garlic and won't keep as long.

Storing

Store garlic in a cool, dry place. For just a few heads, a ventilated ceramic container or garlic keeper is perfect. If you buy a large amount of garlic, hang it in a mesh sack in your basement or garage—as long as it's cool and dry there. Never store garlic in a plastic bag, and keep it out of the fridge, unless you have a low-humidity drawer.

Prepping

To peel a clove of garlic, first break the skin. Set the clove on a cutting board and cover it with a flat side of a chef's knife. With the heel of your hand, apply light pressure to the knife blade— enough to split the skin but not so much to crush the clove (unless, of course, you want it smashed). Remove the germ (the sprout in the center of the clove), especially if it's pronounced and especially for recipes that call for raw or quickly cooked garlic.

For quick-cooking, chunky dishes, like pasta sauces and sautéed vegetables, finely mince or thinly slice garlic to get the best release of flavor. For long-cooking braises and stews, roughly chop or thickly slice garlic so it slowly melds with the other ingredients.

creamy potato soup with pancetta croutons

**MAKES ABOUT 8 CUPS;
SERVES 6 AS A MAIN COURSE
OR 8 AS A FIRST COURSE**

- 2 **Tbs. unsalted butter**
- 2 **medium onions (8 oz. total), chopped (about 2 cups)**

  Kosher salt and freshly ground black or white pepper
- 3 **large cloves garlic, thinly sliced**
- 2 **lb. russet potatoes (3 to 4 medium), peeled and cut into ¾- to 1-inch chunks**
- 4 **cups homemade or lower-salt chicken broth**
- 2 **bay leaves, preferably fresh**
- 1 **cup whole milk**
- ½ **cup light or heavy cream; more as needed for garnish**

  Pancetta Croutons (recipe below)

Here's a soup that's utterly pleasing—smooth and full-bodied without being heavy, thanks to starchy russet potatoes and just a little cream to enrich the flavor. Pair it with a green salad for a simple but satisfying meal.

1. Melt the butter in a 4-quart saucepan over medium heat. Add the onion, season with salt and pepper, and cook gently, stirring occasionally, until translucent but not at all browned, 8 to 10 minutes. Add the garlic and cook for another 2 minutes. Add the potatoes, stir, pour in the broth, and add the bay leaves. Bring to a simmer over medium-high heat, partially cover, reduce the heat to medium low or low, and simmer gently until the potatoes are very tender, 25 to 30 minutes. Discard the bay leaves.

2. Working in batches, purée the soup in a blender (being careful to fill the blender only half full and vent the lid; hold a folded dishtowel over the top). If the soup is too thick to blend, add a little of the milk. Pulse the blender in short bursts and avoid overworking the soup.

3. Rinse the soup pot and return the soup to it. Add the remaining milk and cream and heat through. Season with salt and pepper to taste. Ladle the soup into bowls and top each with a generous handful of the pancetta croutons. Garnish with a thread of cream, if you like.
—Molly Stevens

PER SERVING BASED ON 8 SERVINGS: 330 CALORIES | 9G PROTEIN | 35G CARB | 17G TOTAL FAT | 8G SAT FAT | 6G MONO FAT | 1.5G POLY FAT | 40MG CHOL | 540MG SODIUM | 3G FIBER

pancetta croutons

MAKES 2 CUPS

- 4 **oz. country-style bread, cut into ½-inch cubes (about 3 cups)**
- 4 **oz. pancetta, cut into ¼- to ½-inch dice (about ¾ cup)**
- 1 **Tbs. extra-virgin olive oil**

  Freshly ground black pepper

These can be made up to 2 hours ahead and kept at room temperature. If you have leftovers, refrigerate them.

Position a rack in the center of the oven and heat the oven to 350°F. Spread the bread cubes and pancetta on a rimmed baking sheet. Sprinkle with the oil and a few grinds of black pepper and toss to combine. Bake, stirring a few times, until the pancetta is crisp and the bread cubes are golden, about 20 minutes. Let cool.

cream of celery and celery root soup

SERVES 4 TO 6

- 2 **Tbs. unsalted butter**
- 6 **cups thinly sliced celery (reserve ¼ cup celery leaves)**
- 1 **medium yellow onion, chopped**
  Kosher salt
- 3 **cups peeled, small-diced celery root**
- 6 **cups homemade or lower-salt chicken broth**
- 3 **sprigs fresh thyme**
- 1 **fresh or ½ dried bay leaf**
- 2 **Tbs. crème fraîche**
  Freshly ground black pepper
  Canola oil, for frying

This soup is smooth and delicate, and its elegant celery leaf garnish makes i a perfect first course for a dinner part Adding celery root (a relative of celery imbues the soup with even deeper celery flavor.

1. In a 4-quart pot, melt the butter over medium heat. Add the celery, onion, and a generous pinch of salt. Cook until tender and just beginning to color, 6 to 8 minutes. Add the celery root and stir to coat with the butter. Pour in the chicken broth and then add the thyme, bay leaf, and ½ tsp. salt. Bring to a boil, then reduce the heat and simmer until the vegetables are very tender, about 15 minutes. Discard the thyme sprigs and bay leaf and purée the soup in a blender until smooth. Pass the soup through a medium-fine–mesh sieve and transfer to a clean pot. Bring the soup back up to a simmer, whisk in the crème fraîche, and season to taste with salt and pepper. Keep hot.

2. Heat ½ inch of canola oil in a 1-quart pot over medium-high heat. Add the celery leaves and cook until crisp, 1 to 2 minutes. Using a slotted spoon, transfer the celery leaves to a plate lined with paper towels.

3. Ladle the soup into bowls and top with the celery leaves.
—*Melissa Pellegrino*

PER SERVING: 170 CALORIES | 7G PROTEIN | 15G CARB | 10G TOTAL FAT | 4.5G SAT FAT | 4G MONO FAT | 1.5G POLY FAT | 15MG CHOL | 330MG SODIUM | 3G FIBER

More about Celery Root

Celery root, also called celeriac, looks like a hairy softball and tastes like a cross between celery and parsley. Try it diced, shredded, or julienned in salads or add it to a soup or stew or to a creamy gratin.

Buying

Choose celery root about the size of a baseball; larger ones can be woody or spongy inside. It should be firm and heavy with no signs of sprouting or shriveling. If its parsley-like leaves are still attached, they should look fresh, not wilted.

Storing

Keep celery root in a dry, cool, dark place for 8 to 12 days; after that it will start to deteriorate.

Prepping

Cut off any leaves and the top and bottom of the root and then slice away the knobby skin until the inner white part of the root appears. Like a potato, peeled celery root turns brown, so drop it in a bowl of cold water or wait to peel until just before you need it.

creamy chickpea soup with crisp chorizo

**MAKES ABOUT 6 CUPS;
SERVES 4**

- **1** **cup dried chickpeas, picked over and rinsed**
- **3** **Tbs. extra-virgin olive oil**
- **1** **yellow onion, diced**
- **1** **medium carrot, peeled and diced**
- **1** **inner rib celery, diced**
- **Kosher salt**
- **1** **clove garlic, minced**
- **2** **tsp. chopped fresh thyme**
- **Freshly ground black pepper**
- **¼** **cup heavy cream**
- **1** **Tbs. sherry vinegar; more as needed**
- **10** **oz. chorizo, cut into ½-inch dice**
- **3** **Tbs. thinly sliced fresh chives**

Puréeing this soup completely gives it a smooth, elegant edge. To add a bit of substance, pureé only a portion of the soup.

1. Cook the chickpeas following the Basic Beans method at right. Be sure they're completely tender; chickpeas take longer to cook than most beans.

2. Heat 1½ Tbs. of the oil in a large saucepan over medium-high heat for 30 seconds. Add the onion, carrot, and celery, season with salt, and cook, stirring occasionally, until the vegetables soften and start to brown, about 7 minutes. Add the garlic and cook for 30 seconds, stirring. Add the chickpeas and their cooking liquid (there should be about 4 cups; if not, add more water to equal this amount) and half of the thyme. Season well with salt and pepper. Bring to a boil, reduce the heat to a bare simmer, and cook for 30 minutes so that the chickpeas soften a little more but don't break up. Working in batches, purée the chickpeas and broth in a blender. Return the puréed soup to the saucepan, stir in the cream, vinegar, and the remaining chopped thyme. Keep warm over low heat, stirring occasionally to prevent scorching. Taste for salt, pepper, and vinegar.

3. Set a large skillet over medium-high heat for 1 minute. Cook the chorizo in the remaining 1½ Tbs. oil until it's brown and crisp, about 8 minutes; reduce the heat if it starts to burn. With a slotted spoon, transfer half the chorizo to a paper-towel-lined plate and stir the rest into the soup. Reserve the cooking oil from the chorizo if you like.

4. Ladle the soup into shallow bowls. Sprinkle with the reserved chorizo and the chives and drizzle with a bit of the reserved chorizo oil, if you like. Serve immediately.   —*Tony Rosenfeld*

PER SERVING: 660 CALORIES | 29G PROTEIN | 36G CARB | 46G TOTAL FAT | 15G SAT FAT | 23G MONO FAT | 5G POLY FAT | 85MG CHOL | 1,140MG SODIUM | 10G FIBER

basic beans

1 CUP DRIED BEANS MAKES ABOUT 3 CUPS COOKED

2   **bay leaves**

2   **cloves garlic, smashed**

2   **to 3 sprigs fresh herbs (such as rosemary, thyme, or flat-leaf parsley)**

1   **to 1½ cups dried beans, picked over and rinsed**

   Kosher salt

1. Wrap the bay leaves, garlic, and herbs in cheesecloth and tie with twine. Put the beans in a large pot and cover with water by 2 inches (about 2 quarts). Add the herb bundle and 1 tsp. salt. Bring to a boil over high heat. Lower the heat to maintain a very gentle simmer, cover, and cook until the beans are tender (try biting into one) but not splitting and falling apart, 1 to 2 hours depending on the type of bean (check occasionally to be sure the beans aren't boiling and are covered with liquid; add water if needed). Discard the herb bundle.

2. Add the beans and their cooking liquid immediately to your soup recipe, or let the beans cool in the liquid and refrigerate for up to 3 days.

More about Chorizo

The word "chorizo" refers to two rather different pork sausages: Spanish chorizo is a hard, dry-cured sausage spiced with pimentón and garlic. Since it's cured, it's ready to eat without further cooking, and it adds a meaty note to stews, pastas, and eggs. Mexican chorizo is a fresh sausage, often sold in bulk rather than in links.

Don't substitute Spanish chorizo for Mexican or vice-versa. A better substitute for Spanish chorizo is another spicy dry-cured sausage; for Mexican, try hot Italian sausage.

If you're not sure whether you're buying Spanish or Mexican chorizo, note its position in the store. If it's in the cheese or deli case, it's probably cured, ready-to-eat Spanish chorizo. If it's in the meat case, it's probably meant to be cooked. If there are cooking instructions on the label, it's likely that it shouldn't be eaten raw.

classic tomato soup

MAKES ABOUT 8 CUPS;
SERVES 8

- **2 Tbs. extra-virgin olive oil**
- **1 Tbs. unsalted butter**
- **1 large white onion, finely chopped**
- **1 large clove garlic, smashed and peeled**
- **2 Tbs. unbleached all-purpose flour**
- **3 cups homemade or lower-salt chicken broth**
- **1 28-oz. can whole peeled plum tomatoes, with their liquid, puréed**
- **1½ tsp. granulated sugar**
- **1 sprig fresh thyme**
- **Kosher salt and freshly ground black pepper**
- **3 Tbs. thinly sliced fresh basil, chives, or dill, or a mixture of all three (omit if using one of the garnishes in the sidebar at right)**

Silky tomato soup is like the little black dress of soups. Unadorned and paired with a grilled cheese sandwich, it's a comforting lunch. Dressed up with simple garnishes, it makes a sophisticated start to a dinner party.

1. In a 5- to 6-quart Dutch oven, heat the oil and butter over medium-low heat until the butter melts. Add the onion and garlic and cook, stirring occasionally, until soft but not browned, about 8 minutes. Add the flour and stir to coat the onion and garlic.

2. Add the broth, tomatoes, sugar, thyme, and ¼ tsp. each salt and pepper. Bring to a simmer over medium-high heat while stirring the mixture to make sure that the flour doesn't stick to the bottom of the pan. Reduce the heat to low, cover, and simmer for 40 minutes.

3. Discard the thyme sprig. Let the soup cool briefly and then purée in batches in a blender or food processor. Rinse the pot and return the soup to the pot. Season to taste with salt and pepper. Reheat if necessary. Serve warm but not hot, garnished with the herbs or dolloped with one of the garnishes in the sidebar below. *—Perla Meyers*

PER SERVING: 110 CALORIES | 3G PROTEIN | 11G CARB | 5G TOTAL FAT | 1.5G SAT FAT | 3G MONO FAT | 0.5G POLY FAT | 5MG CHOL | 430MG SODIUM | 2G FIBER

Garnishes

Try one of these in place of the herbs.

Sour cream, goat cheese & Parmesan
In a small bowl, combine ½ cup sour cream with ¼ cup crumbled goat cheese. Add 1 Tbs. freshly grated Parmigiano-Reggiano, 1 Tbs. thinly sliced chives, and 1 Tbs. extra-virgin olive oil. Mix thoroughly and season to taste with kosher salt and freshly ground black pepper. Add a dollop to each serving.

Crème fraîche, herb & horseradish garnish
In a small bowl, combine ½ cup crème fraîche with 1 Tbs. minced fresh dill and 1 Tbs. minced scallion. Add ½ Tbs. well-drained prepared white horseradish and mix well. Season to taste with kosher salt and freshly ground black pepper. Add a dollop to each serving.

Make Ahead

This soup stores beautifully and tastes better the second day. You can keep it in the refrigerator for a few days or freeze for up to 3 months.

chestnut soup with crisp prosciutto

MAKES ABOUT 10 CUPS; SERVES 8 TO 10

- **3** lb. fresh chestnuts
- **2** Tbs. unsalted butter
- **2** Tbs. plus 1 tsp. extra-virgin olive oil
- **4** medium leeks (white and light green parts only), halved lengthwise, rinsed, and thinly sliced crosswise
- **1½** Tbs. chopped fresh thyme; more for garnish
- **10** cups homemade or lower-salt chicken broth

  Kosher salt and freshly ground black pepper
- **2** oz. thinly sliced prosciutto, cut into thin strips

For an ultrasilky texture, use a regular blender rather than a hand blender to purée the soup.

1. Position a rack in the center of the oven and heat the oven to 400°F. In a medium bowl, cover the chestnuts with warm water and soak for 25 minutes. Drain and dry with paper towels. Score an X into the flat side of each chestnut, cutting all the way through the shell. Put them flat side up on a rimmed baking sheet and roast until the Xs curl back into a crown shape and the chestnuts are tender when squeezed, about 30 minutes. Peel while still warm, removing both the shell and the inner skin. If a shell resists peeling, spoon out the nutmeat instead. Roughly chop the chestnuts and set aside in a medium bowl.

2. In a 6-quart pot, melt the butter with 2 Tbs. of oil over medium-low heat. Add the leeks and cook, stirring occasionally, until softened, 7 to 8 minutes. Add the chestnuts and 1 Tbs. of the thyme; cook until fragrant, about 1 minute. Add the broth and ½ tsp. salt; bring to a boil over medium-high heat. Reduce the heat to low and simmer until the chestnuts are extremely tender, about 30 minutes, skimming off any foam that rises to the surface. Let cool briefly. Working in batches, purée the soup, either in a regular blender or with a hand blender. Strain the soup through a fine-mesh sieve into a clean 4-quart pot. Set the soup back over medium-low heat and gently reheat. Season to taste with salt and pepper.

3. Meanwhile, in an 8-inch nonstick skillet, heat the remaining 1 tsp. oil over medium heat. Add the prosciutto and cook, stirring frequently, until crisp, 2 to 3 minutes. Add the remaining ½ Tbs. thyme and cook for another 30 seconds. Drain on a paper-towel-lined plate.

4. Ladle the soup into bowls and garnish with some of the prosciutto and thyme. —*Melissa Pellegrino*

PER SERVING: 330 CALORIES | 10G PROTEIN | 54G CARB | 10G TOTAL FAT | 3G SAT FAT | 4G MONO FAT | 1.5G POLY FAT | 10MG CHOL | 290MG SODIUM | 5G FIBER

More about Chestnuts

The aroma of chestnuts roasting (preferably over an open fire) signals a delicious beginning to the cold-weather months. These hearty brown tree nuts, which are available only from late fall through winter, are like no other nut—they're slightly sweet, with a deep, rich flavor and a dense, starchy texture.

Chestnut trees *(Castanea sativa)* are found in many countries, including China, Italy, Spain, Japan, and the United States. On the tree, the chestnuts are contained in a sharp, spiky husk, or burr, which can hold up to seven nuts at a time. Each chestnut has a hard brown outer shell and a bitter inner skin that must be removed before eating. Low in fat, chestnuts are also an excellent source of fiber and vitamin C. Because they contain twice as much starch as a potato, they're used in Asia, Africa, and parts of Europe as a primary source of carbohydrates.

Buying and storing

Look for chestnuts that are plump, firm, glossy, and heavy for their size. Avoid those with bruises or cracks and those that rattle when you shake them, which means they have begun to dry out. Store them in a sealed plastic bag in the refrigerator for up to 2 weeks, or freeze them for up to 3 months.

Cooking

Never eat fresh chestnuts raw—they're very tannic and tart, and their shells are almost impossible to remove. To eat or cook with a chestnut, you must first peel the shell and remove the inner skin. This is usually done by boiling or roasting. Boiling chestnuts mellows them, so use this method if you want to pair them with other flavors. Roasting yields a concentrated flavor, so use this method if you want to eat the chestnuts alone or if they're meant to be the star of a finished dish.

To boil chestnuts, use a sharp paring knife to score an X on the flat side of each nut. Bring them to a boil in a pot of cold water, boil until they're tender when squeezed (or poke them with a skewer, if you like), about 15 minutes, and then drain. When they're cool enough to handle (but still warm), peel the shells and inner skin.

To roast chestnuts, follow the method described in the recipe for the soup. After peeling the chestnuts, you can eat them or cook with them. Chestnuts pair well with cabbage, mushrooms, carrots, sage, and pork in savory preparations, and with apples, cream, dried fruit, and chocolate in sweet dishes.

cheddar and cauliflower soup

**MAKES 8 CUPS;
SERVES 6 TO 8**

Kosher salt

½ **head cauliflower
(about 1 lb.), cored and
cut into 1½-inch florets**

2 **Tbs. unsalted butter**

1 **medium yellow onion, small
diced**

1 **medium clove garlic, minced**

2 **Tbs. unbleached
all-purpose flour**

¼ **tsp. packed freshly grated
nutmeg**

⅛ **tsp. cayenne**

2 **cups homemade or lower-
salt chicken broth**

½ **cup heavy cream**

3 **sprigs fresh thyme**

4 **cups grated sharp or extra-
sharp white Cheddar (about
14 oz.)**

Freshly ground black pepper

*To dress up this rustic soup for a special occasion, garnish with a
combination of 3 Tbs. toasted chopped walnuts, 1 Tbs. chopped fresh
parsley, and 1½ tsp. finely grated lemon zest.*

1. Bring a large pot of salted water to a boil. Boil the cauliflower until
tender, about 4 minutes. Drain and let cool slightly. Trim the stems
from 18 of the cauliflower pieces and cut the crowns into mini florets
about ½ inch wide; set aside. Reserve the trimmed stems with the
remaining larger pieces.

2. Melt the butter in a 4-quart saucepan over medium-low heat. Add
the onion and ¼ tsp. salt and cook, stirring frequently, until soft, 10 to
12 minutes.

3. Add the garlic and cook until the aroma subsides, 2 to 3 minutes.
Increase the heat to medium, add the flour, nutmeg, and cayenne and
cook for 3 minutes, stirring constantly. Whisk in the broth, cream, and
2 cups water. Add the thyme and bring to a simmer. Stir in the cheese
until melted and simmer for 5 minutes to develop the flavors.

4. Remove and discard the thyme stems and stir in the larger cauliflower pieces and reserved stems. Working in batches, purée the soup
in a blender. Return the soup to the pot and season with salt and pepper to taste. Add the mini cauliflower florets and reheat gently before
serving. *—Allison Ehri Kreitler*

PER SERVING: 340 CALORIES | 17G PROTEIN | 7G CARB, 28G TOTAL FAT | 17G SAT FAT |
8G MONO FAT | 1G POLY FAT | 90MG CHOL | 540MG SODIUM | 2G FIBER

cauliflower soup with marcona almond and piquillo pepper relish

SERVES 8

Kosher salt

1¾ lb. (6 to 7 cups) cauliflower florets (from 1 medium head)

4 Tbs. unsalted butter

¼ cup Marcona or regular almonds (roasted and salted), finely chopped

¼ cup jarred piquillo peppers or roasted red peppers, rinsed, seeded, and finely diced

2 Tbs. extra-virgin olive oil

1 Tbs. thinly sliced fresh mint

1 medium clove garlic, minced

½ tsp. crushed red pepper flakes

Freshly ground black pepper

If you can find it, use orange cauliflower; it won't change the soup's flavor but will give it a lovely golden color.

1. Bring 6 cups water to a boil in a 4-quart pot over high heat. Add 1 tsp. salt, then add the cauliflower and boil until very tender, 10 to 12 minutes. Drain the cauliflower in a colander set over a large bowl to catch the cooking liquid and let the cauliflower cool slightly.

2. Working in 2 batches, carefully purée each batch of cauliflower with 2 cups of the cooking liquid and 2 Tbs. of the butter in a blender until very smooth. Season to taste with salt. (The soup can be made up to 4 hours ahead.)

3. In a small bowl, combine the almonds, piquillo peppers, oil, mint, garlic, and red pepper flakes. Season to taste with salt and black pepper. (The relish can be made up to 1 hour ahead.)

4. When ready to serve, gently reheat the soup over medium-low heat. Garnish each serving with a spoonful of the almond relish.
—*Nancy Oakes*

PER SERVING: 140 CALORIES | 3G PROTEIN | 7G CARB | 12G TOTAL FAT | 4.5G SAT FAT | 5G MONO FAT | 1.5G POLY FAT | 15MG CHOL | 460MG SODIUM | 3G FIBER

carrot and coriander soup

- **6** Tbs. unsalted butter
- **2** yellow onions, thinly sliced
- **3** lb. carrots, peeled and cut into 1-inch pieces
- **1** bunch cilantro (about 3 oz.), roots attached, washed well; reserve a handful of leaves for garnish
- **1** fresh jalapeño, stemmed, halved, and seeded
- **1** Tbs. coriander seeds, ground

  Kosher salt

- **8** cups homemade or lower-salt chicken broth or water
- **½** cup crème fraîche or sour cream

If you can find cilantro with its roots attached, add the roots, well washed, to the soup for an even stronger cilantro flavor.

1. In a large saucepan, melt 4 Tbs. of the butter over medium-high heat. Add the onion and sauté until soft, about 5 minutes. Add the carrots, cilantro (except for the reserved leaves), jalapeño, ground coriander, and 1 tsp. salt. Continue to cook the vegetables for about 10 minutes, stirring occasionally. Add the broth and simmer until the vegetables are completely tender, about 35 minutes.

2. Carefully purée the soup in batches in a blender until smooth. (For less heat, remove one half of the jalapeño before puréeing.) Stir in the remaining 2 Tbs. butter and taste for seasoning. If the soup seems too thick, add a little water.

3. Ladle into bowls and garnish each serving with a drizzle of crème fraîche and the reserved cilantro leaves. —*Seen Lippert*

PER SERVING: 230 CALORIES, 5G PROTEIN | 21G CARB | 15G TOTAL FAT | 9G SAT FAT | 4G MONO FAT | 1G POLY FAT | 40MG CHOL | 390MG SODIUM | 6G FIBER

carrot-ginger soup

SERVES 8

2	Tbs. vegetable oil
½	cup medium-diced onion
⅓	cup thinly sliced leeks (white and light greens parts only), well washed
¼	cup thinly sliced celery (halve lengthwise then slice crosswise)
1	Tbs. minced fresh ginger
2	tsp. minced garlic
	Kosher salt
1¾	lb. carrots, peeled, halved (or quartered lengthwise if thick), and sliced ¼ inch thick
5	cups vegetable broth, preferably homemade
3	Tbs. orange juice
¼	cup plain thick whole yogurt, preferably Greek
½	tsp. fresh lime juice; more as needed
	Freshly ground black pepper
⅓	cup thinly sliced fresh chives

Tangy yogurt and lime juice give a little snap to the sweetness of the carrot purée in this creamy soup.

1. In a 4- to 5-quart saucepan or Dutch oven, heat the vegetable oil over medium-low heat. When hot, add the onion, leeks, celery, ginger, garlic, and a pinch of salt. Stir well, cover, reduce the heat to low, and cook, stirring occasionally, until the aromatics are softened, 8 to 10 minutes. Stir in 1 tsp. salt.

2. Add the carrots, vegetable broth, and orange juice, stir well, and bring to a simmer over medium heat. Cook, uncovered, stirring occasionally, until the vegetables are very tender and the soup is full-flavored, 7 to 20 minutes.

3. Take the pan off the heat and let the soup cool for 5 minutes. Working in batches, pureé the soup in a blender (fill the jar no more than half full and vent the lid, topping it with a folded kitchen towel to prevent hot splashes). Wipe the pan clean and pour the soup back into the pan.

4. Add the yogurt and lime juice. Season the soup with salt and pepper. Taste and adjust the seasonings with more salt, pepper, or lime juice as needed.

5. Ladle into 8 soup bowls and garnish each serving with 1 to 2 tsp. of the chopped chives. —*Susie Middleton*

PER SERVING: 90 CALORIES | 1G PROTEIN | 13G CARB | 3.5G TOTAL FAT | 1.5G SAT FAT | 1.5G MONO FAT | 0G POLY FAT | 5MG CHOL | 310MG SODIUM | 3G FIBER

carrot and leek soup with herbed croutons

SERVES 6

- 6 Tbs. unsalted butter
- 1 medium yellow onion, chopped
- 2 small leeks (white and light green parts only), sliced and well washed
- 2 large cloves garlic, chopped

   Kosher salt and freshly ground black pepper
- 3 cups homemade or lower-salt chicken broth
- 2 lb. carrots, peeled and sliced ¼ inch thick
- 3 fresh or 2 dried bay leaves
- 2 sprigs fresh thyme
- 4 oz. crusty bread, cut into ½-inch cubes (2 cups)
- 1½ Tbs. chopped fresh chervil
- 1 cup plain full-fat or low-fat yogurt

Adding yogurt to the soup makes it smooth and creamy. If you can't find chervil (a relative of the carrot), use dill instead.

1. Position a rack in the center of the oven and heat the oven to 350°F.

2. In a 4- to 5-quart saucepan, melt 3 Tbs. of the butter over medium heat. Add the onion, leeks, garlic, ½ tsp. salt, and ¼ tsp. pepper; cook until the aromatics are softened and light golden brown, about 10 minutes. Add the broth, carrots, bay leaves, thyme sprigs, and ½ cup water; bring to a boil over medium-high heat. Reduce the heat to medium and simmer until the carrots are tender, about 15 minutes.

3. Meanwhile, melt the remaining 3 Tbs. butter in a 3-quart saucepan over medium heat. Add the bread cubes and chopped chervil and toss to coat evenly. Spread on a rimmed baking sheet, season with salt, and bake until golden, 8 to 10 minutes.

4. When the vegetables are tender, discard the bay leaves and thyme sprigs. With a regular or hand blender, purée the soup (work in batches if using a stand blender). Stir in the yogurt. If you prefer a thinner texture, add a little water. Season to taste with salt and pepper, and serve garnished with the chervil croutons. *—Samantha Seneviratne*

PER SERVING: 290 CALORIES | 8G PROTEIN | 34G CARB | 15G TOTAL FAT | 8G SAT FAT | 3.5G MONO FAT | 1G POLY FAT | 35MG CHOL | 360MG SODIUM | 6G FIBER

butternut squash soup with garam masala, yogurt & lime

- 2 **Tbs. unsalted butter**
- ½ **cup finely chopped shallot**
- ½ **cup thinly sliced leeks (white and light green parts only), well washed**
- ¼ **cup thinly sliced celery (halve lengthwise then slice crosswise)**
- 2 **tsp. minced garlic**

 Kosher salt

- 1 **tsp. garam masala**
- 2 **lb. butternut squash, peeled, seeded, and cut into ½-inch dice**
- 5 **cups homemade or lower-salt vegetable or chicken broth**
- 3 **Tbs. apple cider**
- ¼ **cup plain thick whole-milk yogurt, preferably Greek**
- 1½ **tsp. fresh lime juice**

 Freshly ground black pepper

- ⅓ **cup chopped fresh cilantro**

Indian flavors meet creamy classic butternut squash soup. The yogurt and lime add an unexpected tang to the silky soup.

1. In a 4- to 5-quart saucepan or Dutch oven, heat the butter over medium-low heat. When hot, add the shallot, leeks, celery, garlic, and a pinch of salt. Stir well, cover, reduce the heat to low, and cook, stirring occasionally, until the aromatics are softened, 8 to 10 minutes. Stir in 1 tsp. salt and the garam masala.

2. Add the butternut squash, vegetable broth, and cider, stir well, and bring to a simmer over medium heat. Cook, uncovered, stirring occasionally, until the vegetables are very tender and the soup is full-flavored, 7 to 20 minutes. Take the pan off the heat and let the soup cool for 5 minutes.

3. Working in batches, pureé the soup in a blender (fill the jar no more than half full and vent the lid, topping it with a folded kitchen towel to prevent hot splashes). Wipe the pan clean and put the soup back into the pan.

4. Add the yogurt and ½ tsp. of the lime juice and season with salt and pepper. Taste the soup and adjust the seasonings with more salt, pepper, or lime juice as needed.

5. Ladle into soup bowls and garnish each serving with 1 to 2 tsp. of the chopped cilantro. —*Susie Middleton*

PER SERVING: 80 CALORIES | 1G PROTEIN | 13G CARB | 3.5G TOTAL FAT | 1.5G SAT FAT | 1.5G MONO FAT | 0G POLY FAT | 5MG CHOL | 260MG SODIUM | 2G FIBER

butternut squash soup with cumin and coriander

MAKES ABOUT 6 CUPS; SERVES 6

- 2 Tbs. extra-virgin olive oil
- 1 Tbs. unsalted butter
- 1 medium onion, diced

  Kosher salt
- ¾ tsp. ground cumin
- ½ tsp. ground coriander
- 1 14½-oz. can diced tomatoes, with their liquid

  Freshly ground black pepper

  Flesh of a roasted 2-lb. butternut squash (see the recipe below)
- 3 cups homemade or lower-salt chicken broth
- 1 Tbs. plain yogurt or heavy cream per serving, for garnish
- 1 Tbs. minced fresh flat-leaf parsley, for garnish

Roasting concentrates the best flavors in squash and turns it into a delicious ingredient to be used in other dishes, like this soup.

1. Heat the oil and butter in a heavy soup pot set over medium heat. Add the onion and ½ tsp. salt and sauté for 2 minutes, then cover and let sweat until translucent, about 3 minutes. Uncover and cook, stirring occasionally, until the onion begins to brown, 3 to 5 minutes. Add the cumin and coriander and cook, stirring, until very fragrant, about 30 seconds. Stir in the tomatoes and their liquid, season with a few grinds of pepper, and cook for 2 minutes. Cover and simmer for another 10 minutes.

2. Peel the roasted squash and add the flesh to the pot, breaking it up with a wooden spoon. Add the chicken broth, cover, and bring to a simmer. Adjust the heat to maintain a simmer and cook, covered, for 30 minutes. Let cool slightly.

3. Purée in small batches in a blender or a food processor (don't fill the jar more than half full and vent the lid, holding a folded dishtowel over it to prevent splashes). Taste and add more salt and pepper if needed. Return the soup to the pot and stir occasionally over low heat until hot.

4. Garnish each serving with a spoonful of yogurt or a drizzle of cream and a sprinkling of the minced parsley. —*Ruth Lively*

PER SERVING: 170 CALORIES | 4G PROTEIN | 21G CARB | 9G TOTAL FAT | 2G SAT FAT | 5G MONO FAT | 1G POLY FAT | 5MG CHOL | 520MG SODIUM | 5G FIBER

roasted butternut squash

MAKES 1¾ CUPS CHUNKS OR 1⅓ CUPS MASHED

- 1 2-lb. butternut squash

  Olive oil

  Kosher salt and freshly ground black pepper

Heat the oven to 400°F. Cut the squash in half lengthwise. Use a soupspoon to scoop out the seeds and scrape out the strings from the hollow. Rub the cut surfaces with oil, season generously with salt and pepper, and roast on a parchment- or foil-lined baking sheet, cut side up, until deeply browned and very tender, 80 to 90 minutes. Let cool before using in other recipes, or cover and refrigerate for up to 2 days.

butternut squash soup with apple and bacon

- **8** slices bacon, cut crosswise into ¼-inch strips
- **2½** lb. butternut squash (about 1 medium), peeled, seeded, and cut into ½-inch dice (to yield about 6 cups)
- **1** small Granny Smith or other tart-sweet apple, peeled, cored, and cut into ½-inch dice (to yield about 1 cup)
- **1½** Tbs. finely chopped fresh sage leaves

  Kosher salt and freshly ground black pepper
- **4** cups homemade or lower-salt chicken or vegetable broth

Smoky bacon, herby sage, and sweet apple give this squash soup layers of flavor.

1. In a 5-quart or larger stockpot set over medium heat, cook the bacon, stirring occasionally, until crisp and golden, 8 to 10 minutes. Use a slotted spoon to transfer the bacon to a paper-towel-lined plate.

2. Increase the heat to medium high. Add the squash to the pot with the bacon fat and cook until lightly browned, 4 to 6 minutes (resist the urge to stir it too often or it won't brown). Stir in the apple, sage, 1 tsp. salt, and ½ tsp. pepper and cook for about 4 minutes (you'll see more browning occur on the bottom of the pot than on the vegetables). Add the broth, scraping up any browned bits in the pot with a wooden spoon. Bring to a boil over high heat, reduce the heat to maintain a simmer, and cook until the squash and apples are very soft, 6 to 8 minutes. Remove from the heat and let cool somewhat.

3. Add about half the bacon to the soup and purée, using a stand or immersion blender (you'll need to work in batches if using a stand blender; vent the top and hold a folded dishtowel over the lid). Taste and add more salt and pepper if needed. Reheat the soup and garnish each serving with the remaining bacon. *—Jill Silverman Hough*

PER SERVING: 130 CALORIES | 7G PROTEIN | 19G CARB | 4G TOTAL FAT | 1.5G SAT FAT | 1.5G MONO FAT | 0.5G POLY FAT | 10MG CHOL | 370MG SODIUM | 4G FIBER

wild mushroom soup with sherry and thyme

MAKES ABOUT 5½ CUPS; SERVES 6

- 2 Tbs. unsalted butter
- 2 Tbs. olive oil
- 1 medium onion, cut into medium dice (to yield about 1½ cups)
- 4 cloves garlic, minced
- ¾ lb. fresh wild mushrooms, wiped clean, trimmed (stems removed from shiitake), and thinly sliced (to yield about 4½ cups)
- 2 Tbs. plus 1 tsp. fresh thyme leaves
  Kosher salt and freshly ground black pepper
- 4 cups homemade or lower-salt chicken or vegetable broth
- ¼ cup half-and-half
- 3 Tbs. dry sherry
- 1 Tbs. soy sauce

If you like, drizzle on a bit of white truffle oil just before serving to make this soup especially fragrant and luxurious. For the mushrooms, try a mix of half chanterelles or cremini and half shiitake.

1. Melt the butter and olive oil in a 5-quart or larger stockpot over medium-high heat. Add the onion and cook until it's beginning to brown (resist the urge to stir too often), about 4 minutes. Stir in the garlic and cook for 1 minute. Add the mushrooms, 2 Tbs. of the thyme, and ½ tsp. each salt and pepper; cook until the mushrooms become limp, 2 to 4 minutes.

2. Add the broth, scraping up any browned bits in the pot with a wooden spoon. Bring to a boil over high heat, reduce the heat to maintain a simmer, and cook until the mushrooms are tender, 7 to 10 minutes. Remove from the heat and let cool slightly.

3. Transfer about half of the soup to a stand blender and process until smooth (vent the lid and hold a folded dishtowel over the top to prevent splashes). Return the mixture to the pot and stir in the half-and-half, sherry, and soy sauce. Add more salt and pepper to taste, if needed, and reheat. Garnish each serving with a small pinch of the remaining 1 tsp. thyme. *—Jill Silverman Hough*

PER SERVING: 160 CALORIES | 5G PROTEIN | 14G CARB | 11G TOTAL FAT | 4G SAT FAT | 5G MONO FAT | 1G POLY FAT | 15MG CHOL | 370MG SODIUM | 2G FIBER

baked potato and leek soup with cheddar and bacon

YIELDS ABOUT 6 CUPS; SERVES 4

- 2 **medium russet potatoes (about ½ lb. each)**
- ¼ **cup unsalted butter**
- 2½ **cups sliced leeks (about 2 medium leeks; white and light green parts only), well washed**
- 2 **medium cloves garlic, minced**
- **Kosher salt**
- 2 **cups homemade or lower-salt chicken broth**
- 4 **thick slices bacon, cut into ½-inch dice**
- ½ **cup milk**
- ½ **cup sour cream**
- 1 **cup grated sharp Cheddar (about ¼ lb.)**
- **Freshly ground black pepper**
- 2 **Tbs. thinly sliced scallion greens or chives**

Russets work for this soup since you'll be pureéing it. Don't use russets in any soup where you want the potatoes to stay in small chunks.

1. Heat the oven to 375°F. Scrub the potatoes in water, pat dry, and pierce in several places with a fork. Set them directly on an oven rack and bake until very tender when pierced with a fork, about 1 hour. Let cool completely on a wire rack.

2. Melt the butter in a soup pot over medium-low heat. Add the leeks and garlic, season with salt, and cook, stirring occasionally, until softened, about 10 minutes. Add the broth and 2 cups water. Bring to a simmer over medium heat and cook until the leeks are very tender, about 20 minutes.

3. Meanwhile, put the bacon in a skillet and cook over medium heat, stirring occasionally, until browned and crisp, 8 to 10 minutes. Transfer the bacon bits with a slotted spoon to a saucer lined with paper towels to drain and cool.

4. When the potatoes are cool, cut one of them in half lengthwise. Use a large spoon to scoop the flesh in one piece from each half. Cut the flesh into ½-inch cubes and set aside. Coarsely chop the potato skin and the entire remaining potato and add to the pot with the leeks. Purée the contents of the pot in a blender until very smooth (you'll need to work in batches). Return the puréed soup to a clean soup pot and reheat over medium low. Whisk the milk and sour cream until smooth and then whisk this into the soup, along with ½ cup of the Cheddar. Stir in the diced potato. The soup should be fairly thick, but if it seems too thick, thin it with a little water. Season to taste with salt and pepper. Serve garnished with the remaining Cheddar, the bacon bits, and the scallions or chives. —*Jennifer Armentrout*

When Is Sharp Cheese Extra Sharp?

Cheeses vary in degree of sharpness, some seeming more like a mild Cheddar than a sharp. As it turns out, there are no federal standards for how to define the degree of sharpness in a Cheddar. The manufacturer ages it anywhere from 5 to 8 months.

Cheddar is traditionally made by packing coagulated milk curds into slabs, then stacking and turning them repeatedly to expel as much liquid (whey) as possible (a process known as "cheddaring"). Most mass-market American brands stir the curds, press out the whey in machine-operated vats, and age the cheese in plastic. The result is often a less complex tasting, more homogeneously textured cheese.

broccoli soup with bacon

- 2 Tbs. extra-virgin olive oil
- ⅔ cup medium-diced onion
- ⅔ cup thinly sliced leeks (white and light green parts only), well washed
- 2 tsp. minced garlic
-    Kosher salt
- 1¾ lb. broccoli, bottom of stems trimmed, florets coarsely chopped, stems sliced very thinly
- 2½ cups homemade or lower-salt chicken broth
- 3 Tbs. dry white wine
- ¼ cup heavy cream
- ½ tsp. fresh lemon juice; more as needed
-    Freshly ground black pepper
- ⅓ cup crumbled cooked bacon

The textural contrast of crisp bacon against the creamy pureé of broccoli, leeks, and onion really makes this soup shine.

1. In a 4- to 5-quart saucepan or Dutch oven, heat the olive oil over medium-low heat. When hot, add the onion, leeks, garlic, and a pinch of salt. Stir well, cover, reduce the heat to low, and cook, stirring occasionally, until the aromatics are softened, 8 to 10 minutes. Stir in 1 tsp. salt.

2. Add the broccoli, chicken broth, wine, and 2½ cups water. Stir well and bring to a simmer over medium heat. Cook, uncovered, stirring occasionally, until the vegetables are very tender and the soup is full-flavored, 7 to 20 minutes. Take the pan off the heat and let the soup cool for 5 minutes.

3. Working in batches, pureé the soup in a blender (fill the jar no more than half full and vent the lid, topping it with a folded kitchen towel to prevent hot splashes). Wipe the pan clean and put the soup back into the pan.

4. Add the cream and lemon juice and season with salt and pepper. Taste and add more salt, pepper, or lemon juice as needed. Ladle into soup bowls and garnish each serving with 2 tsp. crumbled bacon.
—*Susie Middleton*

PER SERVING: 120 CALORIES | 6G PROTEIN | 9G CARB | 7G TOTAL FAT | 3.5G SAT FAT | 3G MONO FAT | 0.5G POLY FAT | 15MG CHOL | 300MG SODIUM | 3G FIBER

buttercup squash and leek soup with herb butter

MAKES 12 CUPS; SERVES 12 AS A FIRST COURSE

FOR THE HERB BUTTER

- 1 shallot, finely chopped (about 2 Tbs.)
- ½ cup dry sherry
- ½ lb. (1 cup) unsalted butter, at room temperature
- 2 Tbs. chopped fresh chives
- 1 tsp. kosher salt
- ¼ tsp. ground white pepper; more to taste

FOR THE SOUP

- 4 cups chopped, well-washed leeks (white and light green parts only; about 3 large)
- 8 cups peeled, seeded, and diced (1-inch cubes) buttercup squash (about 3 medium)
- ½ cup dry white wine
- 6 cups homemade or lower-salt chicken broth
-   Kosher salt
- 1 tsp. ground white pepper; up to another 2 tsp. more as needed to taste
-   Chopped fresh chives, for garnish

The earthy flavor of buttercup squash is particularly nice, but you can substitute butternut.

MAKE THE HERB BUTTER

1. Heat a small nonstick sauté pan over medium heat. When hot, add the shallots and heat to release their aroma and lightly toast them, about 30 seconds. Remove from the heat and add the sherry. Set the pan back on the heat and reduce the liquid to 2 Tbs., about 8 minutes. Let cool.

2. In a small bowl, blend the butter, chives, sherry-shallot mixture, salt, and white pepper. Line a baking sheet with parchment or waxed paper and spread the butter ¼ inch thick to cover about 8x6 inches. Cover and chill.

3. With a small cookie cutter or a knife, cut out 12 small shapes; freeze the remainder. If not using right away, wrap the shapes in plastic and freeze for up to 2 weeks.

MAKE THE SOUP

1. Put the leeks in a heavy 8-quart stockpot. Put the squash over the leeks; add the wine and broth. Cover and bring to a boil. Reduce to a simmer and cook until the squash is fork-tender, about 25 minutes. Let cool for 15 minutes.

2. Add 1 Tbs. salt and the white pepper; purée in batches in a blender or food processor. Cover and freeze (or refrigerate for up to 3 days).

TO SERVE

Thaw the herb butter shapes if they've been frozen. Reheat the soup over low to medium heat, stirring frequently. Ladle the hot soup into shallow bowls and garnish with the herb butter shapes and the chives.

—Michael Brisson

PER SERVING: 150 CALORIES | 3G PROTEIN | 16G CARB | 8G TOTAL FAT | 5G SAT FAT | 2G MONO FAT | 0G POLY FAT | 20MG CHOL | 160MG SODIUM | 4G FIBER

grilled yellow tomato bisque
(recipe on p. 69)

bisques & chowders

creamy seafood chowder with bacon, thyme & jalapeño

SERVES 4

- **4** slices bacon, cut crosswise into ¼-inch strips
- **1** medium shallot, minced
- **1** large jalapeño, seeded and very finely chopped (about 2 Tbs.)
- **2** Tbs. unbleached all-purpose flour
- **2** 6½-oz. cans chopped clams, clams and juice separated (about 1 cup juice)
- **2** 8-oz. bottles clam juice
- **1** cup heavy cream
- **8** to 10 oz. unpeeled red potatoes (about 2 medium), scrubbed and cut into ½-inch dice
- **½** tsp. dried thyme
- **¾** lb. skinless haddock or cod fillets

  Kosher salt and freshly ground black pepper

The quick-cooking fish and store-bought canned clams will speed up the time it takes to make this chowder. Because this dish doesn't get a lot of stove time to intensify flavor, the bright addition of jalapeño makes a big impact. The cream in the soup tempers most of the jalapeño's heat, but you can still taste its bright, fresh flavor.

1. In a heavy 4-quart saucepan or Dutch oven, cook the bacon over medium heat, stirring occasionally, until browned and crisp, about 8 minutes. Transfer the bacon to a small dish lined with paper towels, leaving the fat behind in the pan. Add the shallot and 1 Tbs. of the jalapeño to the bacon fat and cook over medium heat, stirring occasionally, until the shallot is softened, about 2 minutes. Add the flour and cook, stirring, for 1 minute. Gradually stir in all the clam juice (from the cans and the bottles). Add the cream, potatoes, and thyme, and bring to a simmer over medium-high heat, stirring occasionally. Reduce the heat as necessary and continue to simmer, stirring occasionally, until the potatoes are tender, about 10 minutes. Add the whole fish fillets and cook for 3 minutes. Stir in the clams and continue stirring until the fish has broken into chunks. Cook until the fish is cooked through and the clams are heated, about another 2 minutes. Season the soup to taste with salt and pepper.

2. Portion into soup bowls and sprinkle each serving with the reserved bacon and the remaining jalapeño. —*Joanne McAllister Smart*

PER SERVING: 310 CALORIES | 17G PROTEIN | 43G CARB | 9G TOTAL FAT | 4.5G SAT FAT | 2.5G MONO FAT | 1G POLY FAT | 35MG CHOL | 540MG SODIUM | 4G FIBER

grilled yellow tomato bisque

MAKES 8 CUPS; SERVES 6

8   large ripe yellow tomatoes
    (about 3½ lb. total)

1   Tbs. olive oil

1   medium-size red onion,
    chopped

1   quart homemade or lower-
    salt chicken broth

1   tsp. granulated sugar

1   cup heavy cream

    Kosher salt and freshly
    ground black pepper

¼   cup chopped fresh mint

This bisque can be made up to 2 days in advance. Although the yellow color is quite charming, red tomatoes can be substituted.

1. Prepare a grill by adjusting the grill grate so that it's 4 to 5 inches from the flame or heat source. Heat a gas grill to high and a charcoal grill to medium hot (the coals should be covered with light ash, and you should be able to hold your hand just over the grate for no more than 3 seconds). Put the whole tomatoes on the grate and grill, turning occasionally, until the skins crack and begin to blacken in some parts and the tomatoes soften, 7 to 9 minutes over charcoal, 12 to 15 minutes on a gas grill. Take them off the grill, core them, and coarsely chop them.

2. Heat the olive oil in a large soup pot over medium-high heat. Add the onion and cook, stirring occasionally, until soft, about 7 minutes. Stir in the chopped tomatoes, chicken broth, and sugar. Increase the heat, and bring to a boil, then turn the heat to medium, and simmer until the soup is reduced by one-quarter, about 20 minutes. Let cool for 10 minutes. In a blender, purée the soup in batches until smooth, 2 to 3 minutes per batch. Strain through a fine-mesh sieve, pressing on the solids, into a clean soup pot and bring to a simmer over medium heat. Turn off the heat and stir in the heavy cream. Taste and season with salt and pepper. Serve garnished with the chopped mint.
—Joanne Weir

PER SERVING: 220 CALORIES | 5G PROTEIN | 12G CARB | 18G TOTAL FAT | 10G SAT FAT | 6G MONO FAT | 1G POLY FAT | 55MG CHOL | 490MG SODIUM | 2G FIBER

lobster bisque

**MAKES ABOUT 6 CUPS;
SERVES 5 OR 6 AS A STARTER**

FOR THE BROTH

    Kosher salt

1 **1½- to 1¾-lb. live lobster,
rinsed**

1½ **oz. (3 Tbs.) unsalted butter**

FOR THE BISQUE

5 **Tbs. unsalted butter**

1 **medium yellow onion,
chopped**

1 **small carrot, peeled and
finely chopped**

1 **large clove garlic, finely
chopped**

¼ **cup unbleached
all-purpose flour**

1 **cup dry white wine**

2 **Tbs. tomato paste**

1 **Tbs. chopped fresh thyme**

1 **dried bay leaf**

1 **cup heavy cream**

2 **Tbs. cream sherry**

    **Kosher salt and freshly
ground black pepper**

*This is a classic soup for
a special occasion. Many
bisques call for upwards of
25 ingredients and a 2-day
cooking method. This stream-
lined version has far less fuss
and yields an opulent bisque
that will make any lobster
lover swoon. For richer flavor
and more intense color, use a
female lobster.*

MAKE THE BROTH

1. In an 8- to 10-quart stockpot, bring 1½ inches of water to a boil over
high heat. Add 1 tsp. salt and the lobster, cover, and steam until bright
red and one of the smaller legs twists off easily, about 18 minutes.
Remove the lobster with tongs and reserve the steaming liquid. When
the lobster is cool enough to handle, twist off the claws and the tail.
Using a nutcracker, crack the knuckles and claws and push out the
meat with your little finger or a pick. Set the tail on a hard surface and
use your hand to press down and crack the shell; push out the meat.
Slice the tail meat in half lengthwise and remove the black intestinal
vein. Dice the meat from one claw and half of the tail and set aside for
garnish. Coarsely chop the remaining meat. Reserve the shells. Rinse
out the tomalley (green matter) from the upper body. Split the body
lengthwise and use your fingers to remove the innards. (If the lobster
is female, you'll see bright-red roe; leave it in the body for additional
color and flavor.)

2. Use kitchen shears or a chef's knife to break the body and reserved
shells into 1- to 2-inch pieces and then use a meat mallet or a small
pot to flatten them.

3. Measure the steaming liquid and add water to total 6 cups of liquid.
Melt the butter in a 4-quart saucepan over medium heat. Add the flattened shells and cook, stirring occasionally, until they begin to blister
and their color intensifies, about 5 minutes. Add the liquid and ½ tsp.
salt and bring to a boil over high heat. Reduce the heat to medium low
and simmer, uncovered, for 30 minutes, skimming off any foam that
rises to the surface. Strain the broth through a fine-mesh sieve into a
large liquid measuring cup. You should have 4 cups—if there's more,
boil until reduced to 4 cups; if there's less, add water.

MAKE THE BISQUE

Clean and dry the saucepan and melt the butter in the pan over low heat. Add the onion, carrot, and garlic and cook until softened, about 15 minutes. Sprinkle in the flour and cook, stirring, until golden and bubbly, about 2 minutes. Add the wine, tomato paste, thyme, and bay leaf; bring to a boil, and cook, stirring, until the liquid is slightly reduced, about 3 minutes. Add the lobster broth and cook uncovered over medium heat until slightly reduced, about 5 minutes. Add the chopped lobster meat and simmer for 2 minutes to heat. Remove the bay leaf. In a blender, purée the mixture in batches until smooth. Strain through a medium-mesh sieve back into the pot, pushing on the solids with a wooden spoon. Stir in the cream and sherry, season to taste with salt and pepper, and cook the bisque over low heat until slightly thickened, about 10 minutes. Serve the bisque garnished with the diced lobster meat. —*Brooke Dojny*

PER SERVING: 470 CALORIES | 25G PROTEIN | 13G CARB | 32G TOTAL FAT | 19G SAT FAT | 9G MONO FAT | 2G POLY FAT | 170MG CHOL | 540MG SODIUM | 1G FIBER

Make Ahead

The bisque and lobster garnish can be refrigerated separately for up to 1 day. Reheat over medium-low heat before serving.

Tips for the Best Bisque

• **Add the steaming liquid to the broth.** The liquid that's left behind from steaming the lobster is full of flavor. Adding it to the broth makes the bisque that much more lobstery.

• **Thicken the bisque with flour.** Although classic bisques are thickened with rice, it gives the bisque a grainy texture. Instead, use flour, which produces a silky-smooth soup.

• **Sauté the shells before using them in the broth.** Cooking the empty lobster shells in butter teases additional flavor from them, which makes for a richer broth. Flattening them before cooking allows more of the shells' surface area to be in contact with the hot pan.

• **Use the lobster meat in the soup and for garnish.** Puréeing some of the meat into the bisque ups the lobster quotient; using diced lobster for garnish makes it extra luxurious.

• **Refrigerate the soup overnight for more intense flavor.** Although the bisque is delicious served immediately, letting it rest for several hours after cooking amplifies its lobster flavor and allows all of its ingredients to marry.

quick clam chowder with bacon, tomatoes & bell peppers

SERVES 4

2 oz. bacon (1 to 3 slices, depending on thickness), cut into ½-inch pieces

1 medium onion, diced

½ large red bell pepper, diced

3 Tbs. unbleached all-purpose flour

4 6½-oz. cans minced clams, clams and juice separated (about 1½ cups minced clams and 2¼ cups juice)

1 8-oz. bottle clam juice

1 14½-oz. can diced tomatoes, with their liquid

¾ lb. boiling potatoes (about 3 small potatoes), cut into medium dice

¼ tsp. dried thyme

2 Tbs. minced fresh flat-leaf parsley

Kosher salt and freshly ground black pepper

Bottled clam juice is the strained liquid of shucked, cooked clams, and its briny, salty flavor helps to flavor this chowder.

1. In a Dutch oven or a large saucepan, fry the bacon over medium heat until the fat renders and the bacon crisps, about 7 minutes. With a slotted spoon, transfer the bacon to a small bowl; set aside. Add the onion and bell pepper to the bacon drippings; sauté until softened, about 5 minutes. Add the flour and stir until lightly colored, about 1 minute. Gradually whisk in the clam juice (from the cans and the bottle) and ½ cup water and then add the tomatoes, potatoes, and thyme. Simmer until the potatoes are tender, about 10 minutes. Add the clams and parsley, season to taste with salt and pepper; and bring to a simmer.

2. Remove the pot from the heat, ladle the chowder into bowls, sprinkle with the reserved bacon, and serve. —*Pamela Anderson*

PER SERVING: 310 CALORIES | 22G PROTEIN | 34G CARB | 10G TOTAL FAT | 3G SAT FAT | 4G MONO FAT | 1G POLY FAT | 55MG CHOL | 880MG SODIUM | 2G FIBER

spicy corn chowder

SERVES 4

½ lb. thick-cut applewood-smoked bacon (6 slices), cut crosswise into ½-inch pieces

1 medium yellow onion, cut into ½-inch dice

3 scallions (white and light green parts only), thinly sliced

2 ribs celery, cut into ½-inch dice

1 red bell pepper, stemmed, seeded, and cut into ½-inch dice

1 tsp. fresh thyme

5 cups fresh corn kernels (from 10 medium ears)

½ tsp. pure chipotle chile powder

2 cups half-and-half

2 cups homemade or lower-salt chicken broth

1 large russet potato, peeled and coarsely grated

Kosher salt

Grated white Cheddar, for garnish (optional)

Don't substitute frozen corn here; the flavor of this quick chowder depends on freshly cut kernels.

1. Cook the bacon in a 5- to 6-quart Dutch oven or other heavy-duty pot over medium-high heat until browned and crisp, about 5 minutes. With a slotted spoon, transfer the bacon to a paper-towel-lined plate. Pour off and discard all but 2 Tbs. of the bacon fat. Return the Dutch oven to medium-high heat and add the onion, half of the scallions, the celery, bell pepper, and thyme. Cook, stirring occasionally, until the vegetables begin to soften, about 5 minutes. Add the corn and cook until softened, about 2 minutes. Stir in the chipotle powder and cook for 30 seconds. Add the half-and-half and chicken broth and bring to a boil. Add the grated potato, lower the heat to medium, and cook, covered, until the potato is cooked through, about 10 minutes.

2. Season to taste with salt and transfer to 4 large soup bowls. Garnish with the reserved bacon and scallions, and the cheese, if using, and serve. —*David Bonom*

PER SERVING: 500 CALORIES | 19G PROTEIN | 69G CARB | 20G TOTAL FAT | 10G SAT FAT | 4.5G MONO FAT | 1.5G POLY FAT | 60MG CHOL | 570MG SODIUM | 8G FIBER

salt cod and corn chowder

MAKES 7 CUPS;
SERVES 4 TO 6

8 oz. dried salt cod

1 tsp. olive oil

2 oz. salt pork, cut into small dice (about ½ cup)

1 small yellow onion, cut into small dice (about 1 cup)

1 medium rib celery, cut into small dice (about ½ cup)

Kosher salt

2 medium red potatoes, cut into small dice (about 2 cups)

1½ cups fresh corn kernels (from 3 ears)

2 8-oz. bottles clam juice

2 sprigs fresh thyme

1 bay leaf, preferably fresh

1 cup heavy cream

¾ cup whole milk

Freshly ground black pepper

Salt-drying improves the flavor and texture of otherwise bland codfish, turning it flaky and toothsome, and making salt cod a staple ingredient in the Mediterranean. Serve this creamy stew with oyster crackers, if you like.

1. One day ahead, rinse the salt cod, put it in a large bowl, and cover with cold water. Cover with plastic and refrigerate for 24 hours, changing the water several times.

2. In a 4-quart saucepan, bring 6 cups water to a boil over high heat. Add the soaked cod and simmer gently over low heat until it flakes easily with a fork, 10 to 20 minutes, depending on thickness. Drain and let cool. Remove and discard the skin, bones, and any spongy ends. Shred the cod into pieces.

3. In a 6-quart Dutch oven, heat the oil over medium heat. Add the salt pork and cook, stirring occasionally, until crisp, 4 to 6 minutes. Transfer with a slotted spoon to a plate lined with paper towels. Add the onion, celery, and a pinch of salt to the pot and cook until the vegetables are tender, 3 to 4 minutes. Stir in the potatoes and corn. Add 2 cups water, the clam juice, thyme, and bay leaf. Adjust the heat as necessary to reach a simmer and cook until the potatoes are just tender, 10 to 12 minutes. Stir in the salt cod, salt pork, heavy cream, and milk. Heat to a gentle simmer, but don't boil. Remove the bay leaf and thyme sprig and season to taste with salt and pepper before serving. —*Melissa Pellegrino*

PER SERVING: 430 CALORIES | 29G PROTEIN | 23G CARB | 25G TOTAL FAT | 13G SAT FAT | 9G MONO FAT | 2G POLY FAT | 125MG CHOL | 620MG SODIUM | 3G FIBER

More about Salt Cod

Salt-dried cod goes by many names in western Europe, where it's a staple: It's *bacalhau* in Portugal, *baccalà* in Italy, *bacalao* in Spain, and *morue* in France.

Some supermarkets carry salt cod—look for it in the seafood section, near the smoked salmon. Stored in a zip-top bag in the fridge, it will keep for a year or more. Regardless of what you're making, you'll need to first rinse and soak it in several changes of cold water for 12 to 36 hours to rehydrate it and remove enough salt to make it palatable. After soaking, give it a quick simmer in water or milk until it's soft enough to flake, remove the skin and bones, and it's ready to use. —*Jennifer Armentrout*

tomato bisque and cheese toasts

SERVES 2

FOR THE BISQUE

2	Tbs. olive oil
1	small onion, diced
1	clove garlic, minced
3	hearty sprigs fresh thyme
1	28-oz. can crushed tomatoes in purée
1½	cups homemade or lower-salt chicken broth
3	Tbs. honey
	Kosher salt and finely ground black pepper
⅓	cup heavy cream
2	Tbs. chopped fresh flat-leaf parsley (optional)

FOR THE TOASTS

4	slices country bread, about ½ inch thick
1	Tbs. Dijon mustard
4	slices Gruyère
1	Tbs. grated Parmigiano-Reggiano

Paired with an adult version of a classic grilled cheese sandwich, this chunky tomato bisque makes a comforting lunch or dinner.

MAKE THE BISQUE

1. In a medium pot, heat the oil. Add the onion and cook over medium heat, stirring frequently, until tender and lightly browned on the edges, about 7 minutes. Add the garlic and thyme; stir until fragrant, about 1 minute. Add the tomatoes, broth, honey, 1½ tsp. salt, and ¼ tsp. pepper. Bring to a boil over high heat. Reduce the heat and simmer, stirring frequently, until reduced by a quarter and thickened, about 15 minutes.

2. Using a stand or immersion blender, purée about half the soup; it will be still be chunky and thick. Return it to the pot and stir in the cream. Heat gently and adjust the seasonings.

MAKE THE TOASTS

Arrange an oven rack to the highest rung and heat the broiler on high. Line a baking sheet with foil. Put the bread on the foil and toast each side until golden brown. Spread the mustard evenly on one side of each toast, cover with the Gruyère, and sprinkle with the Parmigiano. Slide the toasts back under the broiler and cook until bubbling and lightly browned on top, about 2 minutes. Cut each toast in half.

TO SERVE

Ladle the hot soup into bowls, sprinkle with the parsley (if using), and serve immediately with the cheese toasts. —*Abigail Johnson Dodge*

PER SERVING: 950 CALORIES | 35G PROTEIN | 100G CARB | 51G TOTAL FAT | 23G SAT FAT | 21G MONO FAT | 3G POLY FAT | 120MG CHOL | 2,280MG SODIUM | 13G FIBER

summer corn chowder with scallions, bacon & potatoes

MAKES ABOUT 5½ CUPS;
SERVES 6 AS A FIRST COURSE

- 5   ears fresh sweet corn
- 7   oz. scallions (about 20 medium)
- 3   slices bacon, cut into ½-inch pieces
- 1   Tbs. unsalted butter
- 1   jalapeño, cored, seeded, and finely diced

  Kosher salt and freshly ground black pepper
- 3½   cups homemade or lower-salt chicken broth
- 1   large Yukon Gold potato (8 to 9 oz.), peeled and cut into ½-inch dice (about 1½ cups)
- 1½   tsp. chopped fresh thyme
- 2   Tbs. heavy cream

Scallions impart their sweet flavor to this soup. Only the white and light green parts go in at the start, as the dark green ends would wilt and overcook if simmered for a long time; they're best added at the very end.

1. Husk the corn and cut off the kernels. Reserve two of the corn cobs and discard the others.

2. Trim and thinly slice the scallions, keeping the dark green parts separate from the white and light green parts.

3. Cook the bacon in a 3- or 4-quart saucepan over medium heat until browned and crisp, about 5 minutes. With a slotted spoon, transfer the bacon to a paper-towel-lined plate. Pour off and discard all but about 1 Tbs. of the bacon fat. Return the pan to medium heat and add the butter. When the butter is melted, add the white and light green scallions and the jalapeño, 1 tsp. salt, and a few grinds of black pepper. Cook, stirring, until the scallions are very soft, about 3 minutes. Add the broth, corn, corn cobs, potato, and thyme and bring to a boil over medium-high heat. Reduce the heat to medium low and simmer until the potato is completely tender, about 15 minutes. Discard the corn cobs.

4. Transfer 1 cup of the broth and vegetables to a blender and purée. Return the purée to the pot and stir in the cream and all but ⅓ cup of the dark green scallions. Simmer, stirring occasionally, for a couple of minutes to wilt the scallions and blend the flavors. Season to taste with salt and pepper and serve sprinkled with the bacon and reserved dark green scallions. *—Tony Rosenfeld*

PER SERVING: 180 CALORIES | 8G PROTEIN | 25G CARB | 7G TOTAL FAT | 3G SAT FAT | 2.5G MONO FAT | 1G POLY FAT | 15MG CHOL | 320MG SODIUM | 3G FIBER

To keep scallions fresh when storing, remove a couple of inches from the green tops when you bring the scallions home. Rinse under cold running water and pull off any bruised or slimy leaves. Wrap whole, trimmed scallions in a paper towel and put them in a zip-top bag in the fridge. They'll keep for up to a week.

spicy tomato broth with
couscous and chicken
(recipe on p. 134)

hearty soups

chicken noodle soup with lemongrass

SERVES 4

2½ Tbs. canola oil

2 small boneless, skinless chicken breast halves (about ¾ lb.), butterflied (cut horizontally almost all the way through and then opened like a book)

Kosher salt and freshly ground black pepper

3 medium shallots (about 4 oz.), thinly sliced into rings

2 stalks lemongrass, trimmed, outer layers discarded, halved lengthwise, and smashed with the side of a chef's knife

1 Tbs. minced fresh ginger

2 tsp. packed light brown sugar

5½ cups homemade or lower-salt chicken broth

3½ oz. fresh shiitake mushrooms, stemmed and quartered (1½ cups)

9 oz. fresh udon noodles

1 Thai bird chile (or 1 small serrano chile), thinly sliced into rings

8 large fresh basil leaves, torn; plus several sprigs for garnish

1 medium lime, half juiced and half cut into wedges

1 Tbs. soy sauce; more as needed

2 medium scallions, trimmed and sliced, for garnish (optional)

1 medium carrot, cut into matchsticks, for garnish (optional)

½ cup fresh cilantro leaves, for garnish (optional)

In this cross between Vietnamese pho and Japanese udon noodle soup, fresh udon noodles are the star. Fat and bouncy in texture, they cook faster and tend to be more delicate than dried.

1. Heat 1½ Tbs. of the oil in a 5- to 6-quart Dutch oven over medium-high heat until shimmering hot. Season the chicken with ½ tsp. each salt and black pepper, and cook without disturbing until it's browned and releases easily from the bottom of the pot, about 2 minutes. Flip and cook until the second side is browned and almost firm to the touch (just short of cooked through), another 1 to 2 minutes. Transfer the chicken to a cutting board to cool.

2. Add the remaining 1 Tbs. oil and the shallot to the pot. Sprinkle with ¼ tsp. salt, reduce the heat to medium and cook, stirring, until the shallot starts to soften, about 2 minutes. Add the lemongrass, ginger, and brown sugar and cook, stirring, until the ginger and lemongrass sizzle and become fragrant, about 1 minute. Add the chicken broth, scraping up any browned bits from the bottom of the pot, and raise the heat to medium high. Bring the broth to a boil and then reduce to a simmer. Add the mushrooms and cook, stirring occasionally, until tender, 5 to 7 minutes.

3. Meanwhile, bring a medium pot of well-salted water to a boil and cook the noodles, stirring, until just tender, about 3 minutes. Transfer to a colander and run under cold water to cool slightly. Drain well. Use your fingers or the tines of a fork to shred the chicken.

4. Add the shredded chicken and the noodles to the broth and cook until the noodles are completely tender and the chicken is cooked through, about 2 minutes. Discard the lemongrass. Stir in the chile, torn basil, lime juice, and soy sauce; season with more soy sauce to taste. Portion the noodles into four large, deep bowls. Ladle the soup over the noodles and garnish with the basil sprigs and scallions, carrot, and cilantro, if using. Serve with the lime wedges for squeezing.
—*Tony Rosenfeld*

PER SERVING: 500 CALORIES | 35G PROTEIN | 9G CARB | 15G TOTAL FAT | 2G SAT FAT | 7G MONO FAT | 3.5G POLY FAT | 45MG CHOL | 930MG SODIUM | 5G FIBER

> This soup is a great destination for shredded, leftover roast chicken. Use it in place of the chicken breast and add it to the soup along with the chiles, basil, lime juice, and soy sauce.

mediterranean kale and white bean soup with sausage

MAKES ABOUT 10 CUPS; SERVES 8

- ½ lb. sweet Italian sausage (about 3 links)
- 2 Tbs. olive oil
- ½ small yellow onion, cut into small dice
- 1 medium carrot, peeled and cut into small dice
- 1 rib celery, cut into small dice
- 5 large cloves garlic, minced (about 2 Tbs.)
- ⅛ tsp. crushed red pepper flakes

  Kosher salt and freshly ground black pepper
- 6 cups homemade or lower-salt chicken broth
- 1 19-oz. can cannellini or white kidney beans, rinsed and drained, or 2 cups cooked dried beans

This garlicky soup is a snap to pull together, and most of the ingredients are basic pantry staples. The whole thing is ready in about an hour, but the soup's complex flavors belie the quick cooking time. You can serve it as soon as the kale is tender, but letting it sit for an hour and then reheating gently makes it even better (wait to add the lemon until just before serving). Crusty cheese toasts make an excellent accompaniment.

1. Remove the sausage from its casing and tear it by hand into bite-size pieces. Heat 1 Tbs. of the olive oil in a 4- or 5-quart heavy pot or Dutch oven over medium heat. Add the sausage and cook, stirring occasionally, until lightly browned, about 5 minutes. With a slotted spoon, transfer the sausage to a plate, leaving any rendered fat in the pot.

2. Add the remaining 1 Tbs. olive oil to the pot, increase the heat to medium high, and add the onion. Cook, stirring frequently, until the onion is fragrant and beginning to soften, about 2 minutes. Add the carrot and celery and cook, stirring frequently, until they begin to soften and brown, about 2 minutes more. Be sure to scrape any browned bits from the bottom of the pan. Stir in the garlic, pepper flakes, ½ tsp. salt, and ¼ tsp. black pepper and cook, stirring, until the garlic is fragrant, about 1 minute. Add the chicken broth and bring to a boil over high heat.

1 lb. kale, rinsed, stems
   removed, leaves torn into
   bite-size pieces (8 cups
   firmly packed)

1 Tbs. fresh lemon juice

½ tsp. finely grated lemon zest
   (optional)

3. When the broth reaches a boil, reduce the heat to medium, add the sausage along with any collected juices, and half the beans. Mash the remaining beans with a fork or wooden spoon and add them to the pot, stirring to distribute. Stir in the kale, adjust the heat as necessary to maintain a gentle simmer, and simmer until the kale is tender, 15 to 20 minutes. Stir in the lemon juice and lemon zest (if using) and season to taste with salt and black pepper. —*Ruth Lively*

PER SERVING: 200 CALORIES | 13G PROTEIN | 21G CARB | 8G TOTAL FAT | 2G SAT FAT | 4G MONO FAT | 1G POLY FAT | 10MG CHOL | 530MG SODIUM | 4G FIBER

Choosing and Prepping Kale

Kale is usually sold in bundles. Choose deeply colored leaves, with no signs of yellowing or bruising. Store kale unwashed in an unclosed plastic bag in the refrigerator's crisper drawer, where it will keep well for 2 or 3 days. If you need to store it longer, wrap the bundle in slightly damp paper towels before putting it in a plastic bag to help prolong its freshness. Try to use kale within 5 to 7 days, because the longer you keep it, the stronger its flavor will become.

Wash kale in a deep sink or a very large bowl of cold water, gently swirling the stalks to encourage any soil or grit to disperse into the water. Shake off the excess water and pat dry with paper towels.

Before cooking kale, you'll need to remove the tough stems and central ribs from all but the smallest leaves. You can cut them out with a knife or simply tear away the leaf from the rib.

barley minestrone

MAKES ABOUT 3 QUARTS

- **2 Tbs. extra-virgin olive oil**
- **¼ cup finely diced pancetta (about 1 oz.)**
- **2 cups large-diced Savoy cabbage**
- **1 cup medium-diced yellow onion**
- **1 cup sliced carrot (¼ inch thick)**
- **¼ cup medium-diced celery**
- **2 cloves garlic, minced**
- **2 quarts homemade or lower-salt chicken broth**
- **1 14½-oz. can diced tomatoes, with their liquid**
- **½ cup pearl barley, rinsed**
- **2 large sprigs fresh rosemary**
- **1 2-inch square Parmigiano-Reggiano rind (optional)**
- **Kosher salt and freshly ground black pepper**
- **1 cup rinsed and drained canned kidney beans**
- **Freshly grated Parmigiano-Reggiano, for serving**

This rendition of the classic Italian vegetable and bean soup uses barley instead of pasta. Simmering a piece of the rind from Parmigiano-Reggiano in the soup is a traditional way of adding flavor. When you finish off a wedge of Parmigiano, just stash the rind in the freezer so you always have it on hand when you need it.

1. Heat the oil in a heavy 6-quart or larger pot over medium heat. Add the pancetta and cook, stirring frequently, until it becomes ever-so-slightly golden, 2 to 3 minutes. Add the cabbage, onion, carrot, celery, and garlic. Cook, stirring frequently, until the vegetables begin to soften, about 6 minutes. Add the broth, the tomatoes with their liquid, the barley, rosemary, Parmigiano rind (if using), ½ tsp. salt, and 1 cup water. Bring to a boil over high heat, and then reduce the heat to a simmer and cook until the barley and vegetables are tender, about 20 minutes. Discard the rosemary sprigs and Parmigiano rind. Stir in the beans and season to taste with salt and pepper.

2. Serve sprinkled with the grated Parmigiano. —*Jennifer Armentrout*

PER 1 CUP: 170 CALORIES | 8G PROTEIN | 20G CARB | 6G TOTAL FAT | 2G SAT FAT | 3G MONO FAT | 1G POLY FAT | 10MG CHOL | 880MG SODIUM | 4G FIBER

More about Barley

In its heyday during ancient times, barley was the most important cereal grain in the world. First cultivated in the Near East at least 8,000 years ago, barley was used not only for food but also as currency, a unit of measure, medicine, and a sacred offering. In modern times, though, barley has lost much of its glamour. It's used mainly for making malt for beer, malt vinegar, and other products. But given its versatility, maybe it's time for a barley renaissance.

Forms of barley

Like most grains, barley is processed into a number of different forms. Hulled barley (barley groats) has had its inedible husk removed but still has its nutritious, fiber-rich bran layer. Pearl barley has been refined to strip it of its bran and germ. It's still nutritious, though not so much as hulled barley; it's to hulled barley as white rice is to brown rice. Pot or scotch barley is a less refined type of pearl barley. Rolled or flaked barley is hulled barley that's been flattened, like rolled oats. Quick-cooking barley is flattened and parcooked, so it cooks faster; nutritionally, it's similar to pearl barley.

Where to find barley

Look in health-food stores for whole hulled barley, pot barley, and rolled barley. In supermarkets, you'll find pearl barley near the dried beans and quick-cooking barley in the hot cereal section.

Cooking with barley

Barley has a mild flavor that's not as nutty as many other grains, but it has an unusually chewy texture—it pops softly as you bite it. It can be used in just about every way that rice is used—in pilafs, soups, and even risottos. Rolled barley is often eaten as a hot cereal. It's usually a good idea to rinse barley before cooking. Whole hulled barley takes about an hour to cook (though a pressure cooker can speed things along). Pearl barley and rolled barley need about 20 minutes to get tender. Quick-cooking barley is usually done in 12 to 15 minutes.

beef and wild rice soup with winter vegetables

SERVES 8

- **2 Tbs. unsalted butter or bacon fat**
- **1 lb. boneless beef chuck, cut into ¾-inch cubes**
- **Kosher salt and freshly ground black pepper**
- **1 medium yellow onion, cut into ⅓-inch dice**
- **2 cloves garlic, minced**
- **1 cup full-bodied red wine**
- **8 cups homemade or lower-salt chicken broth**
- **2 cups ½-inch-diced butter-nut squash (from a small squash, about 1½ lb.)**
- **1 cup ½-inch-diced medium purple turnip**
- **1 cup wild rice, rinsed**
- **2 Tbs. tomato paste**
- **1 tsp. dried thyme**
- **1 bay leaf**
- **¼ cup chopped fresh flat-leaf parsley**

Thanks in part to its wild rice, this dish has a wonderful nutty, earthy fragrance. It simmers on the stove for up to an hour and serves eight, making it the perfect easy dinner for your family.

1. In a Dutch oven or heavy soup pot, melt the butter or bacon fat over medium-high heat. Season the beef generously with salt and pepper. Put the beef in the pan in a single layer; don't stir for about 1½ minutes. Then stir occasionally until the meat is well browned on all sides, about 5 minutes.

2. With a slotted spoon, transfer the meat to a plate. Reduce the heat to medium low, add the onion and garlic to the pot, and cook, stirring and scraping the bottom of the pot occasionally with a wooden spoon, until they're softened, about 5 minutes. Add the wine, bring to a boil, and cook until the wine is reduced by about half, about 5 minutes. Add the broth, squash, turnip, wild rice, tomato paste, thyme, and bay leaf and bring to a boil over high heat. Add the beef and any accumulated juices, reduce the heat to medium low, cover, and simmer until the wild rice is soft and most of the grains have popped open and are tender, 40 to 60 minutes. (Check occasionally to be sure the soup isn't simmering too quickly or too slowly; it should be a moderate simmer.) Discard the bay leaf. Season the soup with salt and pepper to taste and serve garnished with the parsley.

—Beth Dooley and Lucia Watson

PER SERVING: 320 CALORIES | 16G PROTEIN | 26G CARB | 15G TOTAL FAT | 6G SAT FAT | 6G MONO FAT | 1G POLY FAT | 50MG CHOL | 610MG SODIUM | 4G FIBER

beet greens and bulgur soup with poached eggs

SERVES 4

2 Tbs. extra-virgin olive oil

1 medium yellow onion, chopped

4 medium cloves garlic, minced

2 quarts homemade or lower-salt chicken or vegetable broth

8 cups lightly packed stemmed beet greens, cut into 1-inch pieces

¾ cup whole-grain, quick-cooking bulgur, such as Bob's Red Mill®

 Kosher salt and freshly ground black pepper

4 large eggs

½ cup freshly grated Parmigiano-Reggiano

This rustic soup is made with just a few ingredients, but don't let its simplicity fool you: It's full-flavored and remarkably comforting. It's also perfect for a weeknight. Bulgur, which is simply wheat kernels that have been steamed, dried, and crushed, cooks about as quickly as rice. Be sure to use a pot that's at least 10 inches wide; otherwise, the poached eggs will sink deep into the soup and you'll have a hard time telling when they're done.

1. Heat the olive oil in a large pot that's about 10 inches wide over medium heat. Add the onion and cook, stirring often until golden brown, about 10 minutes. Stir in the garlic and cook for 1 minute. Add the broth, raise the heat to medium high, and bring to a simmer. Stir in the beet greens and bulgur. Cover and simmer vigorously, adjusting the heat as needed, until the greens and bulgur are tender, about 24 minutes. Season to taste with salt and pepper. Adjust the heat as needed to achieve a gentle simmer.

2. Crack one of the eggs into a small bowl and pour it onto the soup near the edge of the pot. Repeat with the remaining eggs, positioning them around the perimeter of the pot. Spoon hot broth over the eggs and cook until the whites are set but the yolks are still soft, about 3 minutes. Carefully ladle the soup and eggs into bowls. Sprinkle with the Parmigiano and serve. —*Jeanne Kelley*

PER SERVING: 370 CALORIES | 25G PROTEIN | 33G CARB | 18G TOTAL FAT | 5G SAT FAT | 9G MONO FAT | 2.5G POLY FAT | 195MG CHOL | 660MG SODIUM | 7G FIBER

More about Beet Greens

Beet greens are similar in flavor to Swiss chard—they add a robust, earthy note to dishes—and can be prepared the same way: sautéed, braised, or cooked and tossed into pasta. Small, tender raw beet leaves make a colorful addition to mesclun mixes or a pretty garnish for sliced beets.

Store beets and their greens separately, as the leaves continue to draw moisture and nutrients from their roots if still attached. Refrigerate washed and dried greens in a plastic bag for up to 2 days; the beets will keep in a plastic bag for up to 3 weeks.

chicken and tortilla soup

SERVES 2 AS A LIGHT MAIN
COURSE OR SUBSTANTIAL
FIRST COURSE

- 1 **Tbs. vegetable or olive oil, plus another ½ to 1 cup for frying the tortillas**
- ¼ **cup finely chopped onion (from about ½ small onion)**
- 1 **Tbs. chili powder; more as needed**
- 1 **Tbs. tomato paste**
- 2 **skinless chicken thighs (bone-in or boneless)**

  Kosher salt
- 4 **cups homemade or lower-salt chicken broth**
- 6 **2-inch stems of fresh cilantro for the broth, plus ¼ cup roughly chopped leaves for the garnish**
- 4 **fresh corn tortillas, 6 inches across, cut into ¼-inch-wide strips**
- ½ **cup corn kernels (canned is fine)**
- ½ **cup canned black beans, rinsed and drained**
- ¾ **cup diced fresh tomatoes**
- 1 **ripe avocado, diced and tossed with a squeeze of lime juice**
- ¼ **cup crumbled queso fresco, feta, or ricotta salata**
- 2 **dollops sour cream**

  Lime wedges

Be sure the broth is very hot so that it heats up the ingredients in the bowl and offers a strong contrast with the cool, smooth chunks of avocado. The spice level is very low—just a slight chile warmth—so if you prefer more of a kick, add more chili powder or use a hotter powder. This recipe is easily doubled.

1. Put 1 Tbs. of the oil in a large saucepan or small soup pot, add the onion, and cook over medium heat until the onion has softened but not browned, about 3 minutes. Add the chili powder and tomato paste and stir with a wooden spoon to mix and cook briefly; take care not to let the chili powder scorch.

2. Season the chicken thighs lightly with salt and nestle them in the chile paste, turning them once so they're entirely coated. Pour in about ½ cup of the broth and adjust the heat to a simmer. Cover the pan and cook the chicken, turning once, until it's extremely tender when pierced with a knife, 30 to 40 minutes (add a little more broth if the pan is drying out). When the chicken is done, remove it from the pan, let it cool a bit, and cut or shred it into bite-size pieces, discarding any bones and bits of fat or gristle; set aside. If there's any visible grease in the pan, spoon it off, add the remaining broth and the cilantro stems, and simmer, uncovered, until the broth has reduced by about one-third and is quite flavorful, 20 to 30 minutes.

3. While the broth is reducing, fry the tortillas. Line a plate or tray with two layers of paper towels. In a small, high-sided saucepan, heat enough oil to come to about a 1-inch depth. Heat the oil over medium heat; when it reaches 375°F or when a strip of tortilla sizzles immediately when dipped in the oil, add 6 to 8 strips of tortilla. With tongs or a long fork, "scrunch" them for a second or two so they take on a wavy shape. Fry until the strips aren't bubbling much and have become pale brown, about 1 minute. Transfer to the paper towels. Repeat with the remaining strips.

4. Divide the shredded chicken, the corn, black beans, tomato, and tortilla strips between two large soup or pasta bowls. Reheat the broth if necessary so it's piping hot and pour it over the ingredients in the bowls. Serve immediately, and let each diner add the avocado, cheese, sour cream, chopped cilantro, and a big squeeze of lime juice at the table. —*Martha Holmberg*

PER SERVING: 670 CALORIES | 34G PROTEIN | 61G CARB | 35G TOTAL FAT | 8G SAT FAT | 15G MONO FAT | 9G POLY FAT | 75MG CHOL | 1,140MG SODIUM | 15G FIBER

chicken coconut soup

MAKES 4¾ TO 5 CUPS;
SERVES 4 AS A STARTER
OR 2 AS A LIGHT MEAL

- **2 stalks fresh lemongrass**
- **2 Tbs. fresh lime juice**
- **2 Tbs. fish sauce**
- **2 scallions (white and green parts), trimmed and very thinly sliced**
- **6 fresh or frozen wild lime leaves (also known as kaffir lime leaves; see the sidebar at right), torn or cut into quarters**
- **10 to 12 thin slices galangal, fresh, frozen, or dried (or 10 to 12 thin slices fresh unpeeled ginger)**

This soup is a quintessentially Thai dish (known as tome kha gai) *that you can make at home simply, quickly, and with great success. Galangal, a relative of ginger, gives this soup a bright, citrusy flavor.*

1. Trim away and discard the root end and the top 3 inches of each stalk of lemongrass, along with any brittle leaves. Pound each stalk lightly with the spine of a cleaver or an unopened can. Cut each stalk crosswise into 2-inch lengths and set aside.

2. In a large serving bowl, combine the lime juice, fish sauce, scallions, and half of the wild lime leaves. Set the bowl by the stove, along with small dishes containing the galangal, lemongrass, and remaining lime leaves; the chiles (if using); the chopped cilantro; and the sliced chicken and mushrooms.

3. In a medium saucepan, combine the coconut milk and broth. Bring to a gentle boil over medium-high heat. Stir in the galangal, lemongrass, and lime leaves. Add the chicken and mushrooms. Return to a

8 to 10 fresh hot red and green Thai chiles, stemmed and lightly pressed with the side of a knife (or 3 or 4 serranos, thinly sliced) for garnish (optional)

2 Tbs. coarsely chopped fresh cilantro

1 boneless, skinless chicken breast half (about 6 oz.), cut into bite-size chunks or sliced across the grain into strips

¼ lb. white mushrooms, cleaned, stems trimmed, and thinly sliced (to yield 1 cup)

1 14-oz. can unsweetened coconut milk (shake the can before opening it)

1¾ cups homemade or lower-salt chicken broth or water

gentle boil, reduce the heat, and simmer for 10 minutes to infuse the flavors and cook the chicken.

4. Remove the pan from the heat, pour the hot soup over the seasonings in the serving bowl, and stir well. Sprinkle with the chopped cilantro and serve hot. Pass around the chiles for those who want them.

—*Nancie McDermott*

PER SERVING: 350 CALORIES | 16G PROTEIN | 25G CARB | 23G TOTAL FAT | 19G SAT FAT | 2G MONO FAT | 1G POLY FAT | 25MG CHOL | 770MG SODIUM | 3G FIBER

More about Wild Lime Leaves

Native to Southeast Asia, wild limes are small, bright green citrus fruits with bumpy, wrinkled skin. Both the peel and the pulp deliver vibrant citrus flavor and are deeply aromatic, but even the leaves are good for cooking. Used widely in Southeast Asian cuisine, especially in curries, wild lime leaves give dishes a refreshing, lingering lift that is intensely floral and citrusy. If you can't find wild lime leaves, you can try substituting lime zest. It doesn't have that same intensely floral aroma, but it will give the dish a similar refreshing citrusy flavor.

Choosing and storing

Fresh lime leaves are often sold in Asian markets; if they're not available fresh, frozen or dried leaves are sometimes sold. Whenever you can, unless otherwise directed, opt for the superior flavor and aroma of fresh lime leaves (frozen are your next-best bet).

Fresh wild lime leaves should be refrigerated in a sealed plastic bag until ready to use. They'll keep this way for several days. Keep frozen lime leaves frozen until just before using.

french onion soup

SERVES 6 TO 8

- ¼ **cup unsalted butter; more for the baking sheet**
- 4 **medium-large yellow onions (about 2 lb.), thinly sliced (8 cups)**
- **Kosher salt and freshly ground black pepper**
- 1 **tsp. granulated sugar**
- 1 **small baguette (½ lb.), cut into ½-inch slices**
- 2 **quarts Roasted Beef Broth (recipe on p. 220) or home-made or lower-salt beef or chicken broth**
- 1 **bay leaf**
- 2 **cups grated Gruyère**

Make Ahead

The soup and croûtes can be made up to 2 days ahead. Store the soup in the refrigerator and the croûtes in an airtight container at room temperature.

This ultimate version of the bistro classic is made with homemade beef broth and caramelized onions. Aged Gruyère is key to getting the traditional bubbling crust of cheese; it's rich, smooth, and melts easily.

1. Melt the butter in a 4-quart pot over medium heat. Stir in the onions and season with 1 tsp. salt and a few grinds of pepper. Reduce the heat to low. Press a piece of foil onto the onions to cover them completely, cover the pot with a lid, and cook, stirring occasionally (you'll have to lift the foil), until the onions are very soft but not falling apart, 40 to 50 minutes. Remove the lid and foil, raise the heat to medium high, and stir in the sugar. Cook, stirring often, until very deeply browned, 10 to 15 minutes.

2. Meanwhile, to make the croûtes (baguette toasts), position a rack in the center of the oven and heat the oven to 350°F. Butter a rimmed baking sheet and arrange the baguette slices on the sheet in a single layer. Bake until the bread is crisp and lightly browned, turning once, 15 to 20 minutes. Set aside.

3. Add the broth and bay leaf to the caramelized onions and bring the soup to a boil over medium-high heat. Reduce the heat to medium low and simmer for 10 minutes to blend the flavors. Discard the bay leaf and season to taste with salt and pepper.

4. To serve, position a rack 6 inches from the broiler and heat the broiler to high. Put six to eight broilerproof soup bowls or crocks on a baking sheet. Put 2 or 3 croûtes in each bowl and ladle the hot soup on top. Sprinkle with the cheese and broil until the top is browned and bubbly, 2 to 5 minutes. Serve immediately. —*Anne Willan*

PER SERVING: 240 CALORIES | 14G PROTEIN | 9G CARB | 16G TOTAL FAT | 10G SAT FAT | 5G MONO FAT | 1G POLY FAT | 45MG CHOL | 270MG SODIUM | 1G FIBER

matzo ball soup

SERVES 6

4 large eggs

¼ cup rendered chicken fat or fat reserved from the Golden Chicken Broth on p. 222, at room temperature

Kosher salt

Ground white pepper

5 oz. (1¼ cups) matzo meal

7 cups Golden Chicken Broth (recipe on p. 222)

¼ cup chopped fresh flat-leaf parsley

The matzo balls can be cooked ahead and then warmed in the broth before serving. To turn this into a more filling meal, add cooked chicken, peas, or carrots. The recipe doubles or triples easily. To render chicken fat, use fat taken from the cavity of a chicken (roasters have a lot), cut into 1-inch pieces, melt over low heat, and then strain.

1. In a large bowl, whisk together the eggs and ⅓ cup cold water. Add the rendered or reserved chicken fat and whisk until the fat blends in. Mix in 1 tsp. salt and ¼ tsp. white pepper. Gradually but quickly stir in the matzo meal with a spoon; the mixture will be thick and stiff, like muffin batter. Don't overmix. Chill for at least 1 hour or up to 3 hours.

2. Line a baking sheet with parchment or waxed paper and fill a bowl with cold water. Dip a large soupspoon in the water and gently scoop up the chilled matzo mixture. Shape it with your hands into 12 medium balls (about 1¾ inches in diameter) or 18 smaller ones (about 1¼ inches in diameter), being careful not to compact them. Put the matzo balls on the lined baking sheet. Cook immediately or refrigerate for up to 1 hour. To cook the matzo balls, bring 1 or 2 large pots of salted water to a boil. Drop in the matzo balls, cover the pots, and reduce the heat after the water returns to a boil. Simmer, covered, until the matzo balls have doubled in size and have lightened all the way through (cut one in half to check), 30 to 40 minutes; drain. They can be held at room temperature for several hours.

3. To serve, bring the chicken broth to a boil. Taste for salt and pepper. Add the matzo balls and heat until they're hot in the middle, 8 to 10 minutes. With a slotted spoon, put 2 medium or 3 small matzo balls in a warm soup bowl. Ladle in the hot broth and sprinkle generously with the parsley. Serve right away. —*Joyce Goldstein*

PER SERVING: 140 CALORIES | 10G PROTEIN | 21G CARB | 13G TOTAL FAT | 4G SAT FAT | 5G MONO FAT | 2G POLY FAT | 150MG CHOL | 690MG SODIUM | 1G FIBER

More about Matzo Meal

Matzo meal, also known as matzah or matzoh meal, is made by grinding matzo, a traditional Jewish unleavened bread. Matzo bread is made by mixing flour and water, rolling it out thin, then baking it in an extremely hot oven. It can be soft and pliable or cracker-crisp. It's the crisp version that is used to make matzo meal.

Prepared matzo meal comes in several types, from course to fine. You can also make your own, either from scratch by making and grinding your own matzo bread or by crushing packaged matzo to your desired consistency.

Like all breadcrumbs, matzo meal acts as a binder and so can be added to casseroles, potato pancakes, and more. You can substitute matzo meal in almost any recipe that calls for breadcrumbs.

spiced tomato and red lentil soup

MAKES ABOUT 14 CUPS; SERVES 8

- 3 Tbs. vegetable oil
- 2 medium yellow onions, chopped

  Kosher salt
- 2 tsp. Madras curry powder or garam masala
- 2 quarts homemade or lower-salt chicken or vegetable broth
- 2 14½-oz. cans petite-diced tomatoes, with their liquid
- 1 lb. (2⅓ cups) dried red lentils, picked over, rinsed, and drained
- 2 medium ribs celery, cut into small dice
- 1 medium carrot, peeled and cut into small dice
- 2 medium cloves garlic, chopped
- ⅛ to ¼ tsp. cayenne

Curry powder and garam masala are both Indian spice blends, which vary in flavor from blend to blend. Experiment to see which you prefer.

1. Heat the oil in a 6-quart Dutch oven over medium heat. Add the onion and a generous pinch of salt and cook, stirring occasionally, until the onion is softened and just starting to brown, 6 to 8 minutes. Add the curry powder or garam masala and cook, stirring constantly, until fragrant, 30 seconds to 1 minute.

2. Add the broth, tomatoes and their liquid, lentils, celery, carrot, garlic, cayenne, ¾ tsp. salt, and 2 cups water. Bring to a boil over high heat, stirring frequently to keep the lentils from sticking; skim any foam as necessary. Reduce the heat and simmer uncovered, stirring occasionally, until the lentils, carrots, and celery are tender, 35 to 40 minutes. Season to taste with salt. You can store leftovers in the refrigerator for up to 5 days. —*Lori Longbotham*

PER SERVING: 320 CALORIES | 22G PROTEIN | 45G CARB | 8G TOTAL FAT | 1G SAT FAT | 3G MONO FAT | 2.5G POLY FAT | 0MG CHOL | 480MG SODIUM | 9G FIBER

chicken noodle soup with carrots and peas

SERVES 4

- **7** cups Golden Chicken Broth (recipe on p. 222)
- **4** boneless, skinless chicken breast halves, cut into 1 x ½-inch strips or ½-inch dice
- **1½** cups diced or julienned carrots
- **3** oz. (about 1½ cups) dried egg noodles
- **1½** cups frozen peas
- **2** Tbs. chopped fresh flat-leaf parsley
- **1** tsp. chopped fresh thyme

    Table salt and freshly ground black pepper

    Freshly grated Parmigiano-Reggiano, for garnish (optional)

Even during their very brief season, English garden peas can be starchy, so this recipe calls for frozen peas, which are consistently sweet and tender. You can thaw them ahead or else defrost them right in the hot broth.

1. Bring the broth to a simmer in a large, heavy saucepan. Add the chicken, reduce the heat to a gentle simmer, and poach until the chicken is firm and just cooked through, 3 to 5 minutes. Remove the chicken and, if the broth is cloudy, strain the liquid through a cheesecloth-lined strainer (this step isn't critical—it's just for looks).

2. Bring the broth back to a simmer in the saucepan, and add the carrots, cooking until they're just tender, about 7 minutes. Remove them with a slotted spoon and set aside with the chicken.

3. Meanwhile, bring a pot of salted water to a boil and cook the egg noodles until they're al dente. Drain them and set aside.

4. When you're ready to serve the soup, bring the broth to a boil. Reduce the heat to a simmer. Add the peas, the cooked carrots, and the chicken and simmer until everything is heated through. Add the cooked noodles, the parsley, and the thyme. Season to taste with salt and pepper. Serve with the grated Parmigiano, if you like.

—Joyce Goldstein

PER SERVING: 310 CALORIES | 38G PROTEIN | 28G CARB | 4G TOTAL FAT | 1G SAT FAT | 1G MONO FAT | 1G POLY FAT | 90MG CHOL | 1,030MG SODIUM | 5G FIBER

chicken soup with rice, lemon & mint

SERVES 4

- **6** cups Golden Chicken Broth (recipe on p. 222)

   Kosher salt

- **½** cup long-grain rice, preferably basmati

- **2** boneless, skinless chicken breast halves, cut into 1½-inch strips or ½-inch dice

- **¼** cup fresh lemon juice

   Freshly ground black pepper

- **6** Tbs. chopped fresh mint leaves

For a variation on this brightly flavored soup, you can add linguiça sausage instead of the chicken or tiny rice-shaped pasta (orzo) instead of rice.

1. Combine ½ cup of the broth, ½ cup water, and ½ tsp. salt in a small, heavy saucepan. Bring to a boil and stir in the rice. Reduce the heat to low, cover the pan, and simmer until all the liquid is absorbed and the rice is just tender, 20 to 22 minutes; set aside.

2. In a large, heavy saucepan, bring the remaining 5½ cups broth to a simmer over medium heat. Add the chicken, reduce the heat to a gentle simmer, and poach until the chicken is firm and just cooked through, 3 to 5 minutes. If the broth is cloudy, you can remove the chicken, strain the liquid through a cheesecloth-lined strainer, and return the chicken to the broth.

3. Add the reserved rice and the lemon juice and season with salt and pepper. Sprinkle on the mint and serve right away. —*Joyce Goldstein*

PER SERVING: 180 CALORIES | 20G PROTEIN | 21G CARB | 2G TOTAL FAT | 0.5G SAT FAT | 0.5G MONO FAT | 0.5G POLY FAT | 35MG CHOL | 970MG SODIUM | 1G FIBER

chicken meatball and escarole soup

SERVES 4

3 Tbs. plain fresh bread-
crumbs

¼ cup finely grated
Parmigiano-Reggiano;
more for serving

2 Tbs. chopped fresh flat-leaf
parsley

Kosher salt and freshly
ground black pepper

½ lb. ground chicken

1 large egg

1 Tbs. extra-virgin olive oil

1 small yellow onion, cut into
small dice

1 small carrot, peeled and cut
into small dice

1 medium rib celery, cut into
small dice

1 quart homemade or lower-
salt chicken broth

1 3- to 4-inch sprig fresh
rosemary

5 cups thinly sliced escarole

*Served with crusty bread, this quick spin on Italian wedding soup
makes a satisfying dinner. Handle the chicken mixture gently; packing
the meat too tightly will make the meatballs tough.*

1. Put the breadcrumbs in a medium bowl and moisten with ½ Tbs.
water. Mix in the Parmigiano, parsley, ¾ tsp. salt, and ½ tsp. pepper.
Add the ground chicken and egg and mix until just combined. Scoop
out 1 Tbs. of the chicken mixture and, with damp hands, roll it into a
¾-inch meatball. Transfer to a plate and shape the remaining meatballs.

2. Heat the oil in a 5-quart pot over medium heat. Add the onion,
carrot, celery, and 1 tsp. salt; cook until tender, 3 to 4 minutes. Add the
chicken broth, rosemary, and 2 cups water; bring to a boil over
medium-high heat. Gently add the meatballs, reduce the heat to
medium low to maintain a gentle simmer, and cook for 10 minutes.
Add the escarole and continue to simmer until the meatballs are
cooked through and the escarole is wilted, about 5 minutes. Discard
the rosemary and season to taste with salt and pepper. Serve
sprinkled with grated Parmigiano. —*Melissa Pellegrino*

PER SERVING: 220 CALORIES | 20G PROTEIN | 10G CARB | 12G TOTAL FAT | 3.5G SAT
FAT | 6G MONO FAT | 2G POLY FAT | 100MG CHOL | 730MG SODIUM | 3G FIBER

cinnamon beef noodle soup

SERVES 6 TO 8

- 1 tsp. peanut or vegetable oil
- 3 cinnamon sticks (about 3 inches each)
- 6 scallions (white and light greens parts), cut into 1½-inch pieces
- 6 cloves garlic, smashed and peeled
- 2 Tbs. minced fresh ginger
- 1½ tsp. aniseed
- 1½ tsp. Asian chile paste
- 4 cups homemade or lower-salt chicken broth
- ½ cup soy sauce
- ¼ cup rice vinegar
- 2½ lb. boneless beef chuck, trimmed and cut into ¾-inch cubes
- 9 oz. fresh udon noodles (or 6 oz. dried)
- 1 1- to 1½-lb. bunch bok choy, bottom trimmed, stalks washed and cut into 1-inch pieces
- ½ cup fresh cilantro leaves

Packaged stewing beef is often made up of irregularly shaped pieces from different cuts. It's best to have pieces cut to a similar size so they cook evenly, so cut your own stew meat using a boneless chuck roast or two ¾-inch-thick chuck steaks.

1. Heat the oil in a heavy soup pot or Dutch oven over medium heat. When very hot, add the cinnamon sticks, scallions, garlic, ginger, aniseed, and chile paste; cook, stirring, for 1 minute. Add 7 cups water, the broth, soy sauce, and vinegar; bring to a boil over high heat. Add the meat and bring to a vigorous simmer. Lower the heat to maintain a gentle simmer and cook, partially covered, until the meat is very tender, about 1½ hours, checking to be sure that the soup doesn't boil or stop simmering.

2. Shortly before the soup is done, bring a large pot of water to a boil. Cook the noodles according to the package directions until just tender. Drain and rinse under cold water.

3. When the meat is tender, remove the cinnamon sticks. Add the bok choy to the soup and simmer until the stalks are crisp-tender and the greens are very tender, 5 to 10 minutes. Stir in the noodles and let them warm through. Serve immediately, garnished with the cilantro leaves. —*Eva Katz*

PER SERVING: 490 CALORIES | 31G PROTEIN | 25G CARB | 29G TOTAL FAT | 11G SAT FAT | 13G MONO FAT | 2G POLY FAT | 100MG CHOL | 1,360MG SODIUM | 2G FIBER

More about Asian Chili Paste

Asian chile pastes are hot sauces made primarily from ground chiles, oil or vinegar, and salt. They may also include other flavors, such as garlic, ginger, sugar, sesame, black beans, or soybeans. Unlike most of the thin, smooth, chile-based hot sauces of the Americas, Asian chile pastes tend to be coarse and on the thick side, full of bits of ground chiles and sometimes whole seeds. Though they won't provide the full flavor spectrum of most chile pastes, you can use hot sauce or crushed red pepper flakes to add some heat (use less than the amount of chile paste called for). You'll find the broadest variety of chile pastes at an Asian grocery store. Be sure the first ingredient listed is chiles. Chile pastes aren't usually labeled as to their heat intensity, so experiment to find a brand you like.

Use the chile paste right out of the can or jar at the beginning of cooking if you want it to really permeate the dish, or add it at the end if you want more of a surface heat.

Some pastes separate during storage, so stir them before using. Once opened, chile pastes will last indefinitely if tightly covered and refrigerated, but transfer canned paste to a jar before storing.

three versatile asian noodles

Udon noodles are a Japanese noodle made with wheat flour and water. Plump, white, and slippery, they're most commonly used in soups and stews. They may be round, square, or flat and are sold both fresh and dried in the Asian or natural-foods section of the supermarket. You can substitute Chinese wheat-flour noodles.

Chinese egg noodles are classic Asian noodles made from wheat flour, water, and egg. Springy with a slight chew, these noodles are made in thin or thick strands. Look for fresh ones in the supermarket's produce department; be sure they contain egg and aren't tinted with food coloring instead. Fresh or dried pasta—angel hair, spaghetti, or linguine—can be substituted.

Rice noodles, made from rice flour and water, have a subtle flavor and an appealing chewy texture. They can be very thin, sometimes called "vermicelli," or flat and narrow to wide.

spicy noodle soup with shrimp and coconut milk

SERVES 4

- **1** small onion, roughly chopped

- **1** 2-inch piece fresh ginger (about 1 oz.), peeled and sliced into disks

- **5** cloves garlic, crushed

- **2** to 3 fresh serrano chiles, stemmed and roughly chopped

- **2** stalks lemongrass, trimmed and roughly sliced

- **1** Tbs. freshly ground coriander seeds

- **1** tsp. freshly ground cumin seeds

- **½** tsp. ground turmeric

continued on p. 108

Don't be intimidated by the long list of ingredients here—this soup comes together in under an hour. The end result is otherworldly: a bowl of rice noodles bathed in a silky, spicy coconut broth and capped with a crunchy, cooling garnish.

1. Put the onion, ginger, garlic, chile, lemongrass, coriander, cumin, turmeric, fish sauce, and brown sugar in a food processor. Purée to make a paste, scraping down the sides as needed.

2. Heat the oil in a heavy soup pot or Dutch oven over medium heat until hot but not smoking. Add the paste mixture and sauté, stirring often, until it softens, becomes very aromatic, and deepens in color, about 8 minutes. Stir in the shrimp shells and cook until they turn pink, about 2 minutes. Add the chicken broth, 3 cups water, the coconut milk, lime juice, and 1 tsp. salt and bring to a boil. Lower the heat so that the broth simmers gently for 30 minutes. Strain the broth through a fine-mesh sieve and discard the solids. Clean the pot; return the broth to the pot, season with salt to taste, and return to a simmer.

continued on p. 108

¼ cup fish sauce

2 tsp. light brown sugar

2 Tbs. peanut or vegetable oil

Shells from the shrimp for the soup

2 cups homemade or lower-salt chicken broth

1 14-oz. can coconut milk

¼ cup fresh lime juice

Kosher salt

6 to 7 oz. wide rice noodles

¼ English (seedless) cucumber

1 cup mung bean sprouts, rinsed and dried

1 fresh chile (serrano, jalapeño, or Thai), stemmed and sliced into thin rounds (optional)

½ cup fresh cilantro leaves, roughly chopped or torn

½ cup fresh mint leaves, roughly chopped or torn

1 lb. shrimp (31 to 40 per lb.), shells removed and reserved; deveined

4 lime wedges

3. While the broth is simmering, bring a large pot of water to a boil and then remove from the heat. Put the rice noodles in the water and let sit until tender, 5 to 10 minutes. Drain, rinse, and distribute among 4 large, shallow soup bowls.

4. Slice the cucumber into ¼-inch rounds, stack the rounds, and slice into thin matchsticks. Put the cucumber sticks in a medium bowl and toss with the bean sprouts, sliced chiles (if using), and herbs.

5. Just before serving, add the shrimp to the broth and gently simmer until they're just cooked through, about 3 minutes. Ladle the hot soup over the noodles. Arrange a mound of the cucumber and bean sprout mixture in the center of the bowl, top with a lime wedge, and serve immediately. —*Eva Katz*

PER SERVING: 560 CALORIES | 24G PROTEIN | 55G CARB | 30G TOTAL FAT | 20G SAT FAT | 5G MONO FAT | 3G POLY FAT | 135MG CHOL | 2,100MG SODIUM | 4G FIBER

More about Lemongrass

While the leaves of lemongrass aren't particularly eye-catching, the stalk, which looks like a large, woody scallion, possesses a complexity of flavors that isn't easy to put into words. Some describe it as citrusy, perhaps a little gingery. Its lemon flavor isn't nearly as overt as lemon juice or zest; it's more delicate, with a slight floral flavor that gives a dish a refreshing, lingering lift.

Buying lemongrass

Many supermarkets, as well as Asian markets, carry lemongrass. Fresh lemongrass is firm, pale to medium green, with a whitish-pinkish bulb. The stalks are usually trimmed to about 12 to 18 inches, and they're sometimes bundled. Avoid stalks that are dry and yellow—that's a sign that they're old and have lost moisture, flavor, and fragrance. Lemongrass keeps for weeks wrapped in plastic and refrigerated. If you know that you won't be using it within a couple of weeks, store it in a plastic bag in the freezer, where it will keep for months with just a slight loss of flavor. For easier handling, cut it into 1- to 2-inch pieces or chop it before freezing. Packaged, frozen lemongrass is an acceptable substitute for fresh, but dried or powdered versions have no resemblance to the real thing.

Using lemongrass

Lemongrass is handled in different ways depending on how it's being used. To infuse broths, teas, and stews, first bruise the stalk lightly. Crush the stalk with the side of a knife to release the aromatic oils; then cut it into 1- to 2-inch pieces. Add the pieces at the start of cooking so that their fragrance gains intensity as they simmer. Most recipes suggest removing the pieces before serving, but you can also leave them in. They're visually interesting, and you might enjoy chewing on some for a more lasting lemongrass effect.

To use in marinades, stir-fries, and salads, finely chop the stalk. This way, the lemongrass can be eaten as part of the dish. Use the bottom whitish part of the stalk, including the bulb; save the more fibrous tops for infusing. To make chopping easier, slice the stalk into very thin rounds first and then finely chop them. If you're chopping a lot of lemongrass, you may want to use a food processor. Either way, remove any long fibers that have resisted the blade.

Peel away the fibrous outer layer of the lemongrass stalk. Trim the root end.

Bruise the stalk lightly to release its aromatic oils. This is only necessary if you're leaving the stalk in bigger pieces to infuse a soup or a stew.

Make lemongrass more manageable for mincing. Slice it into very thin rounds before you start to chop. Remove any long fibers that resist chopping before adding the herb to your dish.

colombian chicken soup (ajiaco)

SERVES 8

FOR THE SOUP

- 3 lb. cut-up chicken, skin removed
- 1 large white onion, peeled and cut into quarters
- 1 leek (white and light green parts only), cut into 1-inch rings and rinsed thoroughly
- 1 green bell pepper, seeded and cut into 1-inch pieces
- 2 ears fresh sweet corn, cut crosswise into quarters
- 2 ribs celery, cut into 1-inch pieces
- 2 large carrots, peeled and cut into 1-inch pieces
- ¾ lb. Yukon Gold potatoes, peeled and cut into 1-inch cubes
- ¾ lb. Idaho potatoes, peeled and cut into 1-inch cubes
- ¾ lb. small red potatoes, peeled and cut into 1-inch cubes
- 6 cloves garlic, peeled
- ½ cup fresh cilantro leaves
- 2 chicken bouillon cubes

  Kosher salt and freshly ground black pepper

Make Ahead

The soup and the aji can be made a day ahead. If the soup is too thick after it's reheated, thin it with a little water.

Three elements set this soup apart: a thick stew-like broth thickened with potato; a spicy condiment called aji (pronounced AH-hee) that adds a fiery punch; and flavorful garnishes like capers and avocado.

MAKE THE SOUP

1. Put the chicken in a large (at least 8-quart) stockpot and add 8 cups water. Bring to a boil over high heat and then reduce the heat to a vigorous simmer. Simmer for 10 minutes, frequently skimming off the foam that floats to the surface.

2. Add all the vegetables, the garlic, the cilantro, and the bouillon cubes to the pot, along with the 1 Tbs. salt and ½ tsp. black pepper. Stir a few times to distribute the vegetables and submerge as many of the solids as possible. When the broth returns to a gentle boil, partially cover the pot and simmer, stirring once or twice, for 1½ hours. Taste for salt and add more if needed. Using tongs or a slotted spoon, pick out the chicken pieces and put them on a large plate. Stir the soup with a large spoon, breaking up some of the potatoes to thicken the soup slightly. Keep hot if serving soon or let cool and refrigerate.

3. When the chicken is cool enough to handle, pull the meat off the bones and shred it by hand, discarding the bones and tendons. Put the shredded chicken in a serving bowl.

FOR THE AJI

- **4** scallions (white and light green parts only)
- **1** medium tomato, peeled and seeded
- **1** small white onion, peeled
- **2** fresh Scotch bonnet or habanero chiles or 2 fresh hot red chiles, stemmed and seeded (wear gloves and don't touch your eyes)
- **3** Tbs. fresh cilantro leaves
- **3** Tbs. white vinegar
- **¼** tsp. kosher salt

FOR THE GARNISHES

- **2** ripe avocados, peeled and cut into ½-inch cubes
- **1** cup sour cream or crème fraîche
- **½** cup nonpareil or other small capers, rinsed and drained (if using large capers, chop them coarsely)
- **½** cup chopped fresh cilantro leaves

MAKE THE AJI

In a food processor, pulse all the aji ingredients until they're finely minced. Transfer to a serving bowl.

FOR THE GARNISH AND TO SERVE

Put the avocados, sour cream or crème fraîche, capers, and cilantro leaves in small bowls and set them on the table, along with the bowls of shredded chicken and the aji. Reheat the soup if necessary and ladle it into large soup bowls, putting a quarter ear of corn in each bowl. Let your guests add the garnishes and the aji to their own servings.
—Tania Sigal

PER SERVING: 440 CALORIES | 26G PROTEIN | 46G CARB | 19G TOTAL FAT | 6G SAT FAT | 8G MONO FAT | 3G POLY FAT | 70MG CHOL | 1,300MG SODIUM | 8G FIBER

ginger chicken soup

1 1-inch piece fresh ginger

2 medium cloves garlic, unpeeled

10 to 12 oz. boneless, skinless chicken thighs, trimmed of excess fat (about 3 medium)

2 cups homemade or lower-salt chicken broth

1 Tbs. soy sauce

2 tsp. fresh lemon juice

¼ tsp. Asian chile paste, like sambal oelek or Sriracha

¼ cup packed fresh cilantro

2 Tbs. thinly sliced scallion (green tops only)

Kosher salt

1 Tbs. mild vegetable oil, like canola or safflower oil

1 cup packed baby spinach (about 2 oz.)

Ample ginger gives this soothing soup some aromatic heat. If you don't have a mortar and pestle, mince the scallions and cilantro, then mash them together with the side of a chef's knife.

1. Peel the ginger and slice it into four ¼-inch coins. Using the flat side of a chef's knife or a meat pounder, smash the coins. Smash the garlic and remove the skin. In a medium saucepan, combine the ginger, garlic, chicken, broth, soy sauce, lemon juice, chile paste, and 1 cup water. Bring to a boil over medium-high heat. Reduce the heat to low and gently simmer until the chicken is cooked through, about 10 minutes. Using a pair of tongs, transfer the chicken to a plate. Use a slotted spoon to remove the ginger and garlic and discard. Keep the broth warm.

2. Finely chop the cilantro and scallion. Put them in a mortar, add a pinch of salt and 2 tsp. of the oil, and pound and mash with the pestle. Once the mixture begins to blend, add the remaining 1 tsp. oil. Continue to grind the pestle into the cilantro mixture until it's aromatic and has the consistency of a paste.

3. Once the chicken is cool, slice it thinly and portion it into 4 soup bowls. Return the broth to a simmer and season with salt to taste. Add the spinach to the broth and continue to simmer until it's wilted, 1 to 2 minutes more. Ladle the broth and spinach evenly over each portion of chicken and then top each with a dollop of the cilantro paste.
—*Maryellen Driscoll*

PER SERVING: 160 CALORIES | 16G PROTEIN | 4G CARB | 10G TOTAL FAT | 2G SAT FAT | 4G MONO FAT | 3G POLY FAT | 45MG CHOL | 700MG SODIUM | 0G FIBER

escarole and white bean soup with rustic croutons

SERVES 4

¼ cup extra-virgin olive oil

1 medium onion (6 oz.), diced

2 oz. very thinly sliced pancetta, diced (about ½ cup)

1 Tbs. minced garlic

1 medium to large head escarole (about 14 oz.), trimmed of outer leaves, 2 inches of root end cut off, leaves sliced across into ¾-inch-wide strips (to yield about 9 to 10 cups), thoroughly washed

Kosher salt and freshly ground black pepper

2 cups homemade or lower-salt chicken broth

1 cup cooked small white beans

1 Tbs. fresh lemon juice

¼ cup freshly grated Parmigiano-Reggiano

2 cups Rustic Croutons (recipe below)

It's hard to believe how quickly this soup comes together because it has such great long-cooked flavors. Escarole is one of the easiest greens to prepare since you don't need to stem it; just slice the whole head across into ribbons before washing.

1. Heat the olive oil in a 4-quart low-sided soup pot or Dutch oven over medium to medium-high heat. Add the onion and pancetta and sauté until the onion is softened and both are browned, about 12 minutes. Add the garlic, stir, and sauté until fragrant, 30 seconds to 1 minute. Add the escarole and stir thoroughly to coat the leaves (and to deglaze the pan slightly with their moisture). Season with ½ tsp. salt and a few grinds of pepper. Add the broth, stir well, and bring to a boil; cover the pot, lower to a simmer, and cook 8 to 10 minutes.

2. Uncover the pot, add the beans, and simmer for another 2 to 3 minutes. Add the lemon juice and turn off the heat. Ladle the soup into 4 shallow soup bowls and top each with 1 Tbs. of the cheese and a quarter of the croutons. —*Susie Middleton*

PER SERVING: 390 CALORIES | 14G PROTEIN | 30G CARB | 25G TOTAL FAT | 5G SAT FAT | 16G MONO FAT | 2G POLY FAT | 15MG CHOL | 1,080MG SODIUM | 9G FIBER

rustic croutons

MAKES 2 CUPS

2 Tbs. extra-virgin olive oil

2 cups (lightly packed) ¾-inch cubes of bread cut from an airy, crusty loaf like ciabatta

Kosher salt

Heat the oil in a nonstick skillet over medium-high heat. Add the cubes of bread and stir to coat with the oil. Season with salt and sauté, stirring constantly, until crisp and browned on most sides, 2 to 4 minutes.

french farmers' soup

MAKES 10 CUPS; SERVES 6

- 8 oz. (1¼ cups) dried flageolets or baby lima beans, picked over and rinsed
- 1 medium clove garlic, smashed and peeled
- 1 bay leaf

  Kosher salt
- 2 Tbs. extra-virgin olive oil
- ¼ lb. bacon or pancetta (optional)
- 1½ cups chopped shallots and leeks

  Freshly ground black pepper
- 4 tsp. fresh thyme, chopped
- 1 cup peeled carrots, cut into ¼-inch-thick half-moons
- 1 cup peeled celery root, cut into ½-inch dice
- 1 cup peeled turnips, cut into ½-inch dice
- 5 to 6 cups homemade or lower-salt chicken broth or vegetable broth
- 1 to 2 tsp. white-wine vinegar
- 1 cup croutons, preferably homemade (see the recipe at left)
- ⅓ cup chopped fresh flat-leaf parsley

This hearty bean soup makes the most of root vegetables. If you're short on time, you can substitute 3 cups canned limas (rinsed and drained) for the dried beans, and skip the steps of soaking and cooking them, though the flavor won't be quite as rich.

1. Put the beans in a large bowl and add enough cold water to cover the beans by 3 inches. Soak for 4 to 12 hours.

2. Drain the beans, rinse them, and transfer to a 3- or 4-quart saucepan. Add the garlic clove, bay leaf, and 6 cups cold water. Partially cover to limit evaporation and simmer gently, stirring every 20 to 30 minutes, until the beans are tender and almost creamy inside, without being mealy or mushy, about 45 minutes to 1 hour. When the beans are about three-quarters done, season with ¾ tsp. salt. If at any time the liquid doesn't cover the beans, add 1 cup fresh water. Drain the beans, reserving the cooking liquid, and discard the bay leaf.

3. Heat the olive oil in a 4- to 5-quart soup pot or Dutch oven over medium heat. Add the bacon or pancetta (if using) and cook until it browns. Pour the meat and fat into a small strainer set over a bowl and set the meat aside. Spoon 2 Tbs. of the fat back into the pot and return it to medium heat. Add the shallots and leeks to the pot, season with a pinch of salt and pepper, and cook until they begin to soften but not brown, 4 to 6 minutes. Stir in the thyme and cook for 1 minute. Add the carrots, celery root, turnips, and 2 cups of the broth. Partially cover and simmer until the vegetables are just barely tender, 10 to 20 minutes. Add the beans and 3 cups of the broth, plus 1 cup of the reserved bean-cooking liquid. If you have less than 1 cup of bean liquid, adjust the broth for a total of 4 cups liquid. Return the cooked meat to the pot, if using. Stir and simmer, partially covered, for 10 minutes. Add the vinegar plus salt and pepper to taste.

4. Serve hot, topping each serving with a small handful of croutons and a sprinkle of parsley. *—Molly Stevens*

PER SERVING: 300 CALORIES | 16G PROTEIN | 40G CARB | 9G TOTAL FAT | 2G SAT FAT | 5G MONO FAT | 1.5G POLY FAT | 5MG CHOL | 470MG SODIUM | 9G FIBER

Make Ahead

Don't have at least 4 hours to soak beans? You can quick-soak them. In a saucepan, add enough cold water to cover the beans by 2 inches, bring to a boil, remove from the heat, and let soak for 1 hour. You can also cook the beans 1 day ahead and refrigerate them in a covered container.

garlicky tortellini, spinach & tomato soup

SERVES 2 OR 3

2 Tbs. unsalted butter

6 to 8 cloves garlic, chopped

1 quart homemade or lower-salt chicken broth

6 oz. fresh or frozen cheese tortellini

1 14-oz. can diced tomatoes, with their liquid

10 oz. spinach, washed and stemmed, coarsely chopped if large

8 to 10 fresh basil leaves, coarsely chopped

Freshly grated Parmigiano-Reggiano, for serving

Served with a crusty piece of bread, this soup makes a delicious lunch or dinner, and it's incredibly easy to make. If you have some of your own broth handy, so much the better. But because you're adding a lot of flavorful garlic, tomatoes, and fragrant basil to the soup, store-bought broth (preferably lower salt) works fine. Serve the soup hot with some grated Parmigiano.

1. Melt the butter in a large saucepan over medium-high heat. Add the garlic and sauté until fragrant, about 2 minutes. Add the broth and bring to a boil. Add the tortellini and cook halfway, about 5 minutes for frozen pasta, less if using fresh. Add the tomatoes and their liquid, reduce the heat to a simmer, and cook just until the pasta is tender.

2. Stir in the spinach and basil and cook until wilted, 1 to 2 minutes. Serve sprinkled with the grated cheese. —*Joanne McAllister Smart*

PER SERVING: 270 CALORIES | 15G PROTEIN | 22G CARB | 15G TOTAL FAT | 9G SAT FAT | 3G MONO FAT | 1G POLY FAT | 35MG CHOL | 560MG SODIUM | 6G FIBER

golden chicken, corn & orzo soup

SERVES 6

Kosher salt

2 Tbs. olive oil

2 large ribs celery, finely diced

1 medium onion, finely diced

1 pinch of saffron threads

½ tsp. dried thyme

2 quarts homemade or lower-salt chicken broth

2 cups finely diced or shredded cooked chicken (such as leftover roast chicken)

½ cup orzo

1 cup frozen corn

¼ cup chopped fresh flat-leaf parsley

3 Tbs. fresh lemon juice; more as needed

Freshly ground black pepper

This quick and delicious weeknight soup is a great way to use up leftover roast chicken.

1. Bring a medium saucepan of well-salted water to a boil over high heat. Meanwhile, heat the oil in a large soup pot over medium heat. Add the celery, onion, saffron, and thyme. Cook, stirring occasionally, until the vegetables start to soften, 5 to 6 minutes. Add the broth and bring to a boil over medium-high heat. Reduce the heat to a simmer, add the chicken, and cook until the vegetables are tender, about 15 minutes. While the soup simmers, cook the orzo in the boiling salted water until tender, 8 to 10 minutes. Drain.

2. Add the drained orzo, corn, and parsley to the soup and cook just until the corn is heated through, about 2 minutes. Stir in the lemon juice and season to taste with salt, pepper, and more lemon juice, if needed. —*Jennifer Armentrout*

PER SERVING: 250 CALORIES | 22G PROTEIN | 19G CARB | 10G TOTAL FAT | 2G SAT FAT | 6G MONO FAT | 2G POLY FAT | 40MG CHOL | 440MG SODIUM | 2G FIBER

lemon chicken soup with spinach and dill

SERVES 6

- **2** Tbs. extra-virgin olive oil
- **1** large yellow onion, cut into medium dice
- **1** lb. boneless, skinless chicken thighs
- **1** quart homemade or lower-salt chicken broth
- **½** cup instant rice
- **1** tsp. dried oregano
- **5** oz. (6 cups lightly packed) baby spinach
- **2** Tbs. minced fresh dill
- **2** Tbs. fresh lemon juice; more as needed

Kosher salt and freshly ground black pepper

This Greek-inspired soup is supereasy to make but comes packed with exciting flavors. Chicken thighs offer all the benefits of chicken breast but cook up moist and tender because they're dark meat.

1. Heat the oil in a 3-quart Dutch oven or soup pot over medium heat. Add the onion and cook until softened, 5 to 7 minutes. Add the chicken thighs, broth, rice, and oregano. Cover, raise the heat to medium high, and bring to a full boil; turn off the heat and let stand, covered, for 5 minutes. With tongs, transfer the chicken to a cutting board and shred it with a table knife and fork, discarding any obvious fat or gristle.

2. Working in two batches, purée the broth, rice, and onion in a blender until very smooth, 30 to 60 seconds (be sure to vent the lid and cover it with a kitchen towel to prevent splashes). Return the chicken and the thickened broth to the pot and bring to a simmer over medium-low heat. Add the spinach and dill; cook until the spinach wilts completely, about 3 minutes. Stir in the lemon juice. Season to taste with salt, pepper, and more lemon juice. *—Pamela Anderson*

PER SERVING: 230 CALORIES | 18G PROTEIN | 14G CARB | 11G TOTAL FAT | 3G SAT FAT | 6G MONO FAT | 2G POLY FAT | 50MG CHOL | 710MG SODIUM | 2G FIBER

thai hot and sour shrimp soup

**MAKES ABOUT 8 CUPS;
SERVES 4**

- **1** Tbs. vegetable oil
- **1** tsp. finely chopped garlic
- **½** tsp. chile paste
- **½** tsp. crushed red pepper flakes
- **3** thin slices fresh or frozen galangal (or 2 thin slices fresh, peeled ginger)
- **1** stalk lemongrass, bruised with the side of a knife and cut into 1-inch pieces on the diagonal
- **6** cups homemade or lower-salt chicken broth
- **2** Tbs. fish sauce
- **4½** tsp. granulated sugar
- **2** wild lime leaves, cut in half (optional)
- **½** cup drained canned straw mushrooms (or 3 oz. fresh white mushrooms, quartered)
- **2** plum tomatoes, seeded and chopped
- **½** lb. raw shrimp, shelled and deveined
- **¼** cup fresh lime juice
- **1** scallion (white and light green parts), coarsely chopped
- **5** fresh basil leaves, chopped
- **5** fresh cilantro sprigs, chopped

A little spicey and a little tangy, this soup is made especially aromatic by the addition of lemongrass. Most of the ingredients used can be found in the supermarket these days.

1. In a saucepan, heat the oil over moderate heat. Add the garlic, chile paste, and red pepper flakes. Stir until fragrant, about 1 minute. Add the galangal and lemongrass; stir until the ingredients are lightly browned, about 2 minutes.

2. Add the chicken broth and simmer for 15 to 20 minutes. Bring the soup to a boil. Add the fish sauce, sugar, wild lime leaves (if using), mushrooms, and tomatoes. Add the shrimp and cook until they just turn pink, about 2 minutes. (The shrimp will continue to cook in the hot broth.) Remove the pan from the heat and add the lime juice, scallion, basil, and cilantro. Serve immediately. —*Mai Pham*

PER 2 CUPS: 150 CALORIES | 15G PROTEIN | 12G CARB | 5G TOTAL FAT | 1G SAT FAT | 3G MONO FAT | 1G POLY FAT | 85MG CHOL | 860MG SODIUM | 1G FIBER

how to peel and devein shrimp

To peel raw shrimp, hold the tail in one hand and start pulling off the shell from underneath, where their legs are attached.

Devein the shrimp by first making a shallow slit down the middle of the back to expose the black intestine. (To butterfly, make the slit deeper.)

Lift out the black vein with the tip of a paring knife and wipe it off on a paper towel. You can also rinse it out under cold running water.

noodle soup with kale and white beans

SERVES 6 TO 8

- 2 Tbs. extra-virgin olive oil
- 3 medium carrots, peeled and chopped
- 1 medium red onion, chopped
- 1 cup broken (2- to 3-inch pieces) dried capellini pasta or fideo noodles
- 2 quarts homemade or lower-salt chicken broth
- 1 small bunch kale, ribs removed, leaves roughly chopped (about 6 cups)
- 1 15-oz. can cannellini beans, rinsed and drained
- 3 Tbs. fresh lime juice; more as needed

  Kosher salt and freshly ground black pepper
- ¼ . cup coarsely chopped fresh cilantro

Cooking the noodles in oil before adding the broth infuses the soup with a tasty flavor. If you can find fideo noodles in the Latin section of your supermarket, try them in place of the capellini.

1. Heat 1 Tbs. of the oil in a large pot over medium-high heat. Add the carrots and onion and cook, stirring occasionally, until the onion is soft and just golden brown, about 10 minutes. With a rubber spatula, scrape the vegetables into a medium bowl and set aside. If necessary, wipe the pot clean.

2. Heat the remaining 1 Tbs. oil in the pot over medium-high heat. Add the pasta and cook, stirring often, until dark golden brown, 3 to 4 minutes. Add the broth and stir, scraping the bottom of the pot to release any stuck-on pasta. Add the carrots, onion, kale, beans, lime juice, ½ tsp. salt, and ¼ tsp. pepper and bring to a boil. Reduce the heat to medium low and simmer until the kale, carrots, and pasta are tender, 8 to 10 minutes.

3. Remove the pot from the heat, stir in the cilantro, and season to taste with more lime juice, salt, and pepper before serving. —*Liz Pearson*

PER SERVING: 200 CALORIES | 11G PROTEIN | 29G CARB | 6G TOTAL FAT | 1G SAT FAT | 3G MONO FAT | 1G POLY FAT | 0MG CHOL | 230MG SODIUM | 4G FIBER

lemony chicken noodle soup
with ginger, chile & cilantro

MAKES 7 CUPS; SERVES 4

- **1 lemon**
- **¼ cup chopped fresh cilantro**
- **1 tsp. finely grated fresh ginger**
- **2 fresh serrano chiles, stemmed, halved, and seeded**
- **6 cups homemade or lower-salt chicken broth**
- **4 oz. fresh Chinese egg noodles (look in the produce section of your supermarket)**
- **2 Tbs. fish sauce; more as needed**
- **1 boneless, skinless chicken breast half, cut into ¼-inch-thick slices (this is easier to do if the chicken is partially frozen)**

Fish sauce varies in its saltiness from brand to brand, so it's a good idea to prepare the soup with the modest amount specified in this recipe. At serving time, pass around the fish sauce so people can season their portions with a touch more if they like.

1. Finely grate 1 tsp. of zest from the lemon and put in a small dish. Add the cilantro and ginger and mix together. Cut the zested lemon in half and squeeze it to get 3 Tbs. juice. Thinly slice 2 of the chile halves crosswise.

2. In a large saucepan, bring the broth to a boil over medium-high heat. Add the lemon juice, noodles, fish sauce, and the 2 remaining chile halves to the boiling broth. Reduce the heat, cover, and simmer the soup until the noodles are almost cooked, about 3 minutes. Remove the chile halves. Stir in the chicken and chile slices and return to a boil. Remove the pan from the heat, making sure the chicken slices are just cooked through. Taste and add a touch more fish sauce, if you like. Portion the soup and the cilantro mixture evenly among four soup bowls, stir, and serve. —*Jennifer McLagan*

PER SERVING: 190 CALORIES | 18G PROTEIN | 23G CARB | 4G TOTAL FAT | 1G SAT FAT | 1.5G MONO FAT | 1G POLY FAT | 40MG CHOL | 820MG SODIUM | 1G FIBER

minestrone with green beans and fennel

**MAKES ABOUT 8 CUPS;
SERVES 4 TO 6**

- 3 Tbs. extra-virgin olive oil
- 2 medium cloves garlic, smashed and peeled
- ½ lb. green beans, trimmed and cut into 1-inch pieces
- 1 small fennel bulb, quartered, cored, and cut into ¼-inch dice

  Kosher salt

- 1 quart homemade or lower-salt chicken broth
- 1 14½-oz. can diced tomatoes, with their liquid
- 1 15½-oz. can cannellini beans, rinsed and drained
- ½ cup dried ditalini pasta or small elbows
- ½ cup freshly grated Parmigiano-Reggiano; more for serving
- 6 large fresh basil leaves, coarsely chopped

  Freshly ground black pepper

For a vegetarian version of this recipe, use vegetable broth—preferably homemade.

1. Heat the oil and garlic in a medium saucepan over medium heat until the garlic begins to brown, 2 to 3 minutes; discard the garlic. Raise the heat to medium high, add the green beans, fennel, and ¾ tsp. salt, and cook, stirring, until the beans and fennel begin to soften and brown in places, 5 to 7 minutes. Add the broth and the tomatoes with their liquid and bring to a boil. Add the cannellini beans and pasta and return to a boil. Reduce the heat to a simmer, cover, and cook until the pasta and green beans are completely tender, 10 to 12 minutes.

2. Stir in the Parmigiano and basil and season to taste with salt and pepper. Serve sprinkled with more Parmigiano. —*Tony Rosenfeld*

PER SERVING: 220 CALORIES | 10G PROTEIN | 27G CARB | 9G TOTAL FAT | 1.5G SAT FAT | 5G MONO FAT | 1.5G POLY FAT | 0MG CHOL | 510MG SODIUM | 6G FIBER

chicken soup with lime and hominy

SERVES 4

- **12** oz. boneless, skinless chicken breasts
- **1** Tbs. vegetable oil
- **1** small white onion (8 oz.), chopped
- **4** medium cloves garlic, minced
- **1** small fresh jalapeño, minced
- **1** quart homemade or lower-salt chicken broth
- **1** 15-oz. can hominy, drained
- **1** tsp. dried Mexican oregano, crumbled if the leaves are large
- **4** to 5 Tbs. fresh lime juice
- Kosher salt and freshly ground black pepper
- **2½** oz. cotija or feta cheese, cut into ¼-inch cubes (½ cup)

This is a quick and easy version of sopa de lima, a comforting yet refreshing Yucatan chicken soup made tangy with fresh lime juice. Tasty garnishes include fried tortilla strips (or tortilla chips), diced avocado, and fresh cilantro.

1. Cut each chicken breast crosswise into 1½-inch-wide pieces. Heat the oil in a 6-quart pot over medium-high heat until shimmering. Add the onion and cook, stirring often, until softened, about 5 minutes. Stir in the garlic and jalapeño and cook, stirring often, until fragrant, about 45 seconds. Add the broth, hominy, oregano, and chicken. Raise the heat to high and bring to a boil. Reduce the heat to medium, cover, and simmer gently, stirring occasionally and adjusting the heat as needed to maintain a simmer, until the chicken is cooked through, about 10 minutes.

2. Transfer the chicken to a plate. Using two forks, shred the meat into bite-size pieces and return to the pan. Bring the soup back to a simmer over medium heat, stir in the lime juice, and season to taste with salt and pepper. Ladle into bowls, top with the cheese, and serve immediately. *—Dawn Yanagihara*

PER SERVING: 320 CALORIES | 29G PROTEIN | 27G CARB | 12G TOTAL FAT | 4G SAT FAT | 4G MONO FAT | 3G POLY FAT | 65MG CHOL | 680MG SODIUM | 4G FIBER

pasta e fagioli

MAKES 16 CUPS; SERVES 8

- 8 slices bacon, cut crosswise into ¼-inch-wide strips
- 3 medium red onions, finely chopped
- 3 medium cloves garlic, minced
- ½ tsp. dried rosemary
- 2 quarts homemade or lower-salt chicken broth
- 2 15½-oz. cans chickpeas, rinsed and drained
- 1 14½-oz. can petite-cut diced tomatoes, with their liquid
- 4 medium carrots, peeled, halved lengthwise, and thinly sliced
- 3 medium ribs celery with leaves, thinly sliced crosswise
- 1 slender 3-inch cinnamon stick

  Kosher salt and freshly ground black pepper
- 8 oz. tubettini (or other small pasta)
- 1½ tsp. red-wine vinegar; more as needed

  Freshly grated or shaved Parmigiano-Reggiano, for garnish

This Italian soup—which has as many variations as there are cooks— is chock full of pasta, beans, and vegetables, making it a hearty one-dish meal.

1. In a 6-quart Dutch oven over medium heat, cook the bacon, stirring occasionally, until partially crisp, about 7 minutes. With a slotted spoon, transfer the bacon to a paper-towel-lined plate. Add the onion to the pot and cook, scraping up any browned bits and stirring occasionally, until softened, 6 to 8 minutes. Add the garlic and rosemary and cook, stirring constantly, until fragrant, about 1 minute. Add the chicken broth, chickpeas, tomatoes and their liquid, carrots, celery, cinnamon stick, ¾ tsp. salt, ½ tsp. pepper, and 1 cup water. Bring to a boil over high heat; skim any foam as necessary. Reduce the heat and simmer, stirring occasionally, until the carrots and celery are very tender, about 30 minutes.

2. Meanwhile, cook the tubettini according to the package directions and drain.

3. Discard the cinnamon stick and add the pasta. Stir in the bacon and vinegar. Season to taste with more salt, pepper, and vinegar. Serve garnished with the Parmigiano. Store leftovers in the refrigerator for up to 2 days. —*Lori Longbotham*

PER SERVING: 370 CALORIES | 21G PROTEIN | 59G CARB | 7G TOTAL FAT | 1.5G SAT FAT | 2.5G MONO FAT | 2G POLY FAT | 5MG CHOL | 720MG SODIUM | 11G FIBER

root vegetable and barley soup with bacon

MAKES 13 CUPS; SERVES 6 TO 8

- **1** oz. dried porcini mushrooms
- **2** medium cloves garlic
  Kosher salt
- **4** slices bacon, cut in half crosswise
- **2** medium red onions, chopped
- **2** small bay leaves
- **¾** tsp. caraway seeds
- **½** tsp. dried thyme
  Freshly ground black pepper
- **2** quarts homemade or lower-salt chicken broth
- **5** medium carrots, peeled and cut into small dice
- **2** medium purple-top turnips, peeled and cut into small dice
- **2** medium Yukon Gold potatoes, peeled and cut into small dice
- **¾** cup pearl barley, picked over, rinsed, and drained
- **4** tsp. fresh lemon juice

Thick and rich flavored, this makes a perfect cool-weather meal. You can store this soup for up to 2 days, but if you store it for more than a day, the barley will absorb some of the liquid and you'll need to thin it with a little water when you reheat it.

1. In small bowl, soak the mushrooms in 1 cup boiling water for 20 minutes. Remove the mushrooms and pour the liquid through a fine-mesh strainer to remove any grit. Reserve the liquid. Rinse the mushrooms, chop them, and set aside.

2. Chop the garlic, sprinkle it with ¾ tsp. salt, and then mash it to a paste with the side of a chef's knife. Set aside.

3. In a 6-quart Dutch oven, cook the bacon over medium heat until crisp, about 8 minutes. Transfer to a paper-towel-lined plate, crumble when cool, and set aside.

4. Add the onion and 1 tsp. salt to the bacon fat and cook, stirring occasionally, until softened, 6 to 8 minutes. Stir in the garlic paste, bay leaves, caraway seeds, thyme, and ¼ tsp. pepper and cook, stirring constantly, until fragrant, about 1 minute. Add the chopped mushrooms, mushroom liquid, chicken broth, carrots, turnips, potatoes, barley, and 1½ cups water. Bring to a boil over high heat; skim any foam as necessary. Reduce the heat, cover, and simmer, stirring occasionally, until the barley and vegetables are tender, 20 to 25 minutes. Add the lemon juice, season with salt and pepper, and discard the bay leaves. Serve garnished with the bacon. *—Lori Longbotham*

PER SERVING: 210 CALORIES | 11G PROTEIN | 37G CARB | 3.5G TOTAL FAT | 1G SAT FAT | 1.5G MONO FAT | 0.5G POLY FAT | 5MG CHOL | 450MG SODIUM | 7G FIBER

roasted vegetable minestrone

MAKES ABOUT 10 CUPS;
SERVES 8

- 1¼ cups mixed dried cannellini and dried kidney beans, sorted through and rinsed

- 1 large bulb fennel, quartered, cored, and cut into ¾-inch slices

- 3 inner ribs celery, cut into 2-inch pieces

- 2 large carrots, peeled and cut into 1-inch pieces

- 3 Tbs. extra-virgin olive oil

  Kosher salt and freshly ground black pepper

- 1 28-oz. can whole tomatoes, with their liquid

- 1 Tbs. plus 1 tsp. chopped fresh rosemary

- ¼ lb. dried ditalini (or other small tubular pasta), cooked until tender, rinsed with cold water, and drained

- 3 Tbs. chopped fresh flat-leaf parsley

- ½ cup finely grated Parmigiano-Reggiano

Roasting the vegetables sweetens their flavor. Feel free to experiment with other vegetables.

1. Cook the cannellini and kidney beans together, following the Basic Beans method on p. 47.

2. Meanwhile, heat the oven to 450°F. In a large bowl, toss the fennel, celery, and carrots with the oil; season generously with salt and pepper. Spread on a rimmed baking sheet lined with foil. Roast, tossing after 10 minutes and every 5 minutes thereafter, until the vegetables are nicely browned and tender when pierced with a fork, about 30 minutes. Let cool for at least 15 minutes. Transfer the vegetables to a cutting board, chop them coarsely, and put them in a large pot. Slice the tomatoes into large pieces and add them and their liquid, the beans, 3 cups of their cooking liquid (or add water to equal this amount), and 1 Tbs. of the rosemary to the pot. Bring to a boil, turn the heat to medium low, cover, and simmer for 40 minutes, stirring occasionally. Thin with water, if necessary, to get the consistency you like.

3. Stir in the cooked pasta, the remaining 1 tsp. rosemary, the parsley, ¼ cup of the Parmigiano, and salt and pepper to taste. Ladle into bowls and serve immediately with a generous sprinkle of the remaining Parmigiano. —*Tony Rosenfeld*

PER SERVING: 260 CALORIES | 12G PROTEIN | 38G CARB | 7G TOTAL FAT | 2G SAT FAT | 4G MONO FAT | 1G POLY FAT | 5MG CHOL | 550MG SODIUM | 7G FIBER

rustic bean and farro soup

**SERVES 6 AS A MAIN DISH
OR 8 AS A FIRST COURSE**

- 3 Tbs. olive oil
- ¾ cup chopped pancetta
- 1 medium onion, chopped
- 2 medium carrots, peeled and chopped
- 2 medium ribs celery, chopped
- 4 large cloves garlic, minced
- 2 tsp. chopped fresh sage, marjoram, or thyme, or a combination
- 1¼ cups dried chickpeas or cannellini beans (or a combination), picked over, soaked overnight, and drained (or 3½ cups canned chickpeas, cannellini beans, or a combination)
- 1½ cups canned diced tomatoes, with their liquid
- 8 cups homemade or lower-salt chicken broth or water

  Kosher salt and freshly ground black pepper
- 1¼ cups uncooked whole-grain farro

  Extra-virgin olive oil, for garnish

  Freshly grated Parmigiano-Reggiano, for garnish

The farro can get soft if it sits in the soup overnight, so cook it separately and add it to the amount of soup you're serving.

1. Heat the olive oil in a soup pot over medium heat. Add the pancetta and sauté until golden brown, about 5 minutes. Add the onion, carrots, celery, garlic, and herbs and sauté until the vegetables soften, about 5 minutes.

2. If using dried beans, add the soaked, drained beans to the soup pot, with the tomatoes and their liquid, broth or water, and 2 tsp. salt, and bring to a boil. Reduce the heat, cover, and simmer until the beans are tender, 1 to 2 hours. (If using canned beans, drain and rinse them, add the tomatoes, broth or water, and 2 tsp. salt to the soup pot and bring to a boil. Reduce the heat, add the beans, and simmer for about 20 minutes.) Season with salt and pepper. For a creamier soup, purée 1 cup of the bean mixture and stir it back into the pot.

3. While the soup simmers, bring 6 cups salted water to a boil. Add the farro, reduce the heat, and simmer until it's just al dente and chewy, 10 to 30 minutes. Drain, add it to the soup, and simmer for another 10 to 15 minutes to let the flavors meld and to finish cooking. Stir to prevent scorching. Ladle into bowls and garnish with a swirl of olive oil, grated cheese, and pepper. *—Joyce Goldstein*

PER SERVING BASED ON 8 SERVINGS: 330 CALORIES | 16G PROTEIN | 43G CARB | 12G TOTAL FAT | 2G SAT FAT | 7G MONO FAT | 2G POLY FAT | 10MG CHOL | 820MG SODIUM | 7G FIBER

More about Farro

Farro has a nutty flavor and a firm, chewy texture that resembles barley more than wheat.

Buying tips

Don't confuse whole-grain farro with the cracked form, which looks like bulgur, has a very different texture, and cooks much faster. You can buy whole-grain farro in specialty food shops or by mail order.

Cooking basics

Simmer 1 part whole-grain farro in 5 parts salted water until it's toothy and chewy but no longer hard; drain any excess water. Unsoaked, it cooks in 15 to 30 minutes. Cooked farro will keep in the fridge for 5 days; reheat it in broth or water.

sausage, cannellini & kale soup

SERVES 4

- 1½ Tbs. extra-virgin olive oil
- 1 medium yellow onion, finely chopped (1½ cups)
- 1 medium carrot, peeled and finely chopped (¾ cup)
- 1 medium rib celery, finely chopped (¾ cup)
- 1½ tsp. minced fresh rosemary
- 2 Tbs. tomato paste
- 2 large cloves garlic, minced (1 Tbs.)
- 1 quart homemade or lower-salt chicken or vegetable broth
- 2 15-oz. cans cannellini beans, rinsed and drained
- 6 oz. Lacinato kale, center ribs removed, leaves chopped (about 4 firmly packed cups)
- 1 Parmigiano-Reggiano rind (1x3 inches; optional)

  Kosher salt and freshly ground black pepper
- ⅔ lb. sweet or hot bulk Italian sausage, rolled into bite-size meatballs
- 1½ tsp. cider vinegar

This hearty Tuscan soup is full of flavor. The crinkly, deep-green leaves of Lacinato kale (also called dinosaur or black kale) are ideal, but any variety of kale will work. Serve with a crusty baguette or garlic crostini.

1. Heat 1 Tbs. of the oil in a 4- to 5-quart pot over medium heat. Add the onion, carrot, celery, and rosemary and cook, stirring occasionally, until the vegetables begin to soften, about 6 minutes. Add the tomato paste and garlic and cook until fragrant, 45 seconds. Add the broth, beans, kale, and Parmigiano rind (if using). Bring to a boil, reduce the heat to medium low, and simmer gently until the vegetables are tender, about 15 minutes.

2. Meanwhile, heat the remaining ½ Tbs. oil in a 10-inch nonstick skillet over medium-low heat. Add the sausage meatballs, sprinkle with a pinch of salt, and cook, stirring occasionally, until browned and cooked through, about 10 minutes.

3. Add the sausage to the soup and bring to a simmer over medium-high heat. Cook for another 5 minutes to meld the flavors. Stir the cider vinegar into the soup and season to taste with salt and pepper.
—Ivy Manning

PER SERVING: 430 CALORIES | 20G PROTEIN | 48G CARB | 18G TOTAL FAT | 5G SAT FAT | 9G MONO FAT | 3G POLY FAT | 25MG CHOL | 1,160MG SODIUM | 12G FIBER

soup of the bakony outlaws

- **3** Tbs. oil
- **2** onions, cut into ¼-inch dice
- **2** oz. bacon, cut into ¼-inch dice
- **1½** Tbs. sweet paprika
- **8** oz. thin veal cutlet, cut into ¼-inch dice
- **2** to 3 cups homemade or lower-salt chicken broth
- **2** medium carrots, peeled and cut into ¼-inch dice
- **2** medium turnips, peeled and cut into ¼-inch dice
- **8** oz. fresh mushrooms, cut into ¼-inch dice
- **2** medium potatoes, peeled and cut into ¼-inch dice
- **2** medium tomatoes, peeled, seeded, and cut into ¼-inch dice or 4 canned seeded, chopped tomatoes
- Kosher salt and freshly ground black pepper
- **1** cup sour cream
- **2** Tbs. unbleached all-purpose flour
- **1** cup heavy cream or crème fraîche
- **3** Tbs. snipped fresh dill, plus small sprigs for garnish

Bakony is a mountainous region near Lake Balaton in Hungary, and the outlaws must have been both gourmet and gourmand to inspire this hearty, flavorful soup. You'll notice that many of the ingredients are diced pretty fine, which gives the soup a wonderful texture and lots of flavor, but if you need to save some time, you can chop a bit more coarsely, though you should keep the bacon and veal very small.

1. Heat the oil in a large saucepan or Dutch oven and cook the onion and bacon over medium heat until the onion starts to color, 10 to 15 minutes. Stir in the paprika and cook, stirring, for another 2 minutes to release and develop its flavor. Add the veal and just enough of the broth to cover it. Cover the pan and simmer for 20 minutes.

2. Add the carrots, turnips, mushrooms, potatoes, tomatoes, and more broth, reserving about 1 cup; don't worry if the liquid doesn't cover the vegetables at this point. Season with salt and pepper. Bring to a boil, reduce the heat, and simmer until the vegetables are tender, another 20 minutes. Add a little more broth if the soup looks too dry during cooking, bearing in mind that more liquid will be added later.

3. Put the sour cream in a small bowl and stir in the flour with a fork or whisk; stir in the cream. Pour this into the soup and bring it to a boil, stirring constantly. Simmer for 2 minutes. Taste and adjust the salt and pepper. Just before serving, stir in the chopped fresh dill and toss some sprigs on top for garnish, if you like. *—Randall Price*

PER FIRST COURSE SERVING: 390 CALORIES | 12G PROTEIN | 18G CARB | 31G TOTAL FAT | 14G SAT FAT | 10G MONO FAT | 5G POLY FAT | 85MG CHOL | 430MG SODIUM | 3G FIBER

tomato soup with fennel, leek & potato

MAKES 5½ CUPS; SERVES 6

- **3** Tbs. olive oil
- **1** tsp. fennel seeds, coarsely crushed or ground in a spice grinder
- **1** medium fennel bulb, trimmed, cored, and cut into small dice (about 2 cups; save some fronds for optional garnish)
- **1** large leek (white and light green parts only), halved lengthwise, rinsed well, and cut into small dice (about 1 cup)
- **1** Tbs. Pernod (optional)
- **3** cups homemade or lower-salt chicken broth
- **1** 28-oz. can whole peeled plum tomatoes, drained (reserve the liquid) and coarsely chopped
- **1** medium red or yellow potato, peeled and cut into medium dice

  Kosher salt and freshly ground black pepper

Loaded with fennel and potatoes, this hearty tomato soup is perfect with a grilled cheese sandwich, but a fresh spinach salad would make the meal, too. Although the Pernod in this recipe is optional, it enhances and deepens the fennel flavor beautifully.

1. In a nonreactive 4-quart saucepan, heat the oil over medium-low heat. Add the fennel seeds and cook until fragrant and lightly brown, about 3 minutes. Add the diced fennel, leek, and Pernod (if using) and cook over low heat, stirring occasionally, until the vegetables are soft, about 10 minutes.

2. Add the broth, tomatoes, and potatoes. Bring to a boil over medium heat. Reduce the heat to low, cover, and simmer until the potato is cooked through, 30 to 40 minutes. Season to taste with salt and pepper. Serve chunky or purée in a blender. If you purée the soup and it's too thick, add some of the reserved tomato liquid. Garnish with chopped fennel fronds, if you like. *—Perla Meyers*

PER SERVING: 150 CALORIES | 5G PROTEIN | 15G CARB | 8G TOTAL FAT | 1G SAT FAT | 5G MONO FAT | 0.9G POLY FAT | 0MG CHOL | 230MG SODIUM | 3G FIBER

spicy tomato broth with couscous and chicken

MAKES ABOUT 12 CUPS

- **1** Tbs. olive oil
- **1** medium yellow onion, finely chopped
- **3** lb. chicken thighs, skinned
- **1½** tsp. ground cumin
- **½** tsp. sweet paprika
- **¼** tsp. turmeric
- **1** cinnamon stick

  Kosher salt and freshly ground black pepper
- **7** cups homemade or lower-salt chicken broth
- **½** tsp. harissa or ⅛ tsp. cayenne; more as needed
- **2** Tbs. tomato paste
- **3** medium red tomatoes, peeled, seeded, and chopped
- **½** cup couscous (not instant)
- **¼** cup chopped fresh mint
- **¼** cup chopped fresh cilantro
- **2** tsp. fresh lemon juice

Harissa is a fiery condiment used in many North African dishes. If you can't find it, use cayenne instead. Stir in the couscous just before serving the soup. If it sits for too long, the couscous will absorb all the broth. Don't use instant couscous—it will turn to mush.

1. In a large soup pot, heat the olive oil over medium-high heat. Add the onion and cook, stirring occasionally, until soft, about 7 minutes. Add the chicken thighs, cumin, paprika, turmeric, cinnamon stick, and ½ tsp. each salt and pepper. Cook, stirring, for about 2 minutes. Add the broth, harissa, tomato paste, and tomatoes. Cover and simmer gently until the chicken is cooked and falls easily from the bone, about 45 minutes.

2. Remove and discard the cinnamon stick. Remove the chicken from the broth and let cool. Skim any fat from the surface of the broth. Pull all the chicken meat from the bones; discard the bones. Tear the meat into 1-inch pieces and stir the chicken back into the soup.

3. Over medium-high heat, bring the soup to a gentle boil. Stir the soup constantly as you slowly add the couscous. Reduce the heat to low, add the mint and cilantro, and simmer, uncovered, until the couscous is tender, about 5 minutes. Stir in the lemon juice. Taste and add salt and pepper if needed. —*Joanne Weir*

PER SERVING: 200 CALORIES | 25G PROTEIN | 10G CARB | 6G TOTAL FAT | 1G SAT FAT | 2G MONO FAT | 1G POLY FAT | 95MG CHOL | 240MG SODIUM | 2G FIBER

turkey soup with ginger, lemon & mint

MAKES 5 CUPS; SERVES 4

- **3** **leeks (white part only), sliced ¼ inch thick (to yield 2 cups)**
- **4½** **cups Turkey Stock (recipe on p. 223)**
- **2** **carrots, peeled and sliced ¼ inch thick**
- **1** **1-inch chunk fresh ginger, peeled and cut into matchsticks (to yield about 2 Tbs.)**
- **1** **cup diced cooked turkey**
- **2** **Tbs. fresh lemon juice**
- **Kosher salt and freshly ground black pepper**
- **¼** **cup finely shredded fresh mint leaves**

The combination of ginger, lemon, and mint gives this soup a light, bright flavor. You could substitute cooked chicken for the turkey.

1. Put the sliced leeks in a large bowl of cold water and let them soak for 10 minutes. Lift them out carefully, making sure to leave the grit at the bottom of the bowl behind, and set aside (there's no need to dry them).

2. Put the turkey stock and carrots in a large saucepan. Bring to a boil, reduce the heat, and cover the pot. Simmer for 5 minutes and then add the leeks and ginger. Continue to cook, covered until the vegetables are just tender, about another 5 minutes. Add the diced turkey, lemon juice, ½ tsp. salt, and pepper to taste. Simmer until the turkey is heated through, about 2 minutes. Adjust the seasonings if needed, add the shredded mint, and serve immediately. —*Jennifer McLagan*

PER SERVING: 160 CALORIES | 15G PROTEIN | 19G CARB | 3G TOTAL FAT | 1G SAT FAT | 0.5G MONO FAT | 1G POLY FAT | 25MG CHOL | 330MG SODIUM | 3G FIBER

spiced lentil soup with herbed yogurt

**MAKES ABOUT 6 CUPS;
SERVES 6**

- **4** oz. bacon (about 4 slices), cut into thin strips
- **2** Tbs. extra-virgin olive oil
- **1** large leek (white and light green parts), cut in half, rinsed of grit, and finely diced
- **2** medium carrots, peeled and finely diced
- **1** rib celery, finely diced
- Kosher salt and freshly ground black pepper
- **2** tsp. ground cumin
- **1** tsp. ground coriander
- **1½** cups dried French green lentils (or brown lentils), sorted through and rinsed
- **6** Tbs. chopped fresh cilantro
- **1** cup plain yogurt
- **2** Tbs. chopped fresh mint

The bacon not only adds salty richness but also cuts through the starchiness of the lentils.

1. Cook the bacon in the oil in a large saucepan or pot over medium heat, stirring occasionally, until it's brown and crisp, about 8 minutes. Using a slotted spoon, transfer the bacon to a plate lined with paper towels. Add the leek, carrots, and celery, season with salt and pepper, and cook, stirring occasionally, until the vegetables soften and just start to brown, about 7 minutes. Stir in the cumin and coriander and cook for 30 seconds. Stir in the lentils and 5 cups water and season with salt and pepper. Bring to a boil, reduce the heat to a gentle simmer, cover, and cook until the lentils become tender but not mushy, about 45 minutes. Stir in ¼ cup of the cilantro and the reserved bacon. Thin with water, if necessary, to get the consistency you like. Taste for salt and pepper.

2. In a small bowl, mix the yogurt with the remaining 2 Tbs. cilantro and the mint and season with salt. Ladle the soup into serving bowls, top with a dollop of the yogurt, and serve immediately. —*Tony Rosenfeld*

PER SERVING: 350 CALORIES | 17G PROTEIN | 34G CARB | 17G TOTAL FAT | 6G SAT FAT | 9G MONO FAT | 2G POLY FAT | 20MG CHOL | 420MG SODIUM | 16G FIBER

More about French Green Lentils

French green lentils hold their shape well and make an attractive salad or warm side dish. They're especially nice as a bed for fatty fish like tuna or salmon. They have a delicate flavor and less starchy texture than the larger, more common brown lentils. Black beluga lentils are another variety that hold their shape well.

Kitchen math

1 lb. French green lentils = about 2¼ cups = about 5 cups cooked

Choosing

French lentils are not as easy to find as their common brown cousin. Look for them in specialty shops or online. Shop for lentils at a store with a high turnover.

Cooking and storing

Pick the lentils over for tiny stones or other debris and rinse well. Lentils don't need soaking, and they cook in about 30 to 45 minutes. Stored airtight in a cool dry place, lentils will last for at least a year.

tortellini in broth with roasted vegetables

SERVES 2

- **3** cups ¾-inch-diced winter vegetables (carrots, parsnips, turnips, cauliflower, broccoflower, winter squash, sweet potatoes)
- **3** Tbs. extra-virgin olive oil

  Kosher salt
- **6** oz. frozen small cheese tortellini
- **1** small shallot, sliced into rings

  Pinch of crushed red pepper flakes
- **1½** cups homemade or lower-salt chicken broth
- **¼** cup (about ½ oz.) freshly and finely grated Parmigiano-Reggiano
- **2** tsp. coarsely chopped fresh flat-leaf parsley

  Freshly ground black pepper
- **½** small lemon, cut into two wedges

This is a great way to use up extra winter vegetables. There's no need to peel most of them, as the skins are perfectly tender when roasted.

1. Heat the oven to 450°F. Put a large pot of water on to boil. In a 9x13-inch Pyrex® baking dish, toss the 3 cups vegetables with 2 Tbs. of the oil and ¼ tsp. salt and spread in one layer. Roast until the vegetables are well browned and shrunken, 28 to 30 minutes, stirring occasionally with a flat metal spatula.

2. After the vegetables have roasted for about 15 minutes, add 2 tsp. salt and the tortellini to the boiling water; cook the pasta until tender. Save some of the water to pour into two large shallow soup bowls to warm them. Drain the tortellini in a colander. In a small saucepan, heat the remaining 1 Tbs. oil over medium heat. Add the shallot and sauté until softened and browned, about 2½ minutes. Stir in the red pepper flakes and add the chicken broth. Bring to a simmer, cover, and simmer for 4 to 5 minutes. Turn off the heat and keep covered.

3. Pour the water out of the soup bowls. Divide the tortellini between the warmed bowls. Spoon the roasted vegetables over the pasta. Pour the broth over the vegetables and garnish with the Parmigiano and parsley. Season to taste with salt and pepper. Serve with a lemon wedge. —*Susie Middleton*

PER SERVING: 670 CALORIES | 25G PROTEIN | 69G CARB | 34G TOTAL FAT | 9G SAT FAT | 20G MONO FAT | 3G POLY FAT | 50MG CHOL | 2,960MG SODIUM | 7G FIBER

turkey soup with dill, parsley & chive dumplings

SERVES 6

FOR THE TURKEY BROTH

- 2 **medium carrots, cut into 2-inch pieces**
- 2 **medium ribs celery, cut into 2-inch pieces**
- 1 **medium yellow onion, cut into quarters**
- 2 **dried bay leaves**
- 1 **cup dry white wine**
- 1 **roasted turkey carcass, broken in half, plus any leftover bones**

FOR THE SOUP

- 2 **Tbs. extra-virgin olive oil**
- ½ **medium yellow onion, finely diced**
- 4 **medium carrots, peeled, quartered lengthwise, and cut into ½-inch pieces**
- 4 **medium parsnips, peeled, quartered lengthwise, cored, and cut into ½-inch pieces**
- 1½ **cups small-diced celery root**
- **Kosher salt and freshly ground black pepper**
- 1 **14½-oz. can diced tomatoes, with their liquid**
- ½ **cup dry white wine**
- 1 **dried bay leaf**
- 3 **cups medium-diced roast turkey**
- 2 **cups chopped Swiss chard leaves (ribs removed)**

continued on p. 140

Although you can make this soup any time of year, it's a perfect way to use your Thanksgiving turkey carcass. Throw the carcass into a soup pot with a few vegetables and you'll be rewarded with a rich broth that can be used in this delicious soup with airy herb-flecked dumplings.

MAKE THE BROTH

In a 10-quart pot, combine the carrots, celery, onion, bay leaves, wine, carcass, and bones. Add 7 quarts water and bring to a simmer over medium-high heat. Reduce the heat and simmer gently until the broth is rich and flavorful, 4 to 6 hours. Strain the broth through a fine-mesh sieve and discard the solids. Let cool; then skim off and discard the fat on the surface. The broth may be refrigerated for up to 2 days or frozen for up to 2 months.

MAKE THE SOUP

1. Heat the oil in a heavy-duty 6- to 8-quart pot over medium-high heat. Add the onion and cook until starting to brown, about 2 minutes. Add the carrots, parsnips, and celery root and cook until the vegetables start to color, about 4 minutes. Season with salt and pepper. Add the tomatoes with their liquid, wine, and bay leaf and bring to a boil. Add 2 quarts of the turkey broth and return to a boil. Reduce the heat and simmer until the vegetables are tender, 10 to 15 minutes. Season to taste with salt and pepper.

2. Add the turkey and Swiss chard and simmer until the chard is wilted, about 5 minutes. (The soup may be cooled and refrigerated for up to 2 days. Bring to a simmer before continuing.) Remove the bay leaf.

continued on p. 140

FOR THE DUMPLINGS

6 Tbs. unsalted butter

Kosher salt

¾ cup unbleached all-purpose flour

3 large eggs

1 Tbs. chopped fresh dill

1 Tbs. chopped fresh flat-leaf parsley

1 Tbs. chopped fresh chives

MAKE THE DUMPLING BATTER

In a 3-quart saucepan, bring ¾ cup water, the butter, and 2 tsp. salt to a boil over medium heat. When the butter melts, remove the pan from the heat and stir in the flour until thoroughly combined. Return the pan to medium heat and stir until the mixture pulls away from the sides of the pan. Scrape the dough into a large bowl. With a sturdy wooden spoon, beat in the eggs, one by one, until the batter is smooth. Fold in the chopped herbs. (The batter may be covered and refrigerated for up to 1 day.)

FINISH THE SOUP WITH THE DUMPLINGS

Using two ½-teaspoon measures, drop spoonfuls of batter into the simmering soup until all of the batter is used. After the dumplings rise to the top, cover the pan and steam the dumplings until they have puffed up to double their size, about 4 minutes. Serve hot.
—*Maria Helm Sinskey*

PER SERVING: 530 CALORIES | 27G PROTEIN | 44G CARB | 26G TOTAL FAT | 11G SAT FAT | 10G MONO FAT | 3G POLY FAT | 180MG CHOL | 1,360MG SODIUM | 7G FIBER

how to remove chard ribs

Though thick Swiss chard stems are good to eat, they take longer to cook than the leaves, so you'll need to remove them and cook them separately (or start them before you add the leaves). To remove the stems, simply lay each leaf flat and run a sharp knife down both sides of the stem.

tortellini soup with carrots, peas & leeks

SERVES 4

- 2 **medium leeks
  (12 oz. untrimmed)**
- 1 **Tbs. unsalted butter**
- 3 **cloves garlic, finely chopped
  (about 1 Tbs.)**
- ½ **medium carrot, peeled and
  finely diced (2 Tbs.)**

  **Kosher salt and freshly
  ground black pepper**
- 5 **cups homemade or lower-
  salt chicken broth**
- 8 **oz. frozen cheese tortellini**
- 1 **cup frozen peas**
- ¼ **cup freshly grated
  Parmigiano-Reggiano
  or Grana Padano**

You can make most of the soup ahead, but don't add the tortellini until you're ready to eat or they'll become mushy.

1. Trim the roots and dark green leaves from the leeks. Slice the white and light green part in half lengthwise and then slice the halves thinly crosswise. Rinse well and drain. Melt the butter in a 4-quart saucepan over medium heat. Add the garlic, leeks, and carrot. Season with a couple of pinches of salt and cook, stirring occasionally, until tender, 5 to 7 minutes. (It's fine if the vegetables brown lightly.) Stir in ¼ tsp. pepper and cook for about 20 seconds, then add the chicken broth and bring to a boil. Add the tortellini and cook for 3 minutes. Reduce the heat to a simmer and add the peas. Continue to simmer until the tortellini are cooked, 3 to 5 minutes.

2. Season to taste with salt and pepper. Portion the soup into warm bowls, top each with some of the cheese, and serve.

—*Joanne McAllister Smart*

PER SERVING: 310 CALORIES | 17G PROTEIN | 43G CARB | 9G TOTAL FAT | 4.5G SAT FAT | 2.5G MONO FAT | 1G POLY FAT | 35MG CHOL | 540MG SODIUM | 4G FIBER

tuscan peasant soup with rosemary and pancetta

MAKES 3½ QUARTS; SERVES 8

- 5 **Tbs. extra-virgin olive oil**
- 1¼ **cups small-diced pancetta (about 6 oz. or 6 thick slices)**
- 4 **cups large-diced Savoy cabbage (about ½ small head)**
- 2 **cups medium-diced onion (10 to 12 oz. or 2 small)**
- 1½ **cups medium-diced carrot (about 4 medium)**

    Kosher salt

- 2 **Tbs. minced garlic**
- 1 **Tbs. plus 1 tsp. minced fresh rosemary**
- 1 **tsp. ground coriander**
- 1 **28-oz. can diced tomatoes, drained**
- 7 **cups homemade or lower-salt chicken broth**
- 2 **15½-oz. cans small white beans, rinsed and drained (about 2½ cups, drained)**
- 1 **to 2 tsp. fresh lemon juice**

    Freshly ground black pepper

- 1 **cup fresh breadcrumbs, toasted**
- 1 **cup freshly grated Parmigiano-Reggiano**

You'll feel like you are in Italy when you have a pot of this soup simmering on the stove.

1. Heat 2 Tbs. of the olive oil in a 4- to 5-quart Dutch oven over medium heat. When hot, add the pancetta and cook, stirring frequently, until quite shrunken, golden brown, and crisp (the oil will also be golden brown), about 6 minutes. Remove the pan from the heat and with a slotted spoon or strainer carefully transfer the pancetta to a paper-towel-lined plate. Pour off and discard all but 2 Tbs. of the fat from the pan.

2. Return the pot to medium-high heat and add the chopped cabbage. Cook the cabbage, stirring occasionally, until limp and browned around the edges, about 3 minutes. Remove the pot from the heat again and transfer the cabbage to another plate.

3. Put the pot back over medium heat and add another 2 Tbs. olive oil. When the oil is hot, add the onion, carrots, and ½ tsp. salt. Cook, stirring occasionally, until the onion is softened and the vegetables are browned around the edges and beginning to stick to the bottom of the pan, 8 to 9 minutes. Add the remaining 1 Tbs. oil, the garlic, 1 Tbs. of the fresh rosemary, and the ground coriander and cook, stirring, until the garlic is fragrant, about 1 minute. Stir in the tomatoes and cook for another 2 to 3 minutes.

4. Return the cabbage to the pan and add the chicken broth. Stir well, bring to a boil, and reduce to a simmer. Cook for 10 to 15 minutes to infuse the broth with the flavor of the vegetables. Add the beans, bring back to a simmer, and cook for a minute or two. Remove the pan from the heat, stir in the remaining 1 tsp. fresh rosemary, and let rest for a few minutes.

5. Taste the soup and add lemon juice to brighten it—you'll want at least 1 tsp. Season with more salt if necessary and a few grinds of black pepper. Serve the soup hot, garnished with the reserved pancetta crisps, the toasted breadcrumbs, and the grated Parmigiano.
—Susie Middleton

PER SERVING: 370 CALORIES | 17G PROTEIN | 37G CARB | 18G TOTAL FAT | 4.5G SAT FAT | 10G MONO FAT | 2G POLY FAT | 20MG CHOL | 1,010MG SODIUM | 8G FIBER

white bean soup with sautéed shrimp and garlic croutons

MAKES ABOUT 6 CUPS; SERVES
4 AS A FIRST COURSE

1½   cups dried cannellini beans,
      sorted through and rinsed

5   Tbs. extra-virgin olive oil;
      plus 1 Tbs. for drizzling

1   large yellow onion, cut into
      ¼-inch dice

1   carrot, peeled and cut into
      ¼-inch dice

1   inner rib celery, cut into
      ¼-inch dice

      Kosher salt

2   cloves garlic, minced

1   Tbs. chopped fresh rosemary

      Freshly ground black pepper

4   tsp. fresh lemon juice; more
      as needed

2½   cups ¾-inch diced country
      bread or baguette (about
      6 oz.)

¾   lb. large shrimp (21 to
      25 per lb.), peeled, deveined,
      rinsed, halved lengthwise,
      and patted dry

      Pinch of cayenne

*The earthiness of rosemary
makes this white bean soup
exciting. The croutons add
texture and crunch.*

1. Cook the cannellini beans
following the Basic Beans
method on p. 47.

2. Heat a large, heavy saucepan over medium-high heat for 30 seconds.
Add 1½ Tbs. of the oil, along with the onion, carrot, and celery. Season
with salt and cook, stirring occasionally, until the vegetables soften
and start to brown, about 7 minutes. Add half the garlic and cook for
30 seconds, stirring. Add the beans and their cooking liquid (there
should be about 4 cups liquid; if not, add more water to equal this
amount) and half the rosemary. Season well with salt and pepper. Bring
to a boil, lower the heat to a bare simmer, and cook for 30 minutes so
that the beans soften a little more but don't break up. Let cool for
10 minutes. Scoop out 1 cup of the beans and set aside.

3. Working in batches, purée the remaining beans and all of the broth
in a blender (be sure to vent the lid and cover the top with a kitchen
towel to prevent splashes). Transfer the puréed soup and the
reserved beans to a clean saucepan and keep warm over low heat.
Add the lemon juice and salt and pepper to taste. Thin with water,
if necessary, to get the consistency you like.

4. Heat a large skillet over medium-high heat for 1 minute. Add another
1½ Tbs. oil and the bread cubes and season well with salt and pepper.
Cook, tossing frequently, until the bread starts to brown around the
edges, 2 to 3 minutes. Toss in the remaining garlic and continue
cooking for 1 minute, tossing well. Transfer to a large plate. Season the
shrimp well with salt and pepper. Add the remaining 2 Tbs. olive oil and
the shrimp to the skillet and sauté, stirring often, until the shrimp is
firm, opaque, and browned slightly, 3 to 4 minutes.

5. Ladle the soup into large, shallow bowls and dust with a pinch of
cayenne. Garnish with a few of the croutons, a portion of the shrimp,
a sprinkling of the remaining rosemary, and a drizzle of oil.
—*Tony Rosenfeld*

PER SERVING: 730 CALORIES | 40G PROTEIN | 84G CARB | 27G TOTAL FAT | 4G SAT
FAT | 16G MONO FAT | 5G POLY FAT | 130MG CHOL | 640MG SODIUM | 15G FIBER

black bean soup with sweet potatoes

**MAKES ABOUT 14 CUPS;
SERVES 8**

 2 **Tbs. vegetable oil**

 2 **medium yellow onions,
    chopped**

 3 **medium cloves garlic,
    coarsely chopped**

1½ **tsp. ground coriander**

 1 **tsp. ground cumin**

 ¼ **tsp. aniseed**

    Freshly ground black pepper

 2 **quarts homemade or lower-
    salt chicken or vegetable
    broth**

 4 **15½-oz. (or two 29-oz.) cans
    black beans, rinsed and
    drained**

 2 **medium sweet potatoes,
    peeled and cut into medium
    dice**

    Kosher salt

 ½ **cup plain yogurt**

 8 **paper-thin lime slices**

The sweet potatoes in this soup contrast nicely with the tang of the yogurt and the tartness of the lime. Aniseed lends an unusual hint of licorice flavor. You can store leftovers in the refrigerator for up to 5 days.

1. Heat the oil over medium heat in a 6-quart Dutch oven. Add the onion and cook, stirring occasionally, until starting to soften and brown slightly, about 8 minutes. Add the garlic, coriander, cumin, aniseed, and ¼ tsp. pepper and cook, stirring constantly, until fragrant, about 30 seconds. Add the broth, beans, sweet potatoes, and ¾ tsp. salt and bring to a boil over high heat; skim any foam as necessary. Reduce the heat and simmer, uncovered, stirring occasionally, until the sweet potatoes are tender, about 15 minutes.

2. Using a slotted spoon, set aside 3 cups of the beans and potatoes. Purée the remaining soup in batches in a blender. Return the solids to the soup and season to taste with salt and pepper. Serve topped with a dollop of the yogurt and a slice of lime. *—Lori Longbotham*

PER SERVING: 310 CALORIES | 17G PROTEIN | 51G CARB | 6G TOTAL FAT | 1G SAT FAT | 2.5G MONO FAT | 2G POLY FAT | 0MG CHOL | 370MG SODIUM | 11G FIBER

wild rice and mushroom soup with almonds

MAKES 8½ TO 9 CUPS SOUP;
SERVES 6 GENEROUSLY AS A
FIRST COURSE

- 1   Tbs. olive oil
- 6   oz. applewood-smoked bacon (about 7 slices), thinly sliced crosswise
- 1   lb. button mushrooms, stems trimmed; wiped clean and quartered (to yield about 5 cups)
- 1   large yellow onion (12 oz.), cut into medium dice (to yield 2 cups)
- 3   medium ribs celery (5 oz. total), cut into medium dice (to yield 1 cup)
- 1   large carrot (5 oz.), peeled and cut into medium dice (to yield 1 cup)
- ½   cup wild rice
- 6   cups homemade or lower-salt chicken broth; more if needed
- 1   smoked ham hock (optional)
- 15   sprigs fresh thyme (¼ oz.)
- 10   sprigs fresh flat-leaf parsley (½ oz.)
- 6   sprigs fresh sage (½ oz.)
- 1   bay leaf
- 5   Tbs. unsalted butter
- ½   cup unbleached all-purpose flour
-     Kosher salt and freshly ground black pepper
- 1½   cups heavy cream

FOR THE GARNISH

- 2   oz. (½ cup) slivered almonds, toasted
- ¼   cup thinly sliced fresh chives

If you can't find a ham hock, just leave it out—the soup will still taste terrific.

1. Heat the oil in a heavy soup pot over medium-high heat. Add the bacon and cook, stirring occasionally, until the fat is rendered and the bacon is crisp, about 5 minutes. Add the mushrooms, stir well to coat in the bacon fat, and then spread out in an even layer. Brown the mushrooms on one side without disturbing them, 4 to 6 minutes. Stir in the onion, celery, and carrot; let cook until the onion is soft, about 5 minutes. Add the rice, stirring to coat. Stir in the chicken broth and ham hock (if using). With kitchen twine, tie together the thyme, parsley, sage, and bay leaf; add the herb bundle to the soup pot. Bring to a boil and then reduce the heat to maintain a gentle simmer. Cook, uncovered, until the rice is tender but still toothsome, 30 to 40 minutes.

2. Meanwhile, melt the butter in a small, heavy saucepan over medium-high heat. Add the flour and whisk constantly until the mixture, called a roux, darkens to a caramel color, 2 to 3 minutes. Set aside.

3. Once the rice is cooked, discard the herbs. If you've used a ham hock, fish it out, and when it's cool enough to handle, take the meat off and return the shredded meat to the soup. Discard the bone. Return the soup to a boil and thoroughly whisk in the roux a little at a time. This amount of roux should thicken the soup perfectly. You can adjust the amount to your taste if it's too thick or thin, but keep in mind that the cream you'll add later will thin the soup. Season to taste with salt and pepper.

4. When ready to serve, heat the soup first and then add the cream. (If you like a lighter soup, you may not want to add all the cream.) Taste for seasoning and adjust if needed, and thin with broth, if you like. Garnish each serving with the toasted almonds and sliced chives.
—*Ris Lacoste*

PER SERVING: 570 CALORIES | 17G PROTEIN | 30G CARB | 44G TOTAL FAT | 22G SAT FAT | 16G MONO FAT | 4G POLY FAT | 115MG CHOL | 480MG SODIUM | 4G FIBER

Make Ahead

You can prepare the soup up to 3 days ahead (to just before you add the cream), or it can be frozen for up to a month. When ready to serve, heat the soup and add the cream and garnishes.

tortellini en brodo

MAKES ABOUT 6 QUARTS
BROTH AND ABOUT
200 TORTELLINI; SERVES 14

FOR THE BROTH

- 1 4-lb. chicken, cut into 6 pieces
- 2 lb. veal bones or veal shank
- 2 lb. beef stew meat or scraps
- 1 medium yellow onion, quartered
- 2 medium carrots, cut into large pieces
- 2 ribs celery, cut into large pieces
- 1 3-inch-square Parmigiano-Reggiano rind (optional)

   Kosher salt

FOR THE FILLING

- 2 Tbs. unsalted butter
- 5 oz. boneless pork loin, trimmed and cut into ½-inch cubes (about 1 cup)
- ½ cup dry white wine
- 3 oz. sliced prosciutto, coarsely chopped (⅔ cup)
- 3 oz. sliced mortadella, coarsely chopped (¾ cup)
- 1 oz. freshly grated Parmigiano-Reggiano (½ cup grated on the small holes of a box grater)
- ½ tsp. freshly grated nutmeg
- 1 large egg, lightly beaten

   Kosher salt

continued on p. 148

This comforting dish of stuffed pasta in a hearty broth is a holiday tradition in northern Italy. It's often served as a first course, followed by a pork or veal roast and lots of winter vegetables. Both the tortellini and the broth can be made ahead.

MAKE THE BROTH

1. Wash the chicken, veal bones, beef, and vegetables under cold running water. Put all of the broth ingredients, except the salt, in a 10-quart pot and add 6½ quarts cold water. Partially cover the pot and bring to a simmer over medium heat. As soon as the water begins to bubble, reduce the heat to low and, with a fine-mesh skimmer or a large spoon, skim off and discard any foam that has risen to the surface. Partially cover the pot and simmer gently until the broth is flavorful, about 2½ hours. Add 1 Tbs. salt during the last few minutes of cooking.

2. Remove the chicken and discard or save the meat for another use. Using a slotted spoon, discard the remaining solids from the broth. Strain the broth through a fine-mesh strainer into a large bowl. Line the strainer with a clean thin kitchen towel or cheesecloth and strain the broth again into another large bowl. You should have about 6 quarts broth. Transfer the broth to storage containers and refrigerate overnight. Remove the fat and reserve the broth. (The broth may be refrigerated for 2 days or frozen for up to 3 months.)

MAKE THE FILLING

1. Melt the butter in a 10-inch skillet over medium heat. Add the pork and cook, stirring, until lightly golden and cooked through, about 4 minutes. Increase the heat to high, pour in the wine, and stir until almost evaporated, 3 to 5 minutes. Let cool slightly. Transfer the pork and its juices to a food processor. Add the prosciutto and mortadella and pulse until the mixture is very finely chopped (but not puréed).

2. Transfer the filling to a medium bowl and add the Parmigiano, nutmeg, egg, and ¾ tsp. salt. Mix well. (The filling should be moist and just a little sticky.) Cover the bowl with plastic wrap and refrigerate. (The filling may be made and refrigerated for up to 2 days or frozen for up to 1 month.)

MAKE THE PASTA DOUGH

1. On a large wooden board or other work surface, shape the flour into a mound. Using your fingers, make a round well in the center of the flour. Carefully crack the eggs into the well, making sure they don't escape the walls of the well. Lightly beat the eggs with a fork. Begin to incorporate flour into the eggs with the fork, starting from the inner rim of the well, until about half of the flour is incorporated and a soft dough begins to form.

continued on p. 148

FOR THE PASTA DOUGH

10½ oz. (2⅓ cups) unbleached all-purpose flour; more as needed

4 large eggs

FOR SERVING

Freshly grated Parmigiano-Reggiano

2. With a dough scraper, push all of the remaining flour to one side of the board. Scrape off and discard the bits and pieces of dough attached to the board. Wash and dry your hands. Begin adding some of the flour you have pushed aside into the soft dough, kneading it gently with the heels of your hands as you incorporate the additional flour and the dough becomes firmer. Keep the board clean and dust it with flour as you knead to prevent the dough from sticking. After kneading for 8 to 10 minutes, the dough should be smooth, elastic, and just a little sticky.

3. Press one finger into the center of the dough; if it comes out barely moist, the dough is ready to be rolled out. If the dough is still quite sticky, add a little more flour and knead it for 2 to 3 minutes longer until soft and pliable.

4. Wrap the dough in plastic wrap and let it rest at room temperature for 20 to 30 minutes.

ROLL THE PASTA

1. Unwrap the dough and knead it for a minute or two. Set the rollers of a pasta machine at their widest. Cut off a piece of dough about the size of a small lemon and flatten it with the palm of your hand to about ½ inch thick. As you work, keep the rest of the dough wrapped in plastic. Dust the piece of dough lightly with flour and run it through the machine. Fold the rolled dough in half and run it through the machine again, pressing it with your fingertips into the rollers. Repeat this step four or five times, dusting the dough with flour if it becomes sticky, until smooth and elastic.

2. Change the rollers to the next setting down and roll out the dough without folding. Repeat rolling the sheet of dough (without folding) through the pasta machine, decreasing the settings until the pasta is ⅛ inch thick. On a floured wooden board, cut the dough into 1½-inch squares. Keep the squares covered with plastic as you shape the tortellini. (See the sidebar at right).

SHAPE THE TORTELLINI

1. Put about ⅛ tsp. of the filling in the center of a pasta square. Bring one corner over the filling toward the corner diagonally opposite and fold into a triangle. Press around the filling to seal. Bend the tortellino around your finger with one corner slightly overlapping the other and press to seal. The tortellino will look like a crown. Transfer to a large rimmed baking sheet lined with a clean kitchen towel. Arrange the tortellini in a single layer without letting them touch (you'll need 2 to 3 baking sheets) and cover with another clean towel.

2. Repeat the filling and shaping with the remaining pasta and filling. (The tortellini can be refrigerated, loosely covered with a towel, for up to 1 day. Or freeze the tortellini on the baking sheets; then transfer to freezer bags and freeze for up to 3 months.)

COOK AND SERVE THE TORTELLINI EN BRODO

You can make as many or as few servings as you like. For each serving, you'll need 1½ cups of broth and 14 tortellini. Bring the broth to a boil in a large pot over medium heat. Gently drop the tortellini into the pot. Cook until they rise to the surface and are tender but still firm to the bite, 2 to 3 minutes for fresh, 4 to 5 minutes for frozen. Remove the pot from the heat. Ladle the tortellini and broth into serving bowls, sprinkle with grated Parmigiano, and serve immediately.

—Biba Caggiano

PER SERVING: 240 CALORIES | 18G PROTEIN | 22G CARB | 9G TOTAL FAT | 3.5G SAT FAT | 3.5G MONO FAT | 1G POLY FAT | 95MG CHOL | 580MG SODIUM | 1G FIBER

how to make tortellini

Add ⅛ tsp. filling to the center of a pasta square, then fold up one corner, forming a triangle.

Press the dough around the filling to seal.

Wrap the tortellino around your finger so that it looks like a crown.

curried lentil soup

MAKES ABOUT 1 QUART;
SERVES 4

- **1** large clove garlic
- **1** ⅓-inch-long piece of peeled fresh ginger
- **½** small bulb fennel, cored and cut into large chunks, or 1 small rib celery, cut into large chunks
- **1** small carrot, peeled and cut into large chunks
- **1** small parsnip, peeled, cored, and cut into large chunks
- **1** large shallot, cut in half
- **3** Tbs. unsalted butter
- **2** tsp. curry powder
- **1** cup brown lentils, picked over and rinsed
- **1** quart homemade or lower-salt chicken or vegetable broth

  Kosher salt and freshly ground black pepper

Garnish with a dollop of plain whole-milk yogurt and chopped fresh mint or cilantro, or both.

1. Pulse the garlic and ginger in a food processor until chopped. Add the fennel or celery, the carrot, parsnip, and shallot and pulse until coarsely chopped.

2. Melt 2 Tbs. of the butter in a 4-quart saucepan over medium-high heat. Add the chopped vegetables and cook, stirring, until softened, about 3 minutes. Add the curry powder and cook, stirring, until the curry powder is fragrant, about 30 seconds. Add the lentils, broth, and ¼ tsp. each salt and pepper. Bring the soup to a boil over high heat, reduce the heat to maintain a brisk simmer, cover, and cook until the lentils are tender, 25 to 30 minutes.

3. Transfer 1½ cups of the soup to a blender or a food processor and purée until smooth. Stir the purée back into the soup along with the remaining 1 Tbs. butter. Season to taste with salt and pepper, and adjust the consistency with water, if you like. —*Allison Ehri Kreitler*

PER SERVING: 330 CALORIES | 19G PROTEIN | 43G CARB | 11G TOTAL FAT | 6G SAT FAT | 3G MONO FAT | 1G POLY FAT | 25MG CHOL | 320MG SODIUM | 14G FIBER

seafood gumbo

MAKES ABOUT 3 QUARTS;
SERVES 8

- 1½ **lb. medium shrimp (41 to 50 or 51 to 60 per lb.) or 2 lb. if using head-on shrimp**
- 2 **cups chopped white onion (about 1 large onion; reserve the skin)**
- 1 **cup chopped celery (about 2 medium ribs; reserve the trimmings)**
- ¼ **cup plus 6 Tbs. vegetable oil**
- 1 **lb. fresh or thawed frozen okra, sliced ¼ inch thick (about 4 cups)**

If you can, buy fresh shrimp with the shells and heads intact. If not, just the shells can be used to make the stock.

1. Remove the shrimp heads, if necessary. Peel and devein the shrimp and refrigerate the shrimp until needed. Combine the shrimp shells and heads and the reserved onion skin and celery trimmings in a 6- to 8-quart pot. Cover with 9 cups cold water and bring to a boil over high heat. Reduce the heat to a vigorous simmer and cook, uncovered, for 10 minutes. Strain and reserve. You should have about 2 quarts.

2. In a 10-inch straight-sided sauté pan, heat ¼ cup of the vegetable oil over medium-high heat until hot. Fry the okra in two batches until it becomes lightly browned on the edges, 3 to 5 minutes per batch (fry undisturbed for the first minute or two until browning begins and then stir once or twice to flip most pieces and brown evenly). With a slotted spoon, transfer each batch of okra to a plate or platter lined with a paper towel.

½ cup unbleached all-purpose flour

1 cup chopped green bell pepper (about 1 medium pepper)

1 cup canned crushed tomatoes

½ lb. fresh or pasteurized lump crabmeat (about 1½ cups), picked over for shells, or 4 to 6 gumbo crabs (about 1 lb. total), thawed (see the sidebar below)

1 Tbs. dried thyme

1 bay leaf

Kosher salt and freshly ground black pepper

1 cup fresh shucked oysters (halved if large)

½ cup thinly sliced scallions (about 8; white and light green parts only)

Louisiana-style hot sauce

¼ cup hot cooked white rice per serving

3. Heat the remaining 6 Tbs. oil over medium-high heat in a 6-quart Dutch oven. Once the oil is hot, add the flour and stir constantly with a wooden spoon or heatproof spatula until the mixture, a roux, reaches the color of caramel, about 5 minutes. Add the onion and stir until the roux deepens to a chocolate-brown, 1 to 3 minutes (see p. 154 for more about roux). Add the celery and bell pepper and cook, stirring frequently, until slightly softened, about 5 minutes. Add the shrimp stock, okra, tomatoes, gumbo crabs (if using), thyme, bay leaf, 2 tsp. salt, and 1 tsp. black pepper. Adjust the heat to medium low or low and simmer uncovered, stirring occasionally, for 45 minutes.

4. Five minutes before serving, add the shrimp, fresh or pasteurized lump crabmeat (if using), oysters, and scallions. Add hot sauce, salt, and black pepper to taste. Remove the bay leaf. Serve in large soup bowls over ¼ cup cooked rice per serving. Pass additional hot sauce at the table. *—Poppy Tooker*

PER SERVING: 370 CALORIES | 24G PROTEIN | 32G CARB | 17G TOTAL FAT | 2G SAT FAT | 7G MONO FAT | 7G POLY FAT | 150MG CHOL | 600MG SODIUM | 4G FIBER

What Are Gumbo Crabs?

Gumbo crabs are small blue crabs that have been cleaned and halved or quartered. They are served in the shell, and you pick out the meat as you eat the gumbo. They're available frozen, usually in 1-lb. packages. Ask your fishmonger to get you some if you can't find them in your grocery. Fresh or pasteurized lump crabmeat is a reasonable alternative. Don't use shredded or imitation crabmeat.

the three essentials to fantastic gumbo flavor

A DARK ROUX

How dark is a question answered in as many ways as there are cooks. Some cooks say that roux should be cooked until it's the color of a pecan shell, a hazelnut, or a brown paper grocery bag; others say chocolate-brown. No matter the final color, all roux starts by stirring flour into fat. It's best to start with a high proportion of fat to flour, which makes stirring the mixture easier. Once you become confident with the roux-making process, you can use less fat if you wish. The traditional roux-mixing tool is a flat-edged wooden spatula or spoon. So much stirring is required before the roux reaches the correct color that lumps are not an issue, and the springy action of a wire whisk could cause the molten roux to splash on the cook, resulting in a serious burn. Today, heatproof silicone spatulas are a wonderful alternative to the old-fashioned wooden spoon.

Stir flour into heated oil to combine.

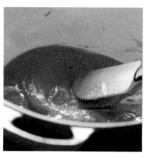

Continue to stir constantly over medium-high heat until the roux turns a caramel color, about 5 minutes.

Add the onion and keep stirring over medium-high heat until the roux turns a chocolate-brown, another 1 to 3 minutes.

OKRA OR FILÉ

Both okra and filé help thicken gumbo and give it a stew-like heartiness. Okra is a green pod, which is sliced into rounds that break down after being cooked. Some people claim an aversion to okra because of its texture, but frying it hot and fast before adding it to the gumbo keeps it from getting slimy.

Filé (pronounced FEE-lay) powder is the ground, dried leaves of the sassafras tree. It smells like eucalyptus and lends an earthy flavor to gumbo. Filé must never be added to boiling gumbo, or it will turn stringy.

CREOLE MIREPOIX

It's easy to understand the religious zeal brought to Creole cooking when you hear people refer to "the holy trinity" of gumbo. What they're talking about is the celery, bell pepper, and onion that make up gumbo's flavor base.

The onion must be added first and by itself to the roux once it turns a caramel color. For some reason, this direction has been omitted from almost every gumbo recipe, although home cooks will confide that they learned this step from their mothers or grandmothers. When you add the onion, it cools the roux slightly as it releases its natural sugars, and this helps prevent burning. Those sugars then caramelize in the roux, bringing it from a caramel color to a chocolate-brown.

The celery and bell pepper release a lot of water when they're heated; if you added them with the onion, the roux would get too light. They're added at the end, when the roux is as dark as you want it to be.

chicken–andouille filé gumbo

**MAKES ABOUT 4 QUARTS;
SERVES 10**

- 1 **lb. andouille sausage or other spicy smoked pork sausage, sliced in half lengthwise, then cut into ⅓-inch-thick half-moons**
- ½ **cup vegetable oil**
- 1 **3- to 4-lb. chicken, cut into 8 pieces**
- **Kosher salt and freshly ground black pepper**
- 1 **cup unbleached all-purpose flour**
- 1 **large white onion, coarsely chopped**
- 3 **ribs celery, coarsely chopped**
- 1 **cup chopped green bell pepper**
- 3 **cloves garlic, minced**
- 2 **quarts homemade or lower-salt chicken broth**
- 2 **bay leaves**
- 2 **tsp. dried thyme**
- 1 **bunch scallions, thinly sliced (dark and light green parts only)**
- **Louisiana-style hot sauce**
- ¼ **cup hot cooked white rice per serving**
- ½ **to 1 tsp. filé powder per serving**

Make Ahead

Store gumbo in the refrigerator for up to 3 days and then reheat gently before serving. As with many stews and braises, gumbo tastes better the second day. You can also freeze it for up to 8 months. Simply transfer to freezer-safe containers.

Don't add filé powder to the entire pot of gumbo. If gumbo is reheated with filé powder in it, the filé will become stringy and unpleasant.

1. Heat a heavy-duty 12-inch skillet over medium-high heat until hot, 1 to 2 minutes. Add the andouille and cook, stirring occasionally with a wooden spoon, until well browned, 4 to 6 minutes. Transfer to a large bowl with a slotted spoon. Add ½ cup water to the skillet and immediately scrape the bottom with a wooden spoon to release any cooked-on bits. Reserve this liquid. Heat the oil in a 7- to 8-quart Dutch oven over medium-high heat. Season the chicken pieces with salt and pepper and sauté the chicken in two batches until golden brown on both sides, 3 to 4 minutes per side. Transfer to the bowl with the sausage.

2. Add the flour to the oil remaining in the Dutch oven and stir constantly with a wooden spoon or heatproof spatula over medium-high heat until the roux reaches the color of caramel, 4 to 8 minutes. Add the onion and stir until the roux deepens to a chocolate-brown, 1 to 3 minutes. Add the celery, bell pepper, and garlic and cook, stirring frequently, until slightly softened, 3 to 4 minutes. Stir in the chicken broth, 1 quart water, the liquid reserved from the sausage pan, and the sausage, chicken, bay leaves, and thyme. Bring to a boil and then reduce the heat and simmer uncovered until the chicken is falling off the bone, about 45 minutes.

3. Transfer the chicken to a plate. If you like, skim the fat from the surface of the gumbo with a large shallow spoon. When the chicken is cool enough to handle, discard the skin and bones, pull the chicken meat into bite-size pieces, and return the meat to the gumbo. Season to taste with salt and pepper if necessary (you may find that the sausage and broth provided enough seasoning). Remove the bay leaves.

4. Five minutes before serving, add the scallions and hot sauce to taste. Serve in large soup bowls over ¼ cup cooked rice per serving. Sprinkle ½ to 1 tsp. of the filé powder on top of each bowl of gumbo and stir to thicken, or pass the filé at the table for everyone to add to taste. —*Poppy Tooker*

PER SERVING: 500 CALORIES | 32G PROTEIN | 28G CARB | 29G TOTAL FAT | 8G SAT FAT | 9G MONO FAT | 7G POLY FAT | 80MG CHOL | 750MG SODIUM | 2G FIBER

mediterranean sausage ragoût
(recipe on p. 196)

stews & chilis

beef stew with red wine and carrots

SERVES 6

1 3-lb. boneless beef chuck roast

2 Tbs. extra-virgin olive oil

2 slices thick-cut bacon, cut into ½-inch pieces

Kosher salt and freshly ground black pepper

8 oz. shallots (8 to 10 medium), thinly sliced (about 2 cups)

2 Tbs. brandy, such as Cognac

2 Tbs. tomato paste

2 to 3 cloves garlic, finely chopped (2 to 3 tsp.)

2 tsp. herbes de Provence

2 cups hearty red wine, such as Côtes de Provence or Côtes du Rhône

Make Ahead

This dish can be made up to 3 days ahead. Reserve the chopped parsley and don't bother skimming the surface fat. Instead, transfer the cooled stew to a bowl or baking dish, cover tightly, and refrigerate. Before reheating, lift off the layer of solid fat that will be on the surface. Reheat gently in a 325°F oven in a covered baking dish, stirring once, until hot, about 30 minutes. Taste for salt and pepper and add the parsley just before serving.

This stew is also known as a daube (pronounced dohb), which is a red-wine–based beef or lamb stew. This type of dish has countless flavor permutations, but the most famous is the Provençal daube, seasoned with local herbs and a bit of orange zest.

Here, the carrots are cut into hefty chunks so they hold their shape during the long cooking, but you could also use a combination of parsnips, baby onions, and celeriac. Mashed potatoes would be a perfect foil for the rich wine sauce, or serve with wide egg noodles tossed with butter and parsley.

1. Using your fingers and a thin knife, pull the roast apart along its natural seams. Trim off any thick layers of fat. Carve the roast into 1½- to 2-inch cubes and arrange them on a paper-towel-lined tray to dry. Position a rack in the lower third of the oven. Heat the oven to 325°F.

2. Heat the oil and bacon together in a 7- or 8-quart Dutch oven over medium heat, stirring occasionally, just until the bacon is browned but not crisp, 5 to 6 minutes. With a slotted spoon, transfer the bacon to a small plate.

3. Season about one-third of the beef with salt and pepper, and arrange the cubes in a sparse single layer in the pot to brown. Adjust the heat so the beef sizzles and browns but does not burn. Cook until all sides are a rich brown, a total of about 10 minutes; transfer to a large plate or tray. Season and brown the remaining beef in 2 more batches.

1. **14½-oz. can whole, peeled tomatoes, with their liquid**

4. **strips orange zest (2½ inches long, removed with a vegetable peeler)**

1. **lb. slender carrots, peeled and cut into ¾- to 1-inch chunks (about 2 cups)**

¼. **cup coarsely chopped fresh flat-leaf parsley**

When buying meat for a daube, your best bet is to select a small chuck roast and cut it yourself. Most butchers and meat markets cut their stew meat way too small.

4. When all the beef chunks are browned, pour off all but about 1 Tbs. of the drippings, if necessary. Set the pot over medium-high heat, add the shallots, season with a large pinch of salt and several grinds of pepper, and sauté until they just begin to soften, about 1 minute. Add the brandy and let it boil away. Add the tomato paste, garlic, and herbes de Provence, stirring to incorporate, and sauté for another 1 minute. Add the wine, stirring and scraping the bottom of the pan with a wooden spoon to dislodge the caramelized drippings, and bring to a boil. Pour in the liquid from the tomatoes, holding the tomatoes back with your hand. Then one by one, crush the tomatoes with your hand over the pot and drop them in. Add the orange zest and return the beef (along with any accumulated juices) and bacon to the pot. Finally, add the carrots, bring to a simmer, cover, and slide into the oven.

5. Cook the stew, stirring every 45 minutes, until the meat is fork-tender (taste a piece; all trace of toughness should be gone), 2 to 3 hours. Before serving, skim off any surface fat, taste for salt and pepper, and stir in the parsley. —*Molly Stevens*

PER SERVING: 580 CALORIES | 49G PROTEIN | 20G CARB | 25G TOTAL FAT | 9G SAT FAT | 12G MONO FAT | 1.5G POLY FAT | 160MG CHOL | 630MG SODIUM | 4G FIBER

beef, barley & butternut squash stew with blue cheese croutons

SERVES 6

1¾ lb. boneless beef chuck, trimmed and cut into 1-inch cubes

Kosher salt and freshly ground black pepper

5 Tbs. unbleached all-purpose flour

4½ Tbs. unsalted butter (1½ Tbs. softened)

1 Tbs. extra-virgin olive oil

2 large leeks (white and light, green parts only), halved thinly sliced, and rinsed well

2 medium carrots, cut into 1-inch pieces

2 medium ribs celery, chopped

1 cup dry white wine, such as Sauvignon Blanc

6 cups homemade or lower-salt chicken broth

⅔ cup pearled barley

3 dried bay leaves

1 Tbs. finely chopped fresh sage

1 tsp. freshly grated nutmeg

1 small butternut squash (about 1½ lb.), peeled, seeded, and cut into ½-inch cubes (about 3⅓ cups)

¼ cup chopped fresh flat-leaf parsley

¼ cup half-and-half

3 oz. blue cheese, crumbled (about ¾ cup)

3 Tbs. finely chopped walnuts

18 ½-inch-thick baguette slices

Top this satisfying stew with the salty blue cheese and walnut croutons, breaking them up into the stew as you eat.

1. Position a rack in the center of the oven and heat the oven to 350°F. Season the beef with 1 tsp. salt and ¼ tsp. pepper and then toss in a large bowl with 2 Tbs. of the flour. Heat 1 Tbs. of the butter and the oil in a 5½- to 6-quart Dutch oven over medium-high heat. Cook half of the beef until browned on several sides, about 5 minutes. Using a slotted spoon, transfer the beef to a plate. Repeat with the remaining beef.

2. In the same pot, melt 2 Tbs. of the butter. Add the leeks, carrots, celery, and a pinch of salt, reduce the heat to medium and cook, stirring occasionally, until softened, about 10 minutes. Add the wine and cook, scraping up any browned bits with a wooden spoon, until evaporated, 7 to 8 minutes. Stir in the remaining 3 Tbs. flour and cook for 1 minute. Whisk in 5 cups of the broth. Stir in the barley, bay leaves, sage, nutmeg, ½ tsp. salt, and the beef along with any accumulated juices. Bring to a boil. Cover the pot snugly with foil and then a tight-fitting lid and braise in the oven until the beef is almost tender, about 1 hour. Stir in the squash and the remaining 1 cup broth. Cover with the foil and lid and continue braising until the beef and squash are very tender, about 30 minutes more. Remove and discard the bay leaves from the stew, and then stir in the parsley and half-and-half. Season to taste with salt and pepper. Keep hot.

3. In a small bowl, combine the softened 1½ Tbs. butter with the blue cheese, walnuts, and ½ tsp. pepper. Spread the mixture evenly onto the baguette slices. Transfer to a baking sheet.

4. Position a rack about 8 inches from the broiler element and heat the broiler on high. Broil the croutons until deep golden-brown and crisp, 2 to 3 minutes. Serve the stew with the croutons. —*Liz Pearson*

PER SERVING: 690 CALORIES | 34G PROTEIN | 54G CARB | 13G TOTAL FAT | 16G SAT FAT | 13G MONO FAT | 3.5G POLY FAT | 95MG CHOL | 750MG SODIUM | 9G FIBER

chicken cacciatore with sautéed mushrooms and zucchini

SERVES 6

6 bone-in, skinless chicken thighs (about 2¼ lb.), large pieces of fat trimmed

Kosher salt and freshly ground black pepper

¼ cup extra-virgin olive oil

1 large red onion, finely diced

½ red bell pepper, cored, seeded, and diced

2 cloves garlic, smashed

⅓ cup dry red wine (like Chianti)

1 28-oz. can whole peeled tomatoes, with their liquid

2 sprigs fresh thyme, plus 1 tsp. chopped

2 small sprigs fresh rosemary

Pinch of crushed red pepper flakes

1 medium zucchini, quartered lengthwise and sliced into ¼-inch pieces

½ lb. white mushrooms, cleaned and thinly sliced

⅓ cup pitted mixed green and black olives, quartered

3 Tbs. chopped fresh flat-leaf parsley; more for garnish

Canned tomatoes give this stew a chunky, full texture, so don't purée the vegetables as you might in the other stews. Serve the stew over white rice, if you like.

1. Season the chicken well with salt and black pepper. Heat 2 Tbs. of the oil in a large Dutch oven or heavy soup pot over medium-high heat. When the oil is hot, add half the thighs and brown them well, 2 to 3 minutes per side. Transfer to a large plate. Brown the remaining thighs and reserve with the rest. Reduce the heat to medium and add the onion, red bell pepper, and garlic. Season generously with salt and cook, stirring often with a wooden spoon and scraping up any browned bits, until the onion softens and browns, about 12 minutes. Turn the heat to high, add the wine, and cook until it's almost completely reduced, about 2 minutes. Reduce the heat to medium and add the tomatoes and their liquid, the thyme sprigs, rosemary, and red pepper flakes. Nestle the chicken into the sauce and add any accumulated juices. Cook, stirring and breaking up the tomatoes with a wooden spoon for 10 minutes. Adjust the heat to maintain a gentle simmer, cover the pot with the lid slightly ajar, and stew the chicken, turning it occasionally, until it's cooked through (check by slicing through the bottom of one of the thighs to the bone), another 25 to 30 minutes. If you like, discard the thyme sprigs, rosemary, and garlic.

2. When the stew is almost done, heat 1 Tbs. of the oil in a large skillet over high heat. When hot, add the zucchini. Season well with salt and black pepper; sauté until the zucchini is tender and lightly browned, 3 to 4 minutes. Transfer to a bowl.

3. Heat the remaining 1 Tbs. oil in the skillet and add the mushrooms. Season with salt and black pepper. Cook, tossing occasionally, until soft and lightly browned, 3 to 4 minutes. Add the olives and chopped thyme, return the zucchini to the pan, and toss. Fold the zucchini mixture and the parsley into the stew. Taste for salt and pepper. Serve immediately with a sprinkling of parsley. —*Tony Rosenfeld*

PER SERVING: 240 CALORIES | 17G PROTEIN | 14G CARB | 13G TOTAL FAT | 2G SAT FAT | 8G MONO FAT | 2G POLY FAT | 55MG CHOL | 460MG SODIUM | 4G FIBER

bouillabaisse

SERVES 8

FOR THE CROUTONS

2 slender baguettes, sliced into forty ½-inch-thick rounds (reserve the remaining baguette for the rouille)

FOR THE FISH BROTH

36 mussels, debearded and scrubbed

¼ cup extra-virgin olive oil

4 large cloves garlic, very roughly chopped

2 medium yellow onions, diced

3 medium fennel bulbs with about 5 inches of stems (about 1½ lb. each), diced

2 medium leeks (white and light green parts only), diced and washed well

1 medium rib celery, sliced

3½ lb. fish skeletons, heads, and trimmings (from firm white fish), gills removed

6 medium-size ripe tomatoes, diced

4 sprigs fresh flat-leaf parsley

3 large sprigs fresh thyme

2 dried bay leaves

Zest of 1 large orange, white pith removed

2 Tbs. pastis, such as Ricard or Pernod

2 tsp. fennel seeds

½ tsp. black peppercorns

Fine sea salt

½ tsp. very loosely packed saffron threads

continued on p. 164

This impressive stew takes 3 to 4 hours to prepare, but each of the elements is easy to make. You can toast the croutons a day ahead, but the other components are best eaten the day they're made. For the full Marseilles experience, serve with a dry rosé from Provence and a tangy lemon tart for dessert.

MAKE THE CROUTONS

Position a rack in the center of the oven and heat the oven to 450°F. Arrange the baguette rounds on a large rimmed baking sheet and bake until crisp and lightly golden, about 10 minutes. Turn off the oven, open the door partially, and let the croutons cool and finish drying in the oven. Store in an airtight container for up to 1 day.

MAKE THE FISH BROTH

1. Put the mussels and 1 cup water in a 4- to 5-quart pot. Cover, bring to a boil over high heat, and cook until all the mussels have opened, about 2 minutes (discard any that don't open). Set a strainer over a small bowl. Shuck the mussels into the strainer, discarding the shells. Press on the mussels to squeeze out any remaining liquid; discard the solids. Strain the mussel-cooking liquid into the bowl and set aside.

2. Heat the oil in a wide 8- to 10-quart pot over medium heat. Add the garlic and onion, cover, and cook, stirring occasionally, until softened but not colored, about 8 minutes. Add the fennel, leeks, and celery and cook, covered, stirring occasionally, until completely soft but not colored, about 20 minutes.

3. While the vegetables cook, use a chef's knife or kitchen scissors to cut the fish skeletons into 4- to 5-inch pieces. Add the fish skeletons, heads, and trimmings to the pot, along with the tomatoes, parsley, thyme, bay leaves, orange zest, pastis, fennel seeds, peppercorns, 2 tsp. salt, and the reserved mussel liquid. Add enough cold water to just cover the solids when you press them down gently (about 1 quart). Bring to a gentle simmer over medium heat and cook, uncovered, until you can easily break the fish parts with a wooden spoon, about 30 minutes. Break apart as many of the fish parts as you can with the spoon.

4. Put a food mill over a large bowl and, working in batches, grind the cooked broth ingredients, discarding the solids left in the food mill between batches. Clean the pot and put a fine-mesh strainer over it. Working in batches, strain the broth, pushing hard on the solids with a ladle to squeeze out all the liquid, and discarding the solids between batches.

5. Crumble the saffron into the broth and bring to a boil to infuse the saffron. Turn off the heat and use an immersion blender to emulsify the broth, or whisk vigorously. Season to taste with salt and set aside. A thin, greasy skin will form on top of the broth as it sits—skim it off before cooking the potatoes. *continued on p. 164*

FOR THE FISH

3½ lb. moderately firm, skin-on, scaled white fish fillets (use 4 types of fish; see the side-bar below for options)

1 Tbs. pastis, such as Ricard or Pernod

Fine sea salt and freshly ground black pepper

FOR THE POTATOES

1¾ lb. small white or yellow potatoes (about 8), peeled and sliced into ⅜-inch-thick rounds, ends discarded

About 3 cups Fish Broth (on p. 163)

FOR THE ROUILLE

2 medium cloves garlic, very coarsely chopped

Fine sea salt

Cayenne

1 cup fresh crustless coarse breadcrumbs (use the reserved baguette from the croutons)

6 Tbs. fish broth (from cooking the potatoes)

3 slices cooked potato

¼ cup extra-virgin olive oil

FOR FINISHING THE STEW

Fine sea salt and freshly ground black pepper

2 Tbs. chopped fresh flat-leaf parsley

PREPARE THE FISH

1. While the broth cooks, cut the fish fillets so you have 8 pieces of each type of fish. Use a scale; each piece should be about 1¾ oz. (If you have more than 14 oz. of any type of fish, first trim off the thinner parts—the tail pieces and belly flaps—and add them to the fish broth.) Put the fish in a large baking dish, keeping the same types of fish together (so you can keep track of each type).

2. Marinate the fish for 45 minutes before you plan to finish the stew: Drizzle the fish with the pastis and sprinkle with 1 tsp. salt and ½ tsp. pepper. Turn the fish to coat evenly, still keeping the same types of fish together. Let the fish marinate in the refrigerator for 30 minutes; then let sit at room temperature for 15 minutes before cooking.

COOK THE POTATOES

Put the potatoes in a 4- to 5-quart pot. Add enough fish broth to cover completely, about 3 cups. Bring to a boil over high heat, reduce the heat, and simmer until slightly undercooked and still a little firm in the centers, about 8 minutes. Set aside off the heat—the potatoes will finish cooking in the hot broth.

choose lean, firm white fish

Any combination of four fresh, lean, moderately firm varieties of white fish will make a delicious bouillabaisse. Here are some ideas:

• Atlantic pollock (wild, domestic or Canadian)

• Barramundi (farmed, domestic)

• Black rockfish (also known as black rock cod and black snapper; hook-and-line caught, Alaska)

• Black sea bass (wild, north- and mid-Atlantic waters)

• Halibut (wild, Pacific)

• Pacific cod (bottom longline-caught, domestic)

• Pacific lingcod (not actually a cod but rather a member of the greenling family; wild, domestic or Canadian)

• Sablefish (also known as black cod; wild, Alaska or British Columbia)

• Scup (wild, Atlantic)

• Striped bass (wild or farmed, domestic)

MAKE THE ROUILLE

In a mortar, mash the garlic and ¼ tsp. each salt and cayenne with a pestle. Mash in the breadcrumbs and broth. Mash in the potato. Mash in the oil a little at a time. The rouille should be fairly thick and spreadable. Don't overmash or it will get gummy. Season to taste with more salt and cayenne; it should be pleasantly spicy. (Alternatively, mash the garlic and salt to a paste on a cutting board with the side of a chef's knife. Transfer the paste to a bowl and use a fork to mash in the remaining ingredients. Don't use a food processor, because it makes a gummy rouille.)

FINISH THE STEW

1. Warm 8 wide, shallow soup bowls and a sauce pitcher in a low oven. Top 16 of the croutons with a thin layer of the rouille (you won't use it all). Transfer the remaining rouille and croutons to two bowls to pass at the table.

2. Reheat the potatoes in their broth, but do not boil or they will break apart.

continued on p. 166

3. Meanwhile, bring the large pot of fish broth to a brisk simmer over medium-high heat. Use a slotted spatula to divide the potatoes among the warm serving bowls. Add the broth remaining from the potatoes to the large pot of fish broth and return to a brisk simmer. Add the thicker pieces of fish to the simmering broth and then add the thinner pieces. If possible, try to keep the same types of fish together for easier plating. Poach until the thinner pieces are just cooked through, about 6 minutes.

4. While the fish poaches, the broth should stay at a bare simmer; adjust the heat as necessary. Working quickly, use the slotted spatula to distribute the thinner pieces of fish, skin side up, among the bowls. Check to make sure the thicker pieces are cooked through and distribute them among the bowls. Each serving should get four types of fish.

5. Return the broth to a boil over high heat. Remove from the heat and use an immersion blender or whisk to emulsify the broth. Season to taste with salt and pepper. Ladle a generous amount of broth over each serving of fish. Transfer any remaining broth to the warm pitcher.

6. Nestle 2 rouille-topped croutons in each bowl and sprinkle with parsley. Serve immediately, passing the remaining croutons, rouille, and broth at the table. —*Allison Ehri Kreitler*

PER SERVING: 660 CALORIES | 54G PROTEIN | 59G CARB | 20G TOTAL FAT | 3.5G SAT FAT | 12G MONO FAT | 3G POLY FAT | 105MG CHOL | 1,200MG SODIUM | 3G FIBER

brazilian chicken and shrimp stew

SERVES 4

3 cloves garlic

Kosher salt

1 large white or yellow onion, coarsely chopped (3 cups)

2 large ripe plum tomatoes, peeled, seeded, and coarsely chopped (1 cup)

½ cup coarsely chopped fresh cilantro stems and leaves, plus ½ cup whole leaves for garnish

¼ cup fresh lime juice

4 fresh Thai bird chiles, coarsely chopped, or jarred malagueta peppers, drained

1 Tbs. minced fresh ginger

Freshly ground black pepper

4 bone-in, skinless chicken thighs (1½ lb.)

1 lb. jumbo shrimp (21 to 25 per lb.), shelled and deveined

2 Tbs. plus ⅓ cup lightly salted cashews, toasted

3 Tbs. olive oil or well-shaken dendê and soy oil blend

¾ cup well-stirred canned coconut milk

Hot cooked white rice, for serving

This take on xim-xim, *a traditional stew from Brazil by way of West Africa, relies on a specific set of ingredients: dendê oil (the Brazilian name for palm oil), coconut milk, and nuts. You can substitute olive oil for the dendê oil.*

1. Peel and chop the garlic. Sprinkle with 1 tsp. salt, and with the side of a heavy chef's knife, mash to a paste. Transfer to a food processor and add the onion, tomatoes, chopped cilantro stems and leaves, lime juice, chiles, ginger, and ¼ tsp. black pepper. Pulse until finely chopped and almost smooth. Put the chicken and shrimp in a large bowl, add the onion mixture, and turn to coat well. Cover and refrigerate for 1 to 2 hours.

2. Meanwhile, pulse 2 Tbs. of the cashews in a spice grinder just until finely ground; do not let them form a paste.

3. Remove the chicken from the marinade, brushing excess marinade back into the bowl. Pat the chicken dry with paper towels. Season on both sides with ¼ tsp. salt. Heat 2 Tbs. of the olive or dendê oil in a 5- to 6-quart Dutch oven over medium heat. Add the chicken and cook, turning once, until very lightly browned on both sides, about 4 minutes per side. Transfer the thighs to a plate as they are browned. Remove the shrimp from the marinade and set them aside.

4. Put the marinade in the Dutch oven, add the coconut milk and ground cashews, and cook over medium heat, stirring and scraping the bottom of the pan, for 3 minutes to cook off the raw onion flavor. Return the chicken to the Dutch oven, reduce the heat to low, cover, and simmer, stirring occasionally and turning the chicken halfway through cooking, until the chicken is tender and cooked through, about 25 minutes total. Increase the heat to medium, stir in the shrimp, and cook, stirring constantly, just until the shrimp are bright pink and nearly opaque throughout, 2 to 3 minutes; they will continue to cook after they're removed from the heat.

5. Off the heat, stir in half the remaining cashews and half of the whole cilantro leaves. Season to taste with salt. Transfer the chicken to a large deep platter and pour the shrimp and sauce over it. Drizzle with the remaining 1 Tbs. dendê or olive oil, top with the remaining cashews and cilantro leaves, and serve hot with the white rice. *—Lori Longbotham*

PER SERVING: 490 CALORIES | 36G PROTEIN | 13G CARB | 33G TOTAL FAT | 13G SAT FAT | 14G MONO FAT | 4G POLY FAT | 215MG CHOL | 650MG SODIUM | 3G FIBER

southwestern spiced chicken and black bean stew

- 2 Tbs. extra-virgin olive oil
- 3 thick slices bacon
- 6 bone-in, skinless chicken thighs (about 2¼ lb.), large pieces of fat trimmed

  Kosher salt and freshly ground black pepper
- 1 large yellow onion, diced
- 1 red bell pepper, cored, seeded, and finely diced
- 2 tsp. chili powder
- 1 tsp. ground cumin
- ¾ cup beer
- 1 15½-oz. can black beans, rinsed and drained (about 2 cups)
- 1 dried chipotle (optional)
- 2 cups homemade or lower-salt chicken broth; more if needed
- 1 lime
- 3 Tbs. chopped fresh cilantro leaves

  Sour cream, for garnish

  Fried tortilla strips (optional)

A dried chipotle gives the broth a wonderful smoky spice. To make fried tortilla strips, cut corn or flour tortillas into long strips and fry in 350°F oil until they start to brown, about 2 minutes.

1. Heat the oil in a large Dutch oven or heavy pot over medium heat. Add the bacon and cook until it renders much of its fat and crisps slightly, about 7 minutes. Transfer the bacon to a paper-towel-lined plate. Season the chicken well with salt and pepper. Add half of the thighs to the pan and brown them well on both sides, 2 to 3 minutes per side. Transfer to a plate. Brown the remaining thighs and reserve with the rest. There should be 2 to 3 Tbs. fat left in the pan; if there's more, spoon out and discard the excess. Add the onion and bell pepper, season well with salt, and cook, stirring often, until the onion softens and caramelizes slightly, about 7 minutes. Raise the heat to high, add the chili powder and cumin, and cook, stirring, for 30 seconds. Add the beer and cook until it's almost completely reduced, about 3 minutes. Add the beans, the chipotle (if using), and the chicken broth. When the mixture comes to a boil, adjust the heat to maintain a simmer and cook for 5 minutes.

2. Transfer 2 cups of the beans and broth (but not the chipotle) to a blender, purée, and then mix it back into the rest of the broth.

3. Return the thighs to the pot, cover with the lid slightly ajar, and simmer until the chicken is cooked through (check by slicing through the bottom of one of the thighs to the bone), about 30 minutes. If the stew is too thick, thin it with more chicken broth. Discard the chipotle. Crumble the reserved bacon. Juice one half of the lime; cut the other half into wedges. Stir the bacon, lime juice, and 2 Tbs. of the cilantro into the stew and season well with salt and pepper.

4. Serve immediately, ladling some of the beans and chicken into each bowl. Sprinkle each serving with the remaining cilantro and a small dollop of sour cream. Serve with the lime wedges and fried tortilla strips, if you like. *—Tony Rosenfeld*

PER SERVING: 350 CALORIES | 22G PROTEIN | 20G CARB | 20G TOTAL FAT | 6G SAT FAT | 10G MONO FAT | 3G POLY FAT | 70MG CHOL | 390MG SODIUM | 6G FIBER

cane vinegar chicken stew with pearl onions, oranges & spinach

- **8** **bone-in, skin-on chicken thighs (2½ to 3 lb. total)**
- **Sea salt and freshly ground black pepper**
- **4** **Tbs. unsalted butter**
- **¾** **lb. fresh pearl onions, peeled**
- **6** **medium cloves garlic, thinly sliced**
- **½** **tsp. smoked sweet paprika (pimentón)**
- **1½** **cups cane vinegar**
- **1½** **cups homemade or lower-salt chicken broth**

Cane vinegar, which is made from sugar cane, adds a malty, sweet-and-sour tang to this stew. If you can't find cane vinegar, you can substitute malt or cider vinegar.

1. Season the chicken on both sides with 1½ tsp. salt and ½ tsp. pepper.

2. Melt the butter in an 8-quart Dutch oven or other heavy pot over medium heat. Working in two batches, cook the thighs until golden on both sides, 4 to 5 minutes per side. Transfer to a plate. Add the onions, garlic, and paprika to the pot and cook until the onions are soft, about 5 minutes. Add the vinegar and use a wooden spoon to scrape up the browned bits from the bottom of the pan. Increase the heat to high and bring to a boil. Reduce the heat to medium high and simmer until the vinegar is reduced by half, 7 to 10 minutes. Increase the heat to high and add the broth. When the liquid comes to a boil, add the chicken to the pot, skin side up, reduce the heat to low, cover, and simmer until the chicken is cooked through and tender, about 30 minutes.

4 large navel oranges

6 oz. fresh spinach, stemmed (4 cups)

2 Tbs. chopped fresh mint

3. Meanwhile, slice the peel off the oranges. Working over a medium bowl to catch the juice, cut the segments free from the membranes. Squeeze any remaining juice from the membranes into the bowl.

4. When the chicken is done, add the orange segments and juice, spinach, and mint to the pot, gently stirring them into the sauce. Portion the chicken and sauce into 4 bowls. Serve immediately.
—*Hugh Acheson*

PER SERVING: 620 CALORIES | 43G PROTEIN | 30G CARB | 36G TOTAL FAT | 14G SAT FAT | 13G MONO FAT | 6G POLY FAT | 170MG CHOL | 1,070MG SODIUM | 6G FIBER

how to peel pearl onions

Their tiny size and tightly wrapped skin make handling pearl onions awkward. And if you sacrifice the more easily peeled first fleshy layer, it doesn't leave you with much onion. Follow the blanching method to peel just the onion's outer skin.

Bring a small saucepan of water to a boil and fill a medium bowl with ice water. Trim both ends of each onion and put them in the boiling water for about 30 seconds. Then transfer the onions to the ice water to stop the cooking.

Once the onions are cool, use a paring knife to slip off the skins.

spicy sausage, escarole & white bean stew

SERVES 4

- 1 Tbs. extra-virgin olive oil
- 1 medium yellow onion, chopped
- ¾ lb. hot Italian sausage, casings removed
- 2 medium cloves garlic, minced
- 2 15-oz. cans cannellini beans, rinsed and drained
- 1 small head escarole, chopped into 1- to 2-inch pieces, washed, and lightly dried
- 1 cup homemade or lower-salt chicken broth
- 1½ tsp. red-wine vinegar; more as needed

  Kosher salt
- ¼ cup freshly grated Parmigiano-Reggiano

Toasted bread rubbed with garlic and drizzled with olive oil makes a nice accompaniment.

1. Heat the oil in a heavy 5- to 6-quart Dutch oven over medium heat. Add the onion and cook, stirring occasionally, until tender, 5 to 6 minutes. Add the sausage, raise the heat to medium high, and cook, stirring and breaking up the sausage with a wooden spoon or spatula until lightly browned and broken into small (1-inch) pieces, 5 to 6 minutes. Add the garlic and cook for 1 minute, then stir in the beans. Add the escarole to the pot in batches; using tongs, toss with the sausage mixture to wilt the escarole and make room for more. When all the escarole is in, add the chicken broth, cover the pot, and cook until the beans are heated through and the escarole is tender, about 8 minutes. Season to taste with the vinegar and salt.

2. Transfer to bowls and sprinkle each portion with some of the Parmigiano. —*Joanne McAllister Smart*

PER SERVING: 390 CALORIES | 20G PROTEIN | 40G CARB | 17G TOTAL FAT | 5G SAT FAT | 8G MONO FAT | 3G POLY FAT | 25MG CHOL | 1,070MG SODIUM | 13G FIBER

More about Escarole

A member of the chicory family, escarole is also known as common chicory, broad chicory, or Batavian endive and has wide, succulent stems and leaves that look more crumpled than curly. Like other chicories, it has a bitter flavor, though somewhat less so than curly endive. Though it can be eaten raw in salads, its hearty leaves benefit from cooking and are delicious with bacon, sausage, and added to white bean soups.

Frisée provides a similar texture and bitter flavor in salads; for cooking, curly endive is a better substitute, since it also has hearty leaves that hold up to heat.

Buying and storing

Avoid escarole with especially thick or tough looking outer leaves and remove any blemished outer leaves as well as the core. Escarole can be quite sandy, so wash it well in a few changes of water. If cooking, you can leave water clinging to the leaves; otherwise dry them well in a salad spinner.

Store escarole in the crisper drawer in the refrigerator and use within a few days.

chicken stew with spinach, potatoes & porcini

SERVES 6

½ oz. dried porcini mushrooms

¼ cup extra-virgin olive oil

2 ⅛-inch-thick slices pancetta or bacon (about 2 oz.), sliced into thin strips

6 bone-in, skinless chicken thighs (about 2¼ lb.), large pieces of fat trimmed

Kosher salt and freshly ground black pepper

1 large yellow onion, cut into ¼-inch dice

2 small cloves garlic, minced

¼ cup dry sherry or dry white wine

2 large Yukon Gold potatoes (1 lb. total), peeled and cut into ½-inch dice

2 sprigs fresh thyme, plus 1½ tsp. chopped

1½ cups homemade or lower-salt chicken broth; more as needed

2 Tbs. sherry vinegar or balsamic vinegar

1 cup coarse fresh bread-crumbs (about 1½ oz.)

2 cups baby spinach leaves (about 2 oz.)

Be sure to buy good-quality dried porcini mushrooms (with large white cross sections). Cheaper ones are dark and shriveled and have an overly pungent aroma, which will give the stew an off taste.

1. Soak the porcini in 1½ cups boiling water for 20 minutes. Strain, then (reserving the soaking liquid) chop them.

2. Heat 2 Tbs. of the oil in a large Dutch oven or heavy soup pot over medium heat. Add the pancetta or bacon and cook, stirring occasionally, until crisp, about 7 minutes; transfer to a paper-towel-lined plate.

3. Season the chicken well with salt and pepper. Add half of the thighs to the pan and brown them well, 2 to 3 minutes per side. Transfer to a large plate. Brown the remaining thighs and reserve with the rest. Add the onion and half of the garlic to the pan and season well with salt. Cook, stirring with a wooden spoon and scraping up any browned bits, until the onion softens and darkens slightly, about 7 minutes. Add the chopped porcini and cook for another 1 minute. Pour in the sherry and cook, stirring occasionally, until it's almost completely reduced, about 2 minutes. Add the potatoes, thyme sprigs, chicken broth, reserved porcini soaking liquid, and vinegar and bring to a boil over high heat. Adjust the heat to maintain a gentle simmer, cover the pan, and cook until the potatoes are just tender, about 15 minutes. Discard the thyme sprigs.

4. Purée 1½ cups of the chunky potato mixture in a blender. Return the puréed mixture to the rest of the broth, nestle in the chicken (and add any accumulated juices), and cover the pot with the lid slightly ajar. Stew the chicken thighs at a bare simmer, turning them occasionally, until they're cooked through (check by slicing through the bottom of one of the thighs to the bone), about 30 minutes.

5. Meanwhile, in a large nonstick skillet, heat the remaining 2 Tbs. oil over medium heat. Add the remaining garlic, sauté until it starts to color, about 20 seconds, and then add the breadcrumbs. Cook, stirring often, until they turn golden brown, about 6 minutes. Stir in ½ tsp. of the chopped thyme, season lightly with salt and pepper, and transfer to a paper-towel-lined plate.

6. When the chicken is done, fold in the spinach and stir until wilted, about 1 minute. Stir in the remaining 1 tsp. chopped thyme and the pancetta; season well with salt and pepper. Serve immediately, sprinkled generously with the breadcrumbs. *—Tony Rosenfeld*

PER SERVING: 280 CALORIES | 18G PROTEIN | 22G CARB | 13G TOTAL FAT | 2G SAT FAT | 8G MONO FAT | 2G POLY FAT | 60MG CHOL | 330MG SODIUM | 2G FIBER

beef bourguignon

SERVES 10

FOR MARINATING THE BEEF

- **2** **750ml bottles full-bodied red wine**
- **2** **shallots, finely chopped (½ cup)**
- **2** **large yellow onions, thinly sliced**
- **1** **medium carrot, peeled and thinly sliced**
- **2** **sprigs fresh thyme or ½ tsp. dried thyme leaves**
- **1** **bay leaf**
- **2** **Tbs. roughly chopped parsley stems**
- **¼** **tsp. ground allspice**
- **¼** **tsp. freshly ground nutmeg**
- **⅛** **tsp. ground cloves**
- **6** **lb. beef blade roast or beef chuck, trimmed of all external fat and cut into 1½-inch cubes**
- **3** **Tbs. olive oil**

FOR THE BRAISE

- **2** **ham hocks, fresh or smoked**
- **Kosher salt**
- **3** **Tbs. olive oil; more as needed**
- **Stems from 1½ lb. fresh button mushrooms; reserve the caps for the garnish**
- **6** **to 8 cups veal or turkey stock or beef stock**
- **1** **bouquet garni of 10 parsley stems, 1 sprig thyme (or ¼ tsp. dried thyme leaves), and 1 bay leaf**
- **2** **large cloves garlic, crushed and coarsely chopped**
- **1½** **cubes beef bouillon, crumbled**

continued on p. 176

This classic French braise is undeniable a project, but it is well worth the time; it's truly a glorious dish, perfect as the centerpiece for a dinner with good friends.

Plan to start the preparations early one evening and finish the braise the next morning. It can be completely prepared up to 3 days ahead, allowed to cool, and refrigerated. To serve, reheat gently but thoroughly to at least 165°F, and let simmer while preparing the croutons.

MAKE THE MARINADE

1. Empty the wine into a large nonreactive saucepan, add the shallots, and slowly bring to a boil. Reduce to a simmer and cook until reduced to 1 quart, about 20 minutes. Let cool completely.

2. In a bowl, toss together the onion, carrot, thyme, bay leaf, and parsley stems. Spread half of this mixture on the bottom of a nonreactive baking dish.

3. Mix the allspice, nutmeg, and cloves in a small dish. Sprinkle the cubes of beef with the spices and then toss with the olive oil. Arrange the meat on top of the aromatics in the baking dish and then cover with the remaining aromatics. Pour the cooled reduced wine over everything, using your fingers to make room between the meat for the wine to enter (don't toss yet). The wine should just cover the meat. Cover with plastic wrap and punch a few holes in the plastic (so sulfur gas from the onions can escape). Refrigerate and marinate for 3 hours. Toss the contents, cover again with the plastic wrap, and refrigerate overnight, or for at least 8 hours.

PREPARE THE BRAISE

1. Cover the ham hocks with cold water in a large saucepan. Bring to a boil with a dash of salt and simmer until softened, about 45 minutes. Meanwhile, drain the marinated meat and aromatics in a colander set over a bowl (reserve the marinade). Remove the beef cubes, dry them thoroughly with a clean dishtowel or paper towels, and set aside. Pat dry the aromatic vegetables. When the hocks are soft, drain them and cut or pull off the rinds. Scrape the rinds of all extra fat. Cut the rinds into 1-inch squares; set aside.

2. In a large skillet, heat the olive oil on medium high. Salt the beef lightly and sear it in batches until browned on all sides, 3 to 5 minutes, adjusting the heat so the meat doesn't burn. Transfer to a plate.

3. In the oil left in the skillet, add the drained aromatic vegetables and the mushroom stems. Sauté on medium high, stirring often, until the vegetables cook down and soften, about 10 minutes. Remove from the heat and transfer the vegetables to a plate. Sop up excess oil in the pan with a wad of paper towels. Add 1 cup of the stock to the skillet and scrape up the caramelized juices. Pour the deglazed juices into a braising pot.

continued on p. 176

Freshly ground black pepper

Prepared parchment and
foil lid (see the sidebar
on p. 178)

FOR THE GARNISHES

12 oz. lean, meaty slab bacon,
    top layer of fat removed and
    fatty ends trimmed

6   Tbs. unsalted butter

36 small white onions

    Table salt and freshly
    ground black pepper

2   Tbs. veal, turkey, or beef
    stock or water

    Reserved button mushroom
    caps (or larger mushrooms,
    quartered)

4. Heat the oven to 325°F. Add the reduced wine marinade to the deglazed skillet (or a saucepan, if the skillet is too small) and bring to a boil, letting the liquid reduce by one-third. Strain the marinade through a fine-mesh strainer directly into the braising pot. Add the reserved pieces of rind to the braising pot, along with the browned meat and vegetables, bouquet garni, garlic, bouillon cubes, and pepper. Pour in enough stock to just cover the meat. Bring to a boil and then reduce to a simmer.

5. Make a parchment and foil lid, called a brazier (see the sidebar on p. 178), and lay them inside, touching the braise. Cover with the pot lid and bake until the meat is extremely tender and a metal skewer penetrates a piece of meat and comes out without resistance (a meat thermometer should read at least 165°F), 2 to 2¾ hours.

PREPARE THE GARNISHES

1. While the beef is in the oven, cut the bacon into strips ⅓ inch thick, and then cut across the strips to create ⅓-inch-thick slices, called lardons. (The bacon will be easier to cut if you put it in the freezer for 15 to 20 minutes.) Cover the lardons with cold water in a saucepan, bring to a boil and simmer for 2 to 3 minutes to remove the smoky flavor and some saltiness. Drain well and pat dry.

2. Heat 2 Tbs. of the butter in a large skillet over medium heat and brown the lardons on all sides until they're golden but not crisp or brittle, 12 to 15 minutes. Transfer the lardons to a paper-towel-lined plate. Discard the fat in the pan but leave the caramelized juices.

3. While the lardons are browning, bring about 1 quart water to a boil. Add the onions, simmer for 1 minute, and turn off the heat. Remove a few onions. When they're cool enough to handle, cut off the root end, slip off the skin, and cut a ⅛-inch-deep cross in the root end to prevent the onion from falling apart during cooking. Repeat with the remaining onions.

4. Add another 2 Tbs. butter to the pan with the caramelized bacon juices and sauté the onions on medium heat until they're golden brown, about 10 minutes. Season lightly with salt and pepper. Add 2 Tbs. stock or water to the pan and roll the onions in the forming glaze. Transfer them to the plate with the lardons.

5. Without cleaning the pan, melt the remaining 2 Tbs. butter and sauté the reserved mushroom caps (or quarters) on medium-high heat until they begin to brown, about 2 minutes. Season with salt and pepper to taste. Cover the pan, turn the heat to medium low, and cook until the mushrooms have given off all their liquid, about 5 minutes. Turn the heat to medium high, uncover the pan, and cook until the liquid concentrates again and the mushrooms turn shiny, about 5 minutes.

continued on p. 178

FOR THICKENING THE SAUCE

> **About 4 Tbs. unsalted butter, at room temperature**
>
> **About 4 Tbs. unbleached all-purpose flour**
>
> **Table salt and freshly ground black pepper**

FOR SERVING

> 5 **⅓-inch-thick slices country French boule, cut in half, a crustless triangle cut from each half**
>
> **About ½ cup olive oil**
>
> 1 **Tbs. chopped fresh flat-leaf parsley, plus more whole leaves for garnish**

Transfer them to the plate with the onions and lardoons. Set aside the skillet, but don't clean it (if there are black or burned bits in the pan, remove them).

TO THICKEN THE SAUCE AND FINISH THE BRAISE

1. Using a slotted spoon, transfer the pieces of meat from the braising pot to a bowl. Strain the sauce that remains through a fine-mesh strainer into a bowl, pressing on the solids. Let stand until the fat has completely surfaced. Remove the fat using a gravy separator, a basting tube, or a spoon. Wipe the braising pot dry.

2. Set the reserved garnish-cooking skillet over medium heat. Deglaze the pan by pouring in some of the defatted sauce and scraping up the caramelized juices. Add this deglazing liquid to the defatted sauce. Return the sauce to the braising pot, passing it through a fine-mesh strainer, and bring to a simmer.

3. Meanwhile, in a small bowl, knead together the butter and flour to a paste, called a beurre manié. Using a whisk, rapidly blend small amounts of the beurre manié into the simmering sauce until it is the consistency you like. You may not need all the beurre manié. Simmer the sauce for about 5 minutes to cook off the raw flour taste.

4. Return the meat and garnishes to the pot with the sauce and season with salt and pepper. Shake the pan back and forth on medium low to blend the elements. Bring to a boil, reduce to a simmer, and cook for 15 to 20 minutes, leaving the lid askew so steam can evaporate (trapping the steam would dilute the sauce). Correct the final seasoning with salt and pepper to taste.

TO SERVE THE BRAISE

1. Heat the oven to 275°F. Set the bread triangles on a baking sheet and top them with a cake rack to prevent buckling. Bake until dry, turning once, about 8 minutes.

2. As close as possible to serving time, heat the olive oil in a large frying pan until it starts shimmering. Fry the bread, a few pieces at a time, until golden, turning once. Drain on a thick layer of paper towels.

3. Transfer the finished braise (well reheated, if necessary) into a deep country dish or platter. Sprinkle with chopped parsley and arrange the croutons alternated with parsley leaves all around the dish.
—*Madeleine Kamman*

PER SERVING: 920 CALORIES | 74G PROTEIN | 18G CARB | 57G TOTAL FAT | 22G SAT FAT | 26G MONO FAT | 4G POLY FAT | 260MG CHOL | 940MG SODIUM | 2G FIBER

continued on p. 178

how to fashion a pot for perfect braising

A few easy steps transform a regular pot into the perfect braising vessel. Begin by setting the lid of the braising pot on a sheet of parchment. Trace the shape of the lid on the paper with a pencil. Cut out the pattern ⅓ inch wider than the template.

Lay two or three sheets of wide, heavy-duty foil on the counter, so the sheets overlap by at least 2 inches. Set the pot on the foil; the amount of foil that extends from under the pot on all sides should be a couple of inches more than the height of the pan. If not, add more foil. Tape the sheets together.

Set the empty pot in the center of the sheet and wrap the foil up and around the sides of the pot, molding it to form a well-defined angle where the bottom meets the sides. Flatten the foil well against the sides, then remove the foil.

Once the meat, aromatic vegetables, and liquid are in the pot, set the parchment over them.

Then insert the prepared foil over the parchment, adjusting as needed to fit tightly all around the pot. Fold down the foil so it hugs the pot's outer walls; trim the excess with scissors.

classic chicken pot pie

This is the definitive pot pie recipe: a creamy chicken stew baked under a rich, flaky crust. It's comfort in a bowl.

SERVES 6

FOR THE CRUST

2	cups unbleached all-purpose flour
¾	tsp. table salt
12	Tbs. cold unsalted butter, cut into 10 pieces

FOR THE FILLING

5	Tbs. olive oil
2½	lb. boneless, skinless chicken thighs or breasts
	Kosher salt and freshly ground black pepper
½	lb. medium cremini mushrooms, quartered (2 cups)
1½	cups frozen pearl onions, thawed and patted dry
4	medium carrots, peeled and sliced ½ inch thick (1½ cups)
3	medium cloves garlic, minced
4	Tbs. unsalted butter, cut into 3 pieces
½	cup unbleached all-purpose flour
3	cups homemade or lower-salt chicken broth
1	cup half-and-half or heavy cream
1¾	lb. red potatoes, cut into ½-inch dice (5 cups)
1	cup frozen petite peas, thawed
¼	cup dry sherry
¼	cup chopped fresh flat-leaf parsley
2	Tbs. chopped fresh thyme
1½	Tbs. Dijon mustard

MAKE THE CRUST

Put the flour and salt in a food processor and pulse to blend. Add the butter and pulse until the butter pieces are the size of peas, 10 to 12 pulses. Drizzle 3 Tbs. cold water over the mixture. Pulse until the dough forms moist crumbs that are just beginning to clump together, 8 or 9 more pulses. Turn the crumbs onto a large piece of plastic wrap and gather into a pile. With the heel of your hand, gently smear the dough away from you until the crumbs come together (two or three smears should do it). Shape the dough into a 4-inch square, wrap tightly in the plastic, and refrigerate until firm, at least 2 hours or up to 2 days. (The dough can also be frozen for up to 1 month. Thaw in the refrigerator overnight or at room temperature for about 1 hour before rolling.)

MAKE THE FILLING

1. Heat 2 Tbs. of the oil in a 7- to 8-quart Dutch oven over medium-high heat until very hot. Generously season the chicken with salt and pepper. Working in two batches, brown the chicken well on both sides, 4 to 5 minutes per side, adding 1 Tbs. oil with the second batch. Transfer the chicken to a cutting board and cut into ¾- to 1-inch pieces (it's fine if the chicken isn't fully cooked; it will finish cooking later). Put the chicken in a large bowl. Add 1 Tbs. oil to the pot and heat over medium-high heat until hot. Add the mushrooms. Cook without stirring for 1 minute. Continue cooking, stirring occasionally, until well browned, 3 to 4 minutes. Transfer the mushrooms to the bowl of chicken.

2. Reduce the heat to medium and add the remaining 1 Tbs. oil and then the onions and carrots to the pot. Cook, stirring occasionally, until the edges are browned, 8 to 9 minutes. Add the garlic and stir constantly until fragrant, about another 30 seconds. Scrape the vegetables into the bowl of chicken and mushrooms.

3. Melt the butter in the same pot over low heat. Add the flour and cook, whisking constantly, until the texture, which will be clumpy at first, loosens and smooths out, about 4 minutes. Slowly whisk in the chicken broth and half-and-half. Bring to a boil over medium-high heat, whisking to scrape up any browned bits from the bottom of the pan. Reduce the heat to low and add the potatoes, chicken-mushroom mixture, onions, and carrots (and any accumulated juice),

continued on p. 180

and a generous pinch each of salt and pepper. Partially cover the pot and simmer gently (adjusting the heat as necessary), stirring occasionally, until the potatoes and carrots are just tender, 15 to 18 minutes. Stir in the peas, sherry, parsley, thyme, and mustard. Season to taste with salt and pepper. (At this point, the filling can be cooled and refrigerated for up to 8 hours before proceeding with the recipe.)

ASSEMBLE THE POT PIES

1. Distribute the filling evenly among six ovenproof bowls or ramekins that are 2 to 3 inches deep and hold at least 2 cups. Let the dough soften slightly at room temperature, about 20 minutes. On a lightly floured surface, roll the dough into a ⅛-inch-thick rectangle. With a round cookie cutter (or using a plate as a guide), cut 6 rounds of dough that are slightly wider than the inner diameter of the bowls (reroll the scraps if necessary). Cut a small X in the center of each round.

2. Top each bowl of stew with a dough round. With your fingertips, gently press the dough down into the edge of the bowl, so that it flares up the sides of the bowl.

BAKE THE PIES

Position a rack in the center of the oven and heat the oven to 425°F. Put the pot pies on a foil-lined rimmed baking sheet. Bake until the filling is bubbling and the crust is deep golden-brown, about 45 minutes. Let cool on a rack for 20 to 30 minutes before serving.

—Abigail Johnson Dodge

PER SERVING: 860 CALORIES | 45G PROTEIN | 64G CARB | 47G TOTAL FAT | 20G SAT FAT | 19G MONO FAT | 4.5G POLY FAT | 195MG CHOL | 770MG SODIUM | 7G FIBER

eggplant ragoût with tomatoes, peppers & chickpeas

SERVES 4 TO 6

- 1½ lb. eggplant, preferably plump round fruits
- 2 Tbs. olive oil; more for brushing the eggplant
- 1 large red onion, cut into ½-inch dice
- 1 large red or yellow bell pepper, cored, seeded, and cut into 1-inch pieces
- 2 plump cloves garlic, thinly sliced
- 2 tsp. paprika
- 1 tsp. ground cumin
- Generous pinch of cayenne
- 2 Tbs. tomato paste
- 5 plum tomatoes, peeled, quartered lengthwise, and seeded
- 1 15-oz. can chickpeas (preferably organic), rinsed and drained
- Kosher salt
- ¼ cup coarsely chopped fresh flat-leaf parsley
- Freshly ground black pepper

Broiling the eggplant first helps it keep its shape in the stew.

1. Heat the broiler. Cut the eggplant crosswise into ¾-inch rounds and brush both sides with olive oil. Broil until light gold on each side, about 2 minutes per side. Let cool and cut into 1-inch pieces.

2. In a medium Dutch oven, heat the 2 Tbs. olive oil over medium-high heat. Add the onion and bell pepper and sauté until the onion is lightly browned, 12 to 15 minutes. During the last few minutes of browning, add the garlic, paprika, cumin, and cayenne. Stir in the tomato paste and cook, stirring, for 1 minute. Stir in ¼ cup water and bring to a boil, using a wooden spoon to scrape up the juices from the bottom of the pan. Add the tomatoes, eggplant, chickpeas, 1 cup water, and 1 tsp. salt. Bring to a boil and then simmer, covered, until the vegetables are quite tender, about 25 minutes, stirring once or twice. Stir in the parsley, taste for salt and pepper, and serve. —*Deborah Madison*

PER SERVING: 220 CALORIES | 6G PROTEIN | 32G CARB | 8G TOTAL FAT | 1G SAT FAT | 5G MONO FAT | 1G POLY FAT | 0MG CHOL | 550MG SODIUM | 8G FIBER

cod stew with chorizo, leeks & potatoes

SERVES 4

- 2 **small leeks (or 1 large leek)**
- 6 **oz. chorizo**
- 1 **lb. red potatoes (4 to 5 medium), scrubbed and cut into ¾-inch cubes**
- **Kosher salt**
- 1 **Tbs. olive oil**
- 3 **cloves garlic, minced**
- 1 **28-oz. can diced tomatoes, with their liquid**
- ½ **cup dry white wine**
- **Freshly ground black pepper**
- ¼ **cup chopped fresh flat-leaf parsley**
- 1 **lb. cod fillet, cut into 4 even portions**

Chorizo, a Spanish smoked pork sausage, is sold in many supermarkets and in Hispanic groceries.

1. Trim off the root, dark greens, and most of the light green parts of the leeks. Chop the leeks into ½-inch pieces and rinse thoroughly to remove all the grit. Cut the chorizo in half lengthwise and slice into half-moons about ⅛ inch thick.

2. Put the potatoes in a large saucepan and cover with cold water by 1 to 2 inches. Salt the water, cover partially, and bring to a boil over high heat. Reduce the heat as needed and boil until the potatoes are tender, 10 to 15 minutes; drain.

3. While the potatoes cook, heat the oil in a large pot (choose one that's wide enough to hold the fish in a single layer) over medium heat for 1 minute. Add the chorizo and leeks and cook, stirring occasionally, until the chorizo has browned slightly and the leeks are soft, about 6 minutes. Add the garlic and cook for 1 minute. Stir in the tomatoes and their liquid, the wine, 1½ cups water, and ½ tsp. salt. Bring to a boil over high heat. Partially cover the pot, reduce the heat to medium, and simmer for 15 minutes.

4. Add the potatoes, season with salt and pepper, and stir in half of the parsley. Season the cod with salt and pepper, set the fillets on top of the stew, cover, and simmer until just cooked through, 6 to 8 minutes. Using a wide spatula, carefully transfer the cod to shallow soup bowls (the fillets may break apart). Spoon the stew over the cod and serve immediately, garnished with the remaining parsley. *—Eva Katz*

PER SERVING: 490 CALORIES | 37G PROTEIN | 38G CARB | 21G TOTAL FAT | 7G SAT FAT | 11G MONO FAT | 2G POLY FAT | 85MG CHOL | 1,340MG SODIUM | 6G FIBER

chicken, lemon & olive stew

SERVES 10 TO 12

6 lb. boneless, skinless chicken thighs (about 25 thighs), trimmed of excess fat

Kosher salt and freshly ground black pepper

¼ cup extra-virgin olive oil

3 large yellow onions, thinly sliced

8 cloves garlic, smashed and peeled

1 Tbs. ground turmeric

2 tsp. ground cumin

2 tsp. ground coriander

3 small dried red chiles, preferably chile de Arbol, stemmed and crumbled

2 3-inch cinnamon sticks

2 fresh bay leaves or 1 dried

1 quart homemade or lower-salt chicken broth

Finely grated zest and juice of 4 lemons

2 cups canned chickpeas, rinsed and drained

2 cups small pitted green olives, such as Picholine or Manzanilla

Saffron Couscous (recipe at right)

3 Tbs. chopped fresh cilantro or mint

Make Ahead

This stew can be prepared ahead and refrigerated for up to 3 days or frozen for up to 1 month. Reheat gently over medium-low heat, adding ½ cup water if the stew seems too thick.

Warm, earthy spices infuse this savory stew, and olives and lemon add brightness. It's perfect for casual entertaining because it tastes even better a day or two after it's made.

1. Season the chicken all over with 2 tsp. salt and 2 tsp. pepper. Heat the oil in an 8-quart Dutch oven over medium-high heat. Working in batches so as not to crowd the pan, brown the chicken well all over, about 3 minutes per side, transferring each batch to a plate or bowl—it will take about 4 batches and 24 minutes total to brown all the chicken. The bottom of the pan will be brown, but that's fine.

2. Reduce the heat to medium, add the onion and garlic, and cook, stirring occasionally, until the onion is softened and golden brown, 5 to 6 minutes. Add the turmeric, cumin, coriander, chiles, cinnamon sticks, and bay leaves and cook, stirring constantly, until fragrant, about 1 minute. Add the chicken broth, lemon zest, and ½ cup of the lemon juice. Cover and simmer over medium-low heat for 30 minutes.

3. Return the chicken and any accumulated juices to the pot. Carefully stir in the chickpeas and olives. Increase the heat to medium high and simmer, uncovered, stirring occasionally, until the sauce has thickened somewhat and the chicken is cooked through, another 6 to 8 minutes. Stir in 1 Tbs. of the remaining lemon juice and season to taste with salt and pepper. Discard the cinnamon sticks and bay leaves.

4. Serve over the Saffron Couscous, sprinkled with the cilantro or mint. *—Heidi Johannsen Stewart*

PER SERVING WITHOUT COUSCOUS: 490 CALORIES | 48G PROTEIN | 18G CARB | 25G TOTAL FAT | 6G SAT FAT | 12G MONO FAT | 5G POLY FAT | 150MG CHOL | 860MG SODIUM | 4G FIBER

saffron couscous

SERVES 10 TO 12

- 3 cups (1½ lb.) couscous
- 3 cups homemade or lower-salt chicken broth
- ¼ cup unsalted butter
- ½ tsp. saffron threads, crumbled

  Kosher salt

- ¼ cup extra-virgin olive oil

Baking the couscous helps it cook evenly and frees up your stovetop, too.

1. Position a rack in the center of the oven and heat the oven to 350°F. Put the couscous in a 9x13-inch baking dish; set aside. In a small saucepan, heat the chicken broth, butter, saffron, and 1 tsp. salt over medium-high heat until the butter is melted and the broth is hot. Pour the mixture over the couscous and mix well.

2. Cover the baking dish with foil and bake until the liquid has been absorbed by the couscous, 10 to 12 minutes. Let sit at room temperature, covered, for 5 minutes. Drizzle the olive oil over the couscous. Using a fork or your fingers, gently mix to coat the couscous in oil and break apart any clumps. Transfer to a serving dish. If not serving immediately, loosely cover the dish and keep warm for up to 30 minutes.

cioppino

SERVES 8

FOR THE GARLIC OIL AND GARLIC CHIPS

- 4   large cloves garlic
- ½   cup extra-virgin olive oil
-     Kosher salt and freshly ground black pepper

FOR THE SHELLFISH STOCK

- 1   lb. large shrimp (16 to 20 per pound)
- 6½ cups homemade or lower-salt chicken broth

FOR THE CIOPPINO BROTH

- ¼   cup olive oil
- 3   cups coarsely chopped yellow onion (about 2 medium)
- 1   cup coarsely chopped carrot (about 2 medium)
- ⅔   cup coarsely chopped celery or fennel (about 2 medium ribs celery or ¼ medium fennel bulb)
- 3   Tbs. coarsely chopped garlic (5 to 6 large cloves)
- 6   cups canned whole peeled tomatoes, broken up, with their liquid, or diced tomatoes with their liquid (two 28-oz. cans)
- 2½ cups (¾ of a 750ml bottle) medium-bodied red wine, such as Zinfandel, Pinot Noir, or Sangiovese
- 6   cups Shellfish Stock (above)
- 3   large bay leaves
- ¼   cup coarsely chopped fresh basil (or 1 Tbs. dried)

continued on p. 188

Californian by way of Italy, cioppino was brought to San Francisco by fishermen from Genoa. Romantic legend has it that fishermen made this stew on board their boats as they returned to Fisherman's Wharf with their catches. Cioppino isn't derived from one specific recipe, but it is all about a tasty broth and a mix of seafood.

MAKE THE GARLIC OIL AND GARLIC CHIPS

Cut the garlic cloves into ⅛-inch slices, put them in a small saucepan with the oil, and season with salt and pepper. Cook over low to medium-low heat until the garlic turns light golden brown, 15 to 20 minutes, adjusting the heat as needed to keep the garlic bubbling gently as it cooks. Remove from the heat and let cool to room temperature. Strain, reserving both the oil and the garlic chips separately. Reserve the garlic chips for garnish (don't leave them at room temperature for more than a day or they'll get soggy). Refrigerate the oil in a clean, sealed container. (You'll use the oil for the sourdough croutons; use any leftover oil for vinaigrettes, roasted vegetables, pasta, or roast chicken.)

MAKE THE SHELLFISH STOCK

Peel the shrimp, reserving the shells. (Refrigerate the shelled shrimp to use later in the stew.) Simmer the shells in the chicken broth for 5 minutes, covered. Strain and refrigerate until ready to use.

MAKE THE CIOPPINO BROTH

1. Heat the olive oil in an 8-quart or larger pot over medium heat. Add the onion, carrot, celery or fennel, and chopped garlic. Cook, stirring occasionally, until the vegetables are lightly browned, 15 to 20 minutes. Add the tomatoes with their liquid, the wine, shellfish stock, bay leaves, basil, oregano, fennel seeds, red pepper flakes, 1 tsp. salt, and several grinds of black pepper. Bring to a boil, then reduce the heat to maintain a simmer and cook for about 20 minutes. Strain through a medium-mesh sieve, pressing on the solids in the sieve. Discard the contents of the sieve.

2. Rinse the pot and return the broth to the pot. Boil the broth until reduced to 8 cups. (If you over-reduce the broth, just add water to compensate.) Taste and add more salt and pepper if needed, remembering that the fish will add some saltiness to the stew. Refrigerate until ready to use.

FINISH THE STEW

1. Position a rack directly under the broiler and heat the broiler. Brush the bread on both sides with the reserved garlic oil. Put the bread on a baking sheet (or directly on the rack) and toast on both sides.

continued on p. 188

1 Tbs. coarsely chopped fresh oregano (or 1 tsp. dried)

2 tsp. fennel seeds

½ tsp. crushed red pepper flakes; more to taste

Kosher salt and freshly ground black pepper

FOR FINISHING THE STEW

8 ¾-inch-thick slices sourdough bread

Garlic Oil (p. 187)

Cioppino Broth (p. 187)

1 to 1½ lb. small hardshell clams, such as mahogany or cherrystones, scrubbed, or 1 whole Dungeness crab (about 2 lb.), cleaned and cut into sections (have the fishmonger do this)

1 to 1½ lb. fresh mussels (18 to 24), scrubbed and debearded

2½ lb. fillets of halibut, monkfish, or other firm-fleshed white fish, cut into 1-inch cubes

Reserved peeled shrimp from the Shellfish Stock

¼ cup chopped fresh flat-leaf parsley

Garlic Chips (p. 187), for garnish

2. Return the broth to a simmer over medium-high to high heat. If using clams, start by adding them to the broth and simmer until they open, 3 to 5 minutes. Add the mussels and crab, if using, and simmer until the mussels have opened, 2 to 3 minutes. Add the fish and shrimp. Stir carefully with a slotted spoon to get all the fish and shrimp into the broth, but try not to break up the pieces. When each batch of seafood is added, it will cause the temperature of the broth to plunge, so you might need to raise and lower the heat to maintain a simmer. Cover and cook until the fish is just barely cooked through, another 3 to 5 minutes, keeping in mind that the fish will continue to cook a little in the time it takes to dish out the servings.

ASSEMBLE THE STEW

Set a piece of toasted sourdough in the bottom of each warm bowl and evenly portion the seafood into the bowls (be sure to discard any unopened clams or mussels). Ladle the broth on top.

GARNISH AND SERVE

Sprinkle the chopped parsley and garlic chips over all and serve immediately. —*John Ash*

PER SERVING: 810 CALORIES │51G PROTEIN │56G CARB │38G TOTAL FAT │7G SAT FAT │ 23G MONO FAT │5G POLY FAT │170MG CHOL │1,600MG SODIUM │4G FIBER

tips for making great-tasting cioppino

• Most cioppino recipes call for fish stock, which can be hard to find or keep on hand. Instead, follow the directions in the recipe to turn ordinary canned chicken stock into a flavorful shellfish stock using shrimp shells. Don't substitute bottled clam juice for fish stock because it's often very salty and sometimes gritty.

• The broth—stock, tomatoes, and wine—can be made a day or two ahead. Then you can finish this recipe in about half an hour.

• Use a balance of fresh fish and shellfish. Dungeness crab—a West Coast crustacean that you occasionally find in other parts of the country—is traditional, but it isn't a requirement. Your best bet is using the freshest seafood you can find.

• When you finish the stew, add the fish and shellfish in stages according to how long each one needs to cook. The recipe direction "until just barely cooked through" is important because the fish will continue to cook as it sits in the warm broth when you portion it out.

farmhouse ragoût with pesto

SERVES 4

FOR THE RAGOÛT

- 3 Tbs. extra-virgin olive oil
- 2 bay leaves
- 2 medium onions, cut into large chunks
- 7 plump cloves garlic, halved
- 3 sprigs fresh thyme
- 6 fresh sage leaves
- ¾ lb. carrots, scrubbed
- ¾ lb. small new potatoes, scrubbed

  Kosher salt and freshly ground black pepper
- ½ lb. wax or green beans (or a mix), ends trimmed and halved crosswise
- 1 yellow bell pepper, cored, seeded, and cut into 1-inch pieces
- 1 lb. summer squash, cut into 1-inch rounds
- 5 plum tomatoes, peeled, seeded, and cut into large chunks
- 1 lb. fresh shelling beans, shucked, or one 15-oz. can top-quality white beans, rinsed and drained

FOR THE PESTO

- 1 cup packed fresh basil leaves
- 2 cloves garlic
- 6 Tbs. extra-virgin olive oil

  Kosher salt
- ½ cup freshly grated Parmigiano-Reggiano (optional)

This humble braise more or less cooks itself as you layer on the vegetables. You'll probably end up with a little extra pesto, but it's great on other vegetables and, of course, on pasta.

START THE RAGOÛT

1. In a large flameproof casserole or Dutch oven with a snug lid, heat the oil with the bay leaves over low heat. When fragrant, add the onion, 6 garlic cloves (if using canned beans instead of fresh, add all 7 cloves), 2 thyme sprigs (if using canned beans instead of fresh, add all 3 sprigs), and the sage, stirring to coat everything thoroughly with oil. Cover and cook over low heat as you prepare the rest of the vegetables.

2. Leave very small carrots whole and unpeeled; if using larger ones, peel them and cut them into 2-inch lengths. Add them to the pot. If the potatoes are the size of large marbles, leave them whole, but quarter larger ones or cut fingerlings in half lengthwise. Add the potatoes to the pot in one layer; season with salt and pepper. Add the wax beans, bell peppers, and summer squash to the pot in layers, seasoning each layer with a little salt and pepper as you go. Add the tomatoes, sprinkling their juices over all. Cover and cook over low heat until the vegetables are tender, 40 to 65 minutes. If tightly covered, the vegetables will produce plenty of flavorful juices. There's no need to stir, but if the pot seems dry, add a few tablespoons of water or dry white wine, if you like.

COOK THE SHELL BEANS

If you're using fresh shell beans, put them in a saucepan with enough water to total 3 cups, beans included. Add the remaining garlic clove, thyme sprig, and a little olive oil. Simmer uncovered until tender, 30 to 45 minutes. Season with salt and pepper.

MAKE THE PESTO

In a blender, process the basil and garlic with the oil, adding a little water to loosen if needed. Add a pinch of salt and the cheese, if using. Taste and adjust the seasonings.

FINISH AND SERVE

Add the beans and their cooking liquid to the pot of vegetables (if using canned beans, add a bit of water or broth); discard the bay leaves. Ladle the soup into shallow bowls, drizzle with the pesto, and serve. *—Deborah Madison*

PER SERVING: 570 CALORIES I 11G PROTEIN I 66G CARB I 32G TOTAL FAT I 4G SAT FAT I 23G MONO FAT I 3G POLY FAT I 0MG CHOL I 200MG SODIUM I 16G FIBER

curried chickpea and summer vegetable stew

SERVES 4 TO 6

- 2 Tbs. peanut or vegetable oil
- 2 cups diced yellow onion
- 2 Tbs. minced fresh ginger
- 1 Tbs. minced garlic
- 1 medium eggplant, cut into ½-inch cubes (4 cups)
- 1 medium yellow summer squash, cut into ½-inch cubes (1¾ cups)
- 1 medium zucchini, cut into ½-inch cubes (1¼ cups)

  Kosher salt
- 1 tsp. garam masala
- ½ tsp. ground coriander
- ½ tsp. ground cumin
- ½ tsp. ground turmeric
- 1 small fresh red hot chile, minced

  Freshly ground black pepper
- 1 15-oz. can chickpeas, with their liquid
- 1½ cups Fresh Tomato Sauce (recipe at right)
- 1 cup light coconut milk
- ¼ cup plus 2 Tbs. chopped fresh cilantro
- ¼ cup unsweetened shredded coconut, lightly toasted (optional)

Transform tomato sauce into an Indian-style vegetable stew that takes advantage of the season's bounty. Serve over basmati rice.

1. Heat the oil in a large, deep skillet over medium heat until shimmering. Add the onion and cook, stirring frequently until soft and golden, about 15 minutes (reduce the heat to medium low, if necessary, to prevent the onion from burning). Stir in the ginger and garlic and cook for 2 minutes. Add the eggplant, yellow squash, zucchini, and ½ tsp. salt; stir to coat thoroughly. Cook over medium heat, stirring occasionally, until the vegetables are barely tender, 7 to 10 minutes. Stir in the garam masala, coriander, cumin, turmeric, chile, 1 tsp. salt, and a few grinds of black pepper. Cook until the spices are fragrant, 1 to 2 minutes.

2. Pour in the chickpeas and their liquid, the tomato sauce, coconut milk, and 2 Tbs. of the cilantro. Raise the heat to medium high and bring the stew to a boil. Reduce the heat to medium low and simmer, uncovered, until the eggplant and zucchini are completely tender but still hold their shape and the sauce has thickened, 15 to 20 minutes.

3. To serve, ladle the stew into shallow rimmed bowls and sprinkle with the remaining ¼ cup cilantro and the toasted coconut (if using).
—Domenica Marchetti

PER SERVING: 300 CALORIES | 11G PROTEIN | 40G CARB | 13G TOTAL FAT | 4.5G SAT FAT | 4G MONO FAT | 2.5G POLY FAT | 0MG CHOL | 520MG SODIUM | 12G FIBER

fresh tomato sauce

MAKES ABOUT 8 CUPS SAUCE

8 lb. ripe Roma tomatoes
   (about 40)

¼ cup extra-virgin olive oil

3 medium cloves garlic,
   smashed and peeled

   Kosher salt

1. Bring a large pot of water to a rolling boil. Rinse the tomatoes in cold water. With a paring knife, cut an X into the bottom of each tomato. (This will make it easier to peel the tomatoes once they're blanched.) Carefully lower about 10 tomatoes into the boiling water and leave them for 20 to 30 seconds. Use a slotted spoon to move them to a large bowl filled with ice water. Continue blanching the tomatoes in batches and transferring them to the ice water. Use a paring knife and your fingers to remove the skin from the tomatoes—it should peel off easily. Cut the tomatoes lengthwise into quarters, core, and remove the seeds. Coarsely chop the tomatoes and transfer them to a bowl.

2. Heat the oil and the garlic in a 5- to 6-quart heavy pot over medium-low heat until the garlic begins to sizzle and very lightly browns, 3 to 4 minutes. Carefully pour in the tomatoes. Raise the heat to medium high and bring the tomatoes to a boil. Stir in 2 tsp. salt, reduce the heat to medium, and let the sauce simmer, stirring occasionally, until the tomatoes have broken down and the sauce has thickened, about 1 hour. Remove from the heat and discard the garlic.

lamb stew with parsnips, prunes & chickpeas

SERVES 4 TO 6

FOR THE LAMB

1   **3-lb. boneless leg of lamb, cut into 1-inch cubes**

    Kosher salt and freshly ground black pepper

2   **medium carrots, cut into 3-inch pieces**

1   **medium yellow onion, peeled and stuck with 1 whole clove**

1   **3-inch cinnamon stick**

1   **bay leaf**

FOR THE STEW

2   **Tbs. unsalted butter or olive oil**

1   **large yellow onion, cut into small dice**

    Kosher salt and freshly ground black pepper

4   **medium cloves garlic, roughly chopped**

1   **Tbs. paprika**

2   **tsp. cumin seeds, toasted and ground**

2   **tsp. coriander seeds, toasted and ground**

½   **tsp. cayenne**

2   **cups cooked chickpeas, rinsed if canned**

18   **pitted prunes, halved**

¼   **cup tomato purée**

1   **lb. medium parsnips, peeled, cored (see the sidebar at right) and cut into 2-inch pieces**

1   **Tbs. chopped fresh cilantro or flat-leaf parsley**

North African in spirit, this hearty sweet-and-savory stew is delicious served with couscous or good crusty bread.

PREPARE THE LAMB

1. Position a rack in the center of the oven and heat the oven to 350°F. Season the lamb with 2 tsp. salt and ½ tsp. pepper.

2. In a 5- to 6-quart Dutch oven, combine the lamb, carrots, onion, cinnamon stick, bay leaf, and enough water to cover. Cover and braise in the oven until the meat is very tender, about 2½ hours. Strain the mixture through a fine-mesh sieve over a large bowl. Discard the vegetables and spices. (The recipe may be prepared to this point up to 2 days ahead. Let the lamb and broth cool, then refrigerate separately. Skim the fat from the broth before continuing.)

MAKE THE STEW

1. In a 5- to 6-quart Dutch oven, heat the butter or oil over medium-high heat. Add the onion, a pinch of salt, and a few grinds of pepper and cook, stirring occasionally, until softened and lightly browned, about 8 minutes. Add the garlic, paprika, cumin, coriander, and cayenne and cook, stirring occasionally, until fragrant (don't let the garlic burn), 1 to 2 minutes.

2. Stir in the chickpeas, prunes, tomato purée, and a pinch of salt. Add the reserved lamb and 4 cups of the broth and bring to a boil. Boil for 5 minutes and then turn the heat to low. Cover and simmer for 10 minutes. Add the parsnips and cook until tender, about 10 minutes. Season to taste with salt and pepper, and serve sprinkled with cilantro or parsley. *—David Tanis*

PER SERVING: 560 CALORIES | 54G PROTEIN | 52G CARB | 16G TOTAL FAT | 6G SAT FAT | 5G MONO FAT | 2G POLY FAT | 155MG CHOL | 950MG SODIUM | 12G FIBER

More about Parsnips

Parsnips are usually harvested in the fall but frost will convert their starches to sugar, concentrating their sweet flavor, so many home gardeners and small growers keep their parsnips in the ground and dig them as needed through winter and early spring.

There are several varieties of parsnips, but most markets don't usually indicate which they're selling, mainly because the differences in flavor, texture, and appearance are minimal. Choose what looks freshest.

fennel, pepper & saffron stew with garlic toast

SERVES 4

- 2 Tbs. extra-virgin olive oil; more for the bread
- 1 medium yellow onion, thinly sliced (2 cups)
- 1 medium fennel bulb, stalks and fronds removed, quartered lengthwise, cored, and thinly sliced crosswise (4 cups)
- 1 medium carrot, peeled and thinly sliced crosswise (¾ cup)
- 1 small red bell pepper, cored, seeded, and thinly sliced lengthwise (1½ cups)
- 3 Tbs. tomato paste
- 2 medium cloves garlic (1 minced, 1 whole)
- ½ cup dry white wine, such as Albariño
- 1 15½-oz. can chickpeas, drained and rinsed
- 1 tsp. chopped fresh thyme
- ⅛ tsp. pimentón (smoked paprika)
- 2 pinches of saffron
- 1 bay leaf
- Kosher salt and freshly ground black pepper
- 4 ¾-inch-thick baguette slices
- 2 Tbs. grated Manchego cheese

A generous handful of chickpeas and a sprinkling of Manchego cheese make this Spanish-inspired stew hearty and satisfying.

1. Heat the oil in a 5-quart saucepan over medium heat. Add the onion, fennel, carrot, and bell pepper and cook, stirring occasionally, until the vegetables are tender but not browned, about 5 minutes. Add the tomato paste and minced garlic and cook, stirring constantly, until the garlic is fragrant, about 45 seconds. Add the wine, bring to a simmer, and cook until the liquid has reduced by half, about 2 minutes. Add 3½ cups water, the chickpeas, thyme, pimentón, saffron, and bay leaf. Bring to a simmer, cover, and cook until the vegetables are tender and the stew has thickened slightly, about 25 minutes. Season to taste with salt and pepper; discard the bay leaf.

2. Position a rack 6 inches from the broiler and heat the broiler on high. Put the bread slices on a rimmed baking sheet and brush both sides with oil. Broil, flipping once, until both sides are golden-brown, about 4 minutes total. Remove from the oven and rub each slice with the whole clove of garlic.

3. Portion the stew into 4 wide, shallow bowls, sprinkle with the Manchego, and serve with the garlic toasts. *—Ivy Manning*

PER SERVING: 380 CALORIES | 15G PROTEIN | 46G CARB | 15G TOTAL FAT | 4G SAT FAT | 6G MONO FAT | 2G POLY FAT | 10MG CHOL | 640MG SODIUM | 13G FIBER

sausage and pepper stew

SERVES 4

3 Tbs. extra-virgin olive oil

1¼ lb. hot Italian sausages, pricked with a fork

1 medium onion, thinly sliced

4 large cloves garlic, finely chopped

3 green bell peppers, cored, seeded, and cut into thin strips

1 28-oz. can tomatoes, drained and chopped

¾ cup uncooked small pasta, such as tubetti, ditali, or shells

5 sprigs fresh basil and 5 sprigs fresh mint, tied together in a bouquet garni

Kosher salt and freshly ground black pepper

Sausage and peppers, a favorite sandwich combination, make a hearty meal as a stew. When cooking the pasta, push it down into the soup to keep it submerged rather than adding more water, which would dilute the stew's flavor.

1. In a large skillet with a lid, heat the olive oil over medium-high heat. Add the sausages and onion and cook, turning the sausages to brown all sides, until the onions are just tender, about 8 minutes. Add the garlic and bell peppers and cook for another couple of minutes. Add the tomatoes, 2 cups water, pasta, basil, mint, and salt and black pepper to taste (be sure the pasta is submerged). Raise the heat to high and cook until the liquid starts to boil.

2. Turn the heat to medium low, cover, and simmer until the sausages feel firm and the pasta is tender, about 25 minutes. Cut the sausages into slices or leave whole for serving. *—Clifford Wright*

PER SERVING: 750 CALORIES | 27G PROTEIN | 39G CARB | 56G TOTAL FAT | 18G SAT FAT | 28G MONO FAT | 7G POLY FAT | 110MG CHOL | 1,600MG SODIUM | 7G FIBER

mediterranean sausage ragoût

- **1** Tbs. olive oil
- **1** lb. Italian sausage (sweet or hot)
- **1** large onion, finely chopped
- **4** large cloves garlic, finely chopped
- **2** Tbs. finely chopped fresh ginger
- Kosher salt
- **1** Tbs. sweet paprika
- **1** tsp. ground coriander
- **½** tsp. crushed red pepper flakes
- **¼** tsp. ground cinnamon
- **5** medium carrots, peeled and sliced on the diagonal ¼ inch thick
- **2** cups homemade or lower-salt chicken broth
- **1½** cups Marinara Sauce (recipe at right)
- **3** cups (two 15½-oz. cans) cooked or canned chick-peas, rinsed
- **2** Tbs. fresh lemon juice

To round out the meal, serve the stew with toasted pita bread seasoned with olive oil, lemon juice, garlic, and parsley. The ragoût is also delicious spooned over couscous.

1. In a Dutch oven or large heavy pot, heat the olive oil over medium heat. Prick the sausages in several places so they release their fat as they cook and put them in the pot. Cook until browned well on all sides, 8 to 10 minutes. If there's more than 2 Tbs. of fat in the pan, spoon out the extra. Stir the onion, garlic, and ginger in with the sausages. Season with salt and cook until the onion is softened, about 5 minutes. Add the paprika, coriander, red pepper flakes, and cinnamon and cook, stirring often, for 2 minutes. Add the carrots and continue to cook, stirring often, for 2 minutes. Pour in the chicken broth, increase the heat to medium high, bring to a boil, and then reduce the heat to a simmer. Cover and simmer until the carrots are almost tender (they should still have a bit of resistance when pierced with a fork), about 10 minutes. Transfer the sausages to a cutting board.

2. Add the marinara sauce and the chickpeas to the pot, bring to a boil, and reduce to a simmer. Simmer uncovered until the carrots are fully tender and the chickpeas are hot, 3 to 5 minutes. Meanwhile, cut the sausages into bite-size pieces and return them to the pot. Stir in the lemon juice, season to taste with salt, and serve. —*Nancy Verde Barr*

PER SERVING: 430 CALORIES | 11G PROTEIN | 38G CARB | 22G TOTAL FAT | 7G SAT FAT | 11G MONO FAT | 3G POLY FAT | 45MG CHOL | 1,550MG SODIUM | 9G FIBER

marinara sauce

MAKES 9½ TO 10 CUPS

6½ lb. canned whole Italian plum tomatoes (three 35-oz. cans), with their liquid

3   Tbs. olive oil; more if needed

5   large cloves garlic, thinly sliced, or 1 medium-large onion, finely chopped

½   tsp. crushed red pepper flakes

¼   cup lightly packed fresh basil leaves, torn into small pieces

    Kosher salt

    Pinch of granulated sugar, if needed

This large batch of sauce freezes well and can be used in any recipe calling for marinara.

1. Empty a can of tomatoes with their liquid into a food processor; pulse until coarsely chopped. Transfer to a bowl and repeat with the remaining two cans of tomatoes (or empty all the tomatoes into a large bowl and break them up with your hands).

2. Heat the oil in a large (at least 4-quart) saucepan or Dutch oven over medium-low heat. Add the garlic or onion. Cook, stirring often, until the garlic or onion is golden and softened, 5 to 10 minutes for garlic (don't let it burn) or about 20 minutes for onion. Stir in the red pepper flakes, let them heat for 15 seconds to release their flavor, and then pour in the tomatoes with their liquid.

3. Bring to a boil over medium high, stirring frequently, and then reduce the heat to maintain a simmer. Add the basil and 1 Tbs. salt and simmer, stirring occasionally, until the sauce is full-flavored and has reduced to a thick, saucy consistency, 20 to 40 minutes (some brands of tomatoes take longer to cook down). Pools of orange may appear on the surface, which means the sauce is done. Taste and add the pinch of sugar only if the sauce lacks the natural sweetness of perfectly ripe, fresh tomatoes.

moroccan vegetable ragoût

SERVES 4

1 Tbs. extra-virgin olive oil

1 medium yellow onion, thinly sliced (about 1¼ cups)

1 3- to 4-inch cinnamon stick

1½ tsp. ground cumin

2 cups peeled and medium-diced (½-inch) sweet potatoes (about ¾ lb.)

1 14- to 16-oz. can chickpeas, rinsed and drained

1 14½-oz. can diced tomatoes, with their liquid

½ cup pitted green Greek or Italian olives

6 Tbs. orange juice, preferably fresh

1½ tsp. honey

2 cups lightly packed very coarsely chopped kale leaves (from about ½ lb. kale)

Kosher salt and freshly ground black pepper

If you don't have an olive-pitting tool, you can use a small skillet or saucepan. Apply pressure with the bottom of the pan until the olives split, exposing the pits enough that they can be plucked away by hand.

This vegetarian stew is enhanced when served with a green salad and couscous studded with toasted almonds.

1. Heat the oil in a 5- to 6-quart Dutch oven or other heavy pot over medium-high heat. Add the onion and cook, stirring frequently, until soft and lightly browned, about 5 minutes. Add the cinnamon stick and cumin and cook until very fragrant, about 1 minute. Add the sweet potatoes, chickpeas, tomatoes and their liquid, olives, orange juice, honey, and 1 cup water; bring to a boil. Reduce the heat to medium low and simmer, covered, stirring occasionally, until the sweet potatoes are barely tender, about 15 minutes.

2. Stir in the kale. Cover and continue cooking until wilted and softened, about another 10 minutes. Discard the cinnamon stick. Season with salt and pepper to taste. —*Kate Hays*

PER SERVING: 290 CALORIES | 9G PROTEIN | 52G CARB | 6G TOTAL FAT | 1G SAT FAT | 4G MONO FAT | 1G POLY FAT | 0MG CHOL | 1,030MG SODIUM | 8G FIBER

red-cooked tofu

SERVES 4

- **4** medium scallions, thinly sliced (white and green parts kept separate)

- **2** medium carrots, cut into small dice

- **1** cup homemade or lower-salt chicken or vegetable broth

- **6** Tbs. reduced-sodium soy sauce; more as needed

- **¼** cup Shaoxing (Chinese cooking wine) or dry sherry

- **1½** Tbs. minced fresh ginger

- **2** tsp. granulated sugar

  Freshly ground black pepper

- **2** 14-oz. packages firm tofu, cut into 1-inch pieces

- **2** Tbs. seasoned rice vinegar

- **2** tsp. arrowroot or cornstarch

Red-cooking is a traditional Chinese braising technique that uses soy sauce, sugar, and rice wine to flavor the food and give it a dark red color. This easy, aromatic stew is delicious served over cooked rice or mustard greens.

1. In a large saucepan, combine the scallion whites, carrots, broth, soy sauce, Shaoxing, ginger, sugar, and ¼ tsp. pepper. Bring to a simmer over medium-high heat, stirring once or twice. Cover, reduce the heat to low, and simmer gently for 5 minutes. Add the tofu, cover, and continue to simmer gently until the tofu is heated through and has absorbed some of the other flavors, 10 minutes.

2. In a small bowl, whisk the vinegar and arrowroot until smooth and then stir the mixture into the stew, taking care not to break up the tofu. Stir gently until thickened, about 1 minute. Add more soy sauce to taste, sprinkle with the scallion greens, and serve.

—Bruce Weinstein and Mark Scarbrough

PER SERVING: 350 CALORIES | 34G PROTEIN | 20G CARB | 18G TOTAL FAT | 2.5G SAT FAT | 4G MONO FAT | 10G POLY FAT | 0MG CHOL | 960MG SODIUM | 6G FIBER

shrimp stew with coconut milk, tomatoes & cilantro

SERVES 6 TO 8

- 3 lb. jumbo shrimp (21 to 25 per lb.), peeled and deveined

  Kosher salt

- 2 Tbs. extra-virgin olive oil

- 1 large red bell pepper, cored, seeded, and sliced into very thin 1½-inch-long strips

- 4 scallions, thinly sliced (white and green parts kept separate)

- ½ cup chopped fresh cilantro

- 4 large cloves garlic, finely chopped

- ½ to 1 tsp. crushed red pepper flakes

- 1 14½-oz. can petite-diced tomatoes, drained

- 1 13½- or 14-oz. can coconut milk

- 2 Tbs. fresh lime juice

This dish is the perfect week-night comfort food. It's quick but soul-satisfying, and since it serves at least six, you'll likely have leftovers—which will be even more flavorful the next day.

1. In a large bowl, sprinkle the shrimp with 1 tsp. salt; toss to coat and set aside.

2. Heat the oil in a 5- to 6-quart Dutch oven over medium-high heat. Add the bell pepper and cook, stirring, until almost tender, about 4 minutes. Add the scallion whites, ¼ cup of the cilantro, the garlic, and the red pepper flakes. Continue to cook, stirring, until fragrant, 30 to 60 seconds. Add the tomatoes and coconut milk and bring to a simmer. Reduce the heat to medium and simmer to blend the flavors and thicken the sauce slightly, about 5 minutes. Add the shrimp and continue to cook, partially covered and stirring frequently, until the shrimp are just cooked through, about another 5 minutes. Add the lime juice and season to taste with salt.

3. Serve sprinkled with the scallion greens and the remaining ¼ cup cilantro. —*Pamela Anderson*

PER SERVING: 270 CALORIES | 29G PROTEIN | 6G CARB | 15G TOTAL FAT | 10G SAT FAT | 3G MONO FAT | 1G POLY FAT | 250MG CHOL | 580MG SODIUM | 1G FIBER

The Difference between Coconut Water, Coconut Milk, and Coconut Cream

What's the difference between coconut water, coconut milk, coconut cream, and "lite" coconut milk? At 4 months old, the young coconut (also called a jelly or green coconut) contains a delicate, clear, slightly sweet liquid called coconut water. Coconut milk, however, is white and thick and is made by blending grated mature coconut with hot water and then straining the liquid. Coconut cream is the thick substance that floats to the top of the coconut milk and may be spooned off. Reduced-fat or "lite" coconut milk is just regular canned coconut milk with water added.

slow-cooker steak and guinness pie

SERVES 4

¼ cup unbleached all-purpose flour; more for rolling

Kosher salt and freshly ground black pepper

2 lb. boneless beef chuck, trimmed of excess fat, cut into 1-inch pieces

2 large carrots, cut into ¼-inch-thick rounds

1 large yellow onion, coarsely chopped

3 large cloves garlic, minced

2 sprigs fresh thyme

1 12-oz. bottle Guinness (or other stout)

1 cup homemade or lower-salt beef broth

2 large russet potatoes (about 1½ lb. total), washed and cut into 1-inch cubes

Nonstick cooking spray

1 sheet frozen puff pastry (about 9 oz.), thawed overnight in the refrigerator

This simple version of the classic Irish dish has the distinctive bitter flavor of Guinness stout. Although it's slow-cooked, the hearty beef stew requires minimal prep time. When it's ready, the puff pastry "tops" are baked separately and served with the stew.

1. In a large bowl, combine the flour, 2 tsp. salt, and 1 tsp. pepper. Toss the beef in the flour mixture to coat. Transfer the mixture (including excess flour) to a 6-quart slow cooker and then add the carrots, onion, garlic, and thyme. Slowly pour in the Guinness and then stir in the beef broth. Cover and cook on low for 6 to 7 hours or on high for 4 to 5 hours. Add the potatoes and continue cooking until the meat and the potatoes are fork-tender, about another 1 hour.

2. Position a rack in the center of the oven and heat the oven to 375°F. Coat a large rimmed baking sheet with cooking spray. On a lightly floured surface, roll the puff pastry sheet into a 10x14-inch rectangle. Put it on the prepared baking sheet and bake until golden-brown, 15 to 18 minutes. Remove from the oven, let cool slightly on a rack, and cut into quarters.

3. To serve, lay the puff pastry quarters in wide, shallow bowls and spoon the stew over the pastry. —*Julissa Roberts*

PER SERVING: 880 CALORIES | 58G PROTEIN | 79G CARB | 34G TOTAL FAT | 7G SAT FAT | 9G MONO FAT | 15G POLY FAT | 80MG CHOL | 860MG SODIUM | 5G FIBER

southwestern beef stew with squash and beans

SERVES 8

- **3** lb. boneless beef chuck

  Kosher salt and freshly ground black pepper

- **3** Tbs. olive or vegetable oil; more as needed

- **2** large or 3 medium onions, diced

- **3** large cloves garlic, minced (about 1 Tbs.)

- **¼** cup chili powder

- **2** tsp. ground cumin

- **1** tsp. dried oregano

- **3** Tbs. unbleached all-purpose flour

- **1** 14½-oz. can diced tomatoes, with their liquid

- **1** cup dry white wine

- **2** cups coarsely chopped yellow squash (cut into bite-size chunks)

- **2** cups coarsely chopped red and green bell peppers (cored, seeded, and cut into bite-size pieces)

- **1** cup canned pinto beans, drained and rinsed

- **2** to 3 Tbs. coarsely chopped fresh cilantro, for garnish

Sort of a cross between beef chili and beef stew, this dish would be at home served with either warm cornbread or mashed or roasted potatoes.

1. Adjust a rack to the lower middle (but not the bottom) of the oven and heat the oven to 450°F. Pat the beef dry with paper towels, trim away any thick pieces of fat, and cut into 1-inch cubes. Season generously with salt and black pepper. Heat 2 Tbs. of the oil over medium-high heat in a heavy Dutch oven that's 9 to 10 inches in diameter. As soon as the oil is very hot, add a quarter of the beef cubes, taking care not to crowd the pan. Sear the beef until two sides form an impressive dark-brown crust, 8 to 10 minutes. Transfer the beef to a bowl and continue to sear the remaining beef in batches, adding more oil to the pan if needed. It's fine for the pan bottom to darken, but if it smells like it's burning, lower the heat just a little. Set all the seared beef aside in a bowl.

2. Reduce the heat to medium and add the onion and garlic to the empty pot, adding another 1 Tbs. oil if the pan is dry. Cook, stirring frequently, until soft, about 5 minutes. Add the chili powder, cumin, and oregano and continue to cook, stirring, until fragrant, 30 seconds to a minute. Season with salt and black pepper. Stir in the flour and then the tomatoes with their liquid, the white wine, and 1 cup water. Return the beef and any accumulated juices back into the pot.

3. Lay a large sheet of heavy-duty foil over the pot and, using a pot-holder or a thick towel, press it down in the center so that it almost touches the stew.

4. Crimp the foil around the pot's rim for a tight seal. Cover snugly with the pot's lid. Turn the burner to medium high until you hear the juices bubble. Put the pot in the oven and cook for 1 hour and 15 minutes. Check the stew: If the meat is fork-tender, it's done; if not, cook for another 15 minutes, adding a little more water to the pan if it looks dry.

5. Meanwhile, heat a large sauté pan over medium-high heat. Add enough oil to cover the bottom of the pan and sauté the squash and red and green bell pepper until just tender and lightly browned. Remove from the heat and set aside. Remove the pot from the oven, carefully remove the foil, and stir in the cooked vegetables and the pinto beans. Remembering that the pot and lid are hot, cover again with the foil and the lid. Let stand so that the meat rests and the vegetables marry, about 15 minutes.

6. Before serving, check to see if the stew juices need thinning to achieve a thin gravy texture. If so, stir in water—¼ cup at a time—as needed. Season with salt and black pepper to taste. Gently reheat, if necessary, and serve garnished with the cilantro. *—Pamela Anderson*

PER SERVING: 450 CALORIES | 38G PROTEIN | 19G CARB | 23G TOTAL FAT | 7G SAT FAT | 12G MONO FAT | 2G POLY FAT | 117MG CHOL | 633MG SODIUM | 5G FIBER

spicy red lentil dal with winter vegetables

SERVES 6

- **1 medium yellow onion, coarsely chopped (1½ cups)**
- **4 medium cloves garlic, chopped**
- **2 Tbs. peeled and chopped fresh ginger (from a 2-inch piece)**
- **1 serrano chile, stemmed and chopped**
- **2 Tbs. vegetable oil**
- **1½ tsp. brown mustard seeds**
- **1 Tbs. garam masala or curry powder**
- **1½ cups red lentils**
- **½ small head of cauliflower, cut into 1½-inch pieces (about 3 cups)**
- **4 medium carrots, peeled and cut into 1-inch pieces (about 2½ cups)**
- **2 large Yukon Gold potatoes (about 8 oz. each), peeled and cut into 1-inch chunks (1¼ cups)**
- **1 tsp. ground turmeric**
- **Kosher salt and freshly ground black pepper**
- **1 cup chopped fresh cilantro**
- **Cooked basmati rice, for serving**

Dal—a thick, spicy Indian stew made with legumes like chickpeas and lentils—is a classic vegetarian dish. It's perfect for nights when you want quick, flavor-packed comfort food.

1. In a food processor, pulse the onion, garlic, ginger, and chile in 1-second intervals until finely chopped. (Don't run the processor constantly or the mixture will become too watery.)

2. Heat the oil in a 4- to 5-quart pot over medium heat. When the oil is hot, add the mustard seeds. When the seeds begin to pop and turn gray, about 1 minute, stir in the garam masala, onion mixture, lentils, cauliflower, carrots, potatoes, turmeric, 6 cups water, and 1½ tsp. salt. Bring to a boil over medium-high heat, reduce the heat to maintain a gentle simmer, and cover. Simmer until the vegetables are tender, stirring occasionally, about 30 minutes. Season to taste with salt and pepper and stir in the cilantro. Serve with basmati rice.   —*Ivy Manning*

PER SERVING: 320 CALORIES | 16G PROTEIN | 515G CARB | 6G TOTAL FAT | 0.5G SAT FAT | 2G MONO FAT | 2G POLY FAT | 0MG CHOL | 610MG SODIUM | 11G FIBER

summer bouillabaisse with smoky rouille

SERVES 4

- **3 Tbs. extra-virgin olive oil; more for the sauce**
- **1½ Tbs. chopped garlic, plus ½ tsp. finely grated or minced garlic**
- **2 lb. ripe tomatoes, cored and cut into large dice (about 4½ cups)**
- **1 cup dry white wine**
- **1 tsp. sweet smoked paprika (Spanish pimentón)**
- **¼ cup mayonnaise**
- **Kosher salt**
- **1¾ cups homemade or lower-salt chicken broth**
- **Large pinch of saffron**
- **1 lb. halibut, cod, or other firm white fish fillets, cut into 1-inch chunks**
- **2 cups fresh sweet corn kernels (from 4 medium ears)**
- **Freshly ground black pepper**
- **1 to 2 Tbs. chopped fresh flat-leaf parsley, for garnish (optional)**

Make Ahead

You can make this soup ahead except for adding the fish, which you should do at the last minute.

To dress this up for entertaining, add ½ lb. peeled medium or large shrimp and ½ lb. Manila clams or mussels. Wash the shellfish well before adding and use only the tightly closed shells. Simmer until the shells open.

1. In a 5- to 6-quart soup pot or Dutch oven, heat the oil over medium heat. Add the 1½ Tbs. chopped garlic and cook until fragrant, about 30 seconds. Add the tomatoes and wine, increase the heat to medium high (if necessary), and simmer vigorously until the tomatoes are broken down and the mixture is slightly soupy, about 15 minutes.

2. While the tomatoes are cooking, whisk the ½ tsp. grated garlic, paprika, and mayonnaise in a small bowl. Whisk in a little olive oil and enough cool water to make a creamy, pourable sauce. Taste and add salt if you like.

3. Add the broth and saffron to the tomato mixture and simmer to slightly reduce the broth and concentrate the flavors, 5 minutes. Add the fish and simmer until it's opaque throughout, another 3 to 5 minutes. Stir in the corn. Season to taste with salt and black pepper.

4. Serve in large bowls with a big drizzle of the sauce on top and a generous sprinkle of parsley, if using. —*Martha Holmberg*

PER SERVING: 490 CALORIES | 30G PROTEIN | 29G CARB | 25G TOTAL FAT | 3.5G SAT FAT | 9G MONO FAT | 2.5G POLY FAT | 40MG CHOL | 480MG SODIUM | 5G FIBER

turkey chili

MAKES 7 CUPS; SERVES 4 TO 6

- 3   Tbs. vegetable oil
- 1   medium onion, chopped
- 1   small green bell pepper, cored, seeded, and chopped
- 8   oz. fresh button mushrooms (about 10 medium-small)
- 2   cloves garlic
- 1   fresh jalapeño, cored
- 2½   Tbs. chili powder
- 1   tsp. dried oregano
- ⅛   to ¼ tsp. cayenne; more as needed

  Kosher salt and freshly ground black pepper

- 1   lb. ground turkey
- 1   29-oz. can tomato purée
- 1   14½-oz. can diced tomatoes, drained
- 1   15½-oz. can small white beans, rinsed and drained
- 1   tsp. balsamic vinegar; more to taste

  Sour cream, for garnish (optional)

  Snipped fresh chives, for garnish (optional)

  Shredded Cheddar cheese, for garnish (optional)

This light but still-hearty chili will warm up any cold winter night. It can be refrigerated for up to 2 days.

1. In a medium Dutch oven, heat the oil over medium heat. Add the onion and bell pepper. Cook, stirring frequently, until they're just limp and some of the edges are browned, about 7 minutes.

2. Meanwhile, slice the mushrooms and mince the garlic and jalapeño. When the onion mixture is ready, add the mushrooms and continue cooking, stirring occasionally, until tender and light brown on the edges, about 5 minutes. Add the garlic, jalapeño, chili powder, oregano, cayenne, 1½ tsp. salt, and a few grinds of black pepper. Stir until well blended and fragrant, about 1 minute. Loosely break apart the ground turkey and add it to the pot. Gently stir until slightly more separated (don't stir too much or the chili will be mealy) and coated with the other ingredients.

3. Stir in the tomato purée and diced tomatoes. Bring to a boil, reduce the heat to medium low or low, and simmer, stirring frequently, until the sauce is slightly reduced and thickened, about 20 minutes. Stir in the drained white beans and the balsamic vinegar. Taste and add more cayenne, salt, and pepper or another 1 tsp. balsamic vinegar to taste.

4. Serve immediately or let cool and refrigerate for up to 2 days. Garnish with the sour cream, chives, and Cheddar, if you like.
—*Abigail Johnson Dodge*

PER SERVING: 310 CALORIES | 27G PROTEIN | 34G CARB | 9G TOTAL FAT | 1G SAT FAT | 2G MONO FAT | 5G POLY FAT | 55MG CHOL | 1,280MG SODIUM | 9G FIBER

texas beef chili with poblanos and beer

MAKES 8 CUPS; SERVES 8

- 3 Tbs. olive oil; more as needed
- 2 large sweet onions, diced (about 4 cups)
- 2 large fresh poblano chiles (or green bell peppers), stemmed, seeded, and diced (about 1½ cups)
- 5 cloves garlic, minced

  Kosher salt
- 4½ lb. boneless beef chuck, cut into 1-inch cubes
- 2 bay leaves
- 2 cinnamon sticks, 3 to 4 inches long
- 3 Tbs. New Mexico chile powder (or 2 Tbs. ancho chile powder)
- 1 Tbs. chipotle chile powder
- 1 Tbs. ground cumin
- ⅛ tsp. ground cloves
- 1 12-oz. bottle amber ale, such as Shiner Bock®, Dos Equis Amber, or Anchor Steam® Liberty Ale®
- 1½ quarts homemade or lower-salt beef broth

continued on p. 208

This chili has a pleasant kick. It thickens as it sits overnight, and the flavors round out and deepen. It is best with chipotle and New Mexico chile powders, but ancho, another pure chile powder, is a good substitute for New Mexico. Look for both ancho and chipotle powders in your supermarket.

1. In a 12-inch skillet, heat 2 Tbs. of the oil over medium-high heat. Add the onion and sauté until softened, translucent, and starting to brown, 8 to 10 minutes. Add the poblanos, reduce the heat to medium, and cook, stirring occasionally, until the poblanos soften, another 8 to 10 minutes. If the pan seems dry, add a little more olive oil. Add the garlic and 1 tsp. salt and sauté for another 5 minutes. Set aside.

2. Meanwhile, heat the remaining 1 Tbs. olive oil in an 8-quart or larger Dutch oven (preferably enameled cast iron) over medium-high heat. Sear the beef cubes until browned and crusty on two sides, working in batches to avoid crowding the pan. With tongs or a slotted spoon, transfer the browned beef to a bowl. During searing, it's fine if the pan bottom gets quite dark, but if it smells like it's burning, reduce the heat a bit. If the pan ever gets dry, add a little more oil. Once all the beef is seared and set aside, add the onion and poblanos to the pan, along with the bay leaves, cinnamon sticks, chile powders, cumin, and cloves and cook, stirring, until the spices coat the vegetables and are fragrant, 15 to 30 seconds. Slowly add the beer while scraping the bottom of the pan with a wooden spoon to dissolve the coating of spices. Simmer until the beer is reduced by about half and the mixture has thickened slightly, 5 to 7 minutes. Add the beef, along with any accumulated juices, and the beef broth. Bring to a simmer and then reduce the heat to medium low. Simmer, partially covered, for 3 hours, stirring occasionally. Test a cube of meat—you should be able to cut it with a spoon. Discard the cinnamon sticks and bay leaves.

3. If not serving immediately, chill overnight. The next day, skim any fat from the top, if necessary, before reheating. To serve, heat the chili gently. Using a slotted spoon, transfer about 2 cups of the beef cubes

continued on p. 208

2 **14-oz. cans kidney beans, rinsed and drained**

1 **medium red onion, chopped**

3 **medium tomatoes, cored, seeded, and chopped**

⅓ **cup coarsely chopped fresh cilantro**

12 **oz. sour cream or whole-milk plain yogurt**

to a plate. Shred the meat with a fork and return it to pot. (The shredded meat will help create a thicker texture.) Taste and add more salt if needed.

4. Heat the beans in a medium bowl in the microwave (or heat them gently in a saucepan). Arrange the beans, chopped red onion, tomatoes, cilantro, and sour cream in small bowls to serve as garnishes with the chili. *—Paula Disbrow and David Norman*

PER SERVING: 590 CALORIES | 58G PROTEIN | 20G CARB | 29G TOTAL FAT | 11G SAT FAT | 13G MONO FAT | 2G POLY FAT | 175MG CHOL | 900MG SODIUM | 6G FIBER

More about Chile Powders

When you see a spice jar labeled simply "chili powder," it's actually a mix of ground chiles with several spices like oregano, garlic powder, and cumin. Blending ground chiles with these spices gives chili powder a balanced flavor and a measure of convenience—it's easier to simply stir chili powder into a dish rather than open up six or seven spice jars.

But when you're looking to add a more nuanced hit of flavor and heat to a soup, stew, or sauce, pure chile powders—ones ground solely from a specific type of chile—are just the thing. You may even already have one in your spice rack: Cayenne is a pure chile powder.

smoky pork chili with black-eyed peas

MAKES ABOUT 2 QUARTS; SERVES 6

FOR THE SOFRITO

- 6 plum tomatoes, cored and coarsely chopped
- 6 medium cloves garlic
- 2 large or 3 medium jalapeños, stemmed, seeded, and coarsely chopped
- 1 medium yellow onion, coarsely chopped
- 1 medium red bell pepper, cored, seeded, and coarsely chopped
- ¼ cup plus 2 Tbs. red-wine vinegar
- 3 Tbs. extra-virgin olive oil
- 1 Tbs. dried oregano
  Kosher salt and freshly ground black pepper
- 2 dried ancho chiles
- 2 dried New Mexico chiles
- 2 canned chipotle chiles in adobo sauce

FOR THE CHILI

- 2 Tbs. vegetable oil
- 2½ lb. ground pork
- 1 Tbs. ground cumin
- 1 tsp. chili powder
  Kosher salt
- 2 cups homemade or lower-salt chicken broth
- 4 cups fresh or thawed frozen black-eyed peas (or three 15-oz. cans, drained and rinsed)
  Sour cream, for serving
  Thinly sliced scallions, for serving

The moderately spicy chiles for this smoky pork and black-eyed pea chili were chosen for their flavor, not their heat, which means you can appreciate all of the flavors in the bowl. The chili will keep in an airtight container in the refrigerator for up to 4 days.

MAKE THE SOFRITO

1. Position a rack in the center of the oven and heat the oven to 500°F. Put the tomatoes, garlic, jalapeños, onion, bell pepper, vinegar, oil, oregano, 1 tsp. salt, and ¼ tsp. black pepper in a 9x13-inch roasting pan and stir to combine. Roast, stirring every 15 minutes and scraping the bottom of the pan, until the vegetables are collapsed and very soft, about 45 minutes. Set aside.

2. While the vegetables roast, heat a 10-inch cast-iron skillet over medium-high heat until hot, 2 to 3 minutes. Put the ancho and New Mexico chiles in the dry pan and toast on both sides until blistered, 2 to 3 minutes per side. Put the chiles in a medium bowl, cover with 2 cups warm water (if they rise to the top, weight them down with a bowl), and soak until soft, about 20 minutes. Drain in a fine-mesh sieve set over a bowl; reserve the soaking water.

3. Stem, seed, and coarsely chop the chiles. Put them in a food processor with the chipotle chiles and the roasted vegetables and purée until the mixture is completely smooth. Set aside.

MAKE THE CHILI

1. Heat the vegetable oil in a 5- to 6-quart Dutch oven or other heavy-duty pot over medium-high heat. Add the pork, cumin, chili powder, and 1 Tbs. plus 1 tsp. salt; cook, stirring, until the meat is lightly browned, 10 to 15 minutes.

2. Add the sofrito and stir until thoroughly combined. Add the reserved chile water, chicken broth, and fresh black-eyed peas. Bring the chili to a boil, reduce the heat to medium low, and simmer until the black-eyed peas are tender, about 45 minutes. (If you're using canned or frozen black-eyed peas, simmer the meat and broth for 30 minutes, add the peas, and continue to cook for another 10 minutes.) Season to taste with salt. Serve with a dollop of sour cream and scallions sprinkled over the top. —*Donald Link*

PER SERVING: 660 CALORIES | 50G PROTEIN | 42G CARB | 34G TOTAL FAT | 9G SAT FAT | 17G MONO FAT | 6G POLY FAT | 110MG CHOL | 1,230MG SODIUM | 11G FIBER

beef and black bean chili with chipotle and avocado

SERVES 4

- 3   **15-oz. cans black beans, rinsed and drained**
- 1   **14½-oz. can diced tomatoes, with their liquid**
- 1   **medium chipotle plus 2 Tbs. adobo sauce (from a can of chipotles in adobo sauce)**
- 2   **Tbs. extra-virgin olive oil**
- 1   **lb. 85%-lean ground beef**
-     **Kosher salt**
- 1   **large red onion, finely diced**
- 1½   **Tbs. chili powder**
- 2   **tsp. ground cumin**
- 1   **lime, juiced**
- ½   **cup chopped fresh cilantro**
-     **Freshly ground black pepper**
- 1   **ripe avocado, cut into medium dice**

Coarsely crumble about 3 handfuls of tortilla chips in a zip-top bag and use them as an additional chili topping.

1. Put one-third of the beans in the bowl of a food processor, along with the tomatoes and their liquid, chipotle, and adobo sauce. Process until smooth and set aside.

2. Heat the oil in a 5- to 6-quart Dutch oven over medium-high heat until it's shimmering hot, about 2 minutes. Add the beef, season with ½ tsp. salt, and cook, using a wooden spoon to break up the meat, until it loses its raw color, about 3 minutes. Using a slotted spoon, transfer the beef to a large plate. Add half of the onion and ¼ tsp. salt to the pot, and cook, stirring, until the onion begins to brown and soften, about 3 minutes. Reduce the heat to medium. Add the chili powder and cumin and cook for 20 seconds. Add the remaining black beans, the puréed bean mixture, and the beef to the pot and simmer for 10 minutes, stirring frequently. Add half of the lime juice, half of the cilantro, and salt and black pepper to taste. If the chili is thicker than you like, it may be thinned with water.

3. Meanwhile, in a small bowl, mix the remaining lime juice and onion with the avocado. Season generously with salt and black pepper. Serve the chili topped with the avocado mixture and the remaining cilantro. *—Tony Rosenfeld*

PER SERVING: 670 CALORIES | 42G PROTEIN | 64G CARB | 29G TOTAL FAT | 7G SAT FAT | 16G MONO FAT | 2.5G POLY FAT | 85MG CHOL | 1,070MG SODIUM | 18G FIBER

spiced roasted chicken and cranberry bean chili

MAKES ABOUT 11 CUPS;
SERVES 6 TO 8

FOR THE SPICE MIX (BAHARAT)

- **4** tsp. dried mint
- **1** Tbs. dried oregano
- **5** bay leaves, roughly torn
- **2** tsp. whole allspice berries
- **2** tsp. yellow mustard seeds
- **1** tsp. green cardamom pods, cracked, black seeds removed and pods discarded
- **1** tsp. whole cloves
- **4** tsp. finely ground black pepper
- **2** tsp. ground cinnamon
- **2** tsp. ground coriander
- **2** tsp. ground cumin
- **2** tsp. ground nutmeg
- **1** tsp. ground ginger

Chicken roasted with baharat, a Middle Eastern aromatic spice blend, adds depth of flavor to this chili. Serve with warm pitas. The chili will keep in an airtight container in the refrigerator for up to 4 days.

MAKE THE SPICE MIX

1. Put the mint and oregano in a fine sieve set over a medium bowl. Rub the herbs against the sieve to crush them into a fine powder.

2. In a spice grinder, grind the bay leaves, allspice, mustard seeds, cardamom seeds, and cloves to a powder and add them to the herb powder. Stir in the black pepper, cinnamon, coriander, cumin, nutmeg, and ginger. Set ¼ cup of the baharat aside. (Save the rest for another use; store in an airtight container in a cool, dark, dry place for up to 3 months.)

MAKE THE CHILI

1. Put the beans in a large bowl, cover with water, and soak for 6 to 8 hours. Drain the beans, put them in a 5- to 6-quart Dutch oven or other heavy-duty pot, and add enough cold water to cover by 2 inches. Bring to a boil over high heat, lower the heat to a gentle simmer, cover partially, and cook until tender, 1 to 2 hours. Drain the beans in a colander and set aside.

2. While the beans cook, roast the chicken: Position a rack in the center of the oven and heat the oven to 400°F. Rinse and pat the chicken dry with paper towels. In a small bowl, combine 2 Tbs. of the baharat with 2 tsp. salt. Rub the spice mixture all over the chicken and then coat the chicken with 2 Tbs. of the oil. Put the chicken in a small roasting pan or large ovenproof skillet and roast until an instant-read thermometer inserted into the thickest part of a thigh registers 170°F, 45 to 50 minutes. Set aside until cool enough to handle. Remove all the meat and shred into bite-size pieces. Discard the skin and bones.

FOR THE CHILI

- **1½** cups dried cranberry beans or small white beans, picked over and rinsed

- **1** 3-lb. chicken

  Kosher salt

- **¼** cup plus 2 tsp. extra-virgin olive oil

- **1** large yellow onion, finely chopped

- **2** medium cloves garlic, minced

- **2** medium green or red bell peppers, halved, cored, and finely chopped

- **1** tsp. pure ancho chile powder

- **4** cups canned chopped tomatoes

- **1** quart homemade or lower-salt chicken broth

- **1** cup low-fat Greek yogurt

- **1** tsp. dried mint

3. Heat 2 Tbs. of the olive oil in a 5- to 6-quart pot over medium heat. Add the onion, reduce the heat to medium low, and cook, stirring occasionally, until soft, about 10 minutes. Stir in the garlic and cook until fragrant, 30 seconds to 1 minute. Stir in the bell peppers, ancho chile powder, the remaining 2 Tbs. baharat, and 1 Tbs. salt. Increase the heat to medium and cook until the bell peppers are soft, stirring occasionally, about 5 minutes. Add the tomatoes, reduce the heat to low, and simmer, stirring occasionally, until thick, about 30 minutes. Stir the chicken broth, chicken meat, and beans into the chili and continue to simmer for 20 minutes to meld the flavors. Season to taste with more salt, if necessary.

4. In a small bowl, whisk the yogurt, dried mint, remaining 2 tsp. olive oil, and ½ tsp. salt. Serve the chili topped with a dollop of the seasoned yogurt. —*Ana Sortun*

PER SERVING: 420 CALORIES | 43G PROTEIN | 34G CARB | 13G TOTAL FAT | 3G SAT FAT | 7G MONO FAT | 2G POLY FAT | 80MG CHOL | 1,060MG SODIUM | 12G FIBER

quick chicken chili

SERVES 8

- **2 Tbs. vegetable oil**
- **1 large onion, cut into medium dice**
- **2 Tbs. ground cumin**
- **2 tsp. dried oregano**
- **3 medium cloves garlic, minced**
- **1 3½- to 4-lb. store-bought rotisserie chicken, meat removed and chopped**
- **1 jar or can (about 4 oz.) diced mild green chiles, drained**
- **1 quart homemade or lower-salt chicken broth**
- **2 15½-oz. cans white beans, rinsed and drained**
- **1 cup frozen corn**

If you like, serve this chili with any combination of the following: tortilla or corn chips, shredded sharp cheese, thinly sliced scallions, cilantro leaves, sliced pickled jalapeños, red or green hot sauce, sour cream, guacamole, red or green salsa, and lime wedges.

1. Heat the oil over medium-high heat in a 5- to 6-quart Dutch oven. Add the onion and cook, stirring, until tender, 4 to 5 minutes. Add the cumin, oregano, and garlic and cook until fragrant, about 1 minute longer. Stir in the chicken and chiles and then add the broth and 1 can of beans. Bring to a simmer. Reduce the heat to low and simmer, partially covered and stirring occasionally, until the flavors blend, about 20 minutes.

2. Meanwhile, purée the remaining can of beans in a food processor. Stir the puréed beans into the chicken mixture along with the corn. Continue to simmer to blend the flavors, about another 5 minutes. Ladle into bowls and serve. —*Pamela Anderson*

PER SERVING: 590 CALORIES | 69G PROTEIN | 32G CARB | 20G TOTAL FAT | 5G SAT FAT | 7G MONO FAT | 5G POLY FAT | 175MG CHOL | 270MG SODIUM | 7G FIBER

vegetable-chickpea chili with fried almonds

MAKES ABOUT 2 QUARTS;
SERVES 4

- 3 Tbs. extra-virgin olive oil
- 3 medium cloves garlic, minced
- 1 large red onion, finely chopped

  Kosher salt
- 1 to 2 Tbs. hot paprika
- 1 Tbs. chili powder
- 1 Tbs. ground cumin
- 1 28-oz. can whole peeled tomatoes, with their liquid
- 2 15-oz. cans chickpeas, drained and rinsed
- 2 cups fresh (or frozen) corn kernels (from about 4 medium ears)
- 1 medium red bell pepper, quartered, cored, and thinly sliced crosswise
- 1 medium jalapeño, thinly sliced crosswise into rounds
- ½ cup sliced or slivered almonds
- ¼ cup small fresh basil leaves
- 6 scallions (white and light green parts only), thinly sliced; more for garnish

  Sour cream, for serving (optional)

This quick vegetarian chili is better after it has mellowed in the fridge for a day or two. Make a batch on the weekend and then enjoy the leftovers later in the week. Serve with basmati rice.

1. Heat 2 Tbs. of the oil in a 5- to 6-quart heavy-duty pot over medium-high heat until shimmering hot, about 2 minutes. Add the garlic and onion, season with 1 tsp. salt, and cook, stirring occasionally, until the onion begins to soften, 3 to 5 minutes. Stir in the paprika, chili powder, and cumin, cook for 1 minute, and then add the tomatoes and their liquid. Stir, smashing the tomatoes against the side of the pot to break them up slightly. Add 2 cups water and bring to a simmer. Stir in the chickpeas, corn, bell pepper, jalapeño, and 1 Tbs. salt and cook until the peppers have lost their raw crunch, 8 to 12 minutes (at this point, if the chili looks too thick, add another 1 cup water).

2. While the vegetables cook, heat the remaining 1 Tbs. olive oil in a 10-inch skillet over medium-high heat. Add the almonds and cook, stirring constantly, until golden brown, 2 to 3 minutes. Using a slotted spoon, transfer them to a paper-towel-lined plate and immediately season them with ½ tsp. salt. Stir the basil and scallions into the chili. Serve the chili with a dollop of sour cream (if using), more scallions, and the almonds. *—Alexandra Guarnaschelli*

PER SERVING: 510 CALORIES | 19G PROTEIN | 65G CARB | 22G TOTAL FAT | 2G SAT FAT | 13G MONO FAT | 5G POLY FAT | 0MG CHOL | 1,900MG SODIUM | 17G FIBER

beef and green chile chili

**MAKES ABOUT 2 QUARTS;
SERVES 6**

FOR THE SPICE MIXTURE

2	dried guajillo chiles
1½	Tbs. ground cumin
1	Tbs. freshly ground black pepper
1	Tbs. granulated sugar
2½	tsp. dried oregano
1½	tsp. dried thyme
1	tsp. kosher salt
½	tsp. ground nutmeg

Green Hatch chiles have a meaty texture and rich, fruity flavor. If you can't find them, use Anaheim or Cubanelle chiles. Garnish this chili with crunchy fried corn tortilla strips, if you like, and serve with more warm tortillas on the side. The chili will keep in an airtight container in the refrigerator for up to 4 days.

MAKE THE SPICE MIXTURE

1. Stem, seed, and grind the dried chiles to a powder; you should have about 1 Tbs.

2. In a medium bowl, combine the chile powder with the remaining spice mixture ingredients.

MAKE THE CHILI

1. Position an oven rack about 4 inches from the broiler and heat the broiler on high. Broil the fresh chiles on a large, heavy-duty rimmed baking sheet, turning with tongs as needed, until charred on all sides, about 10 minutes total. Transfer the chiles to a large bowl, cover with plastic wrap, and set aside until cool enough to handle. With gloved hands, peel, seed, and finely chop the chiles; set aside.

FOR THE CHILI

- 8 large fresh Hatch chiles (or Anaheim or Cubanelle chiles)
- 1½ lb. 85%- to 90%-lean ground beef
- ½ cup vegetable oil
- 2 6-inch fresh corn tortillas, quartered
- 2 medium yellow onions, finely chopped
- 1 large green bell pepper, cored, seeded, and coarsely chopped
- 2 to 3 medium jalapeños, finely chopped
- 2 small cloves garlic, minced
- 3 Tbs. unbleached all-purpose flour
- 5 cups homemade or lower-salt chicken broth, heated

  Kosher salt

2. Put the ground beef in a large bowl. Mix in 3 Tbs. of the spice mixture. Line a plate with paper towels. Heat the oil in a 5- to 6-quart heavy-duty pot over high heat. Add the beef and cook, stirring often, until browned, 4 to 5 minutes. Use a slotted spoon to transfer the beef to a medium bowl and set aside. Put the tortillas in the hot oil and fry on both sides, turning occasionally with tongs, until golden-brown and crisp, 3 to 5 minutes. Transfer the tortillas to the paper-towel-lined plate and set aside.

3. Reduce the heat to medium. Add 1½ cups of the onion and the remaining spice mixture to the pot. Cook for 15 seconds, stirring and scraping the bottom of the pan constantly. Add ½ cup of the roasted chiles, half of the bell peppers, and half of the jalapeños. Cook the mixture, stirring frequently, until the green peppers are softened, about 8 minutes. Stir in the garlic and cook, stirring, for 30 seconds. Stir the flour into the vegetables and cook for 2 minutes, stirring constantly and scraping any browned bits from the bottom of the pan. Add 1 cup of the broth, stirring and scraping the bottom of the pan until no lumps remain. Add the remaining 4 cups broth and 1 Tbs. salt, stir, and return to a boil.

4. While the mixture comes to a boil, transfer 1 cup of the broth mixture to a food processor. Crumble in the fried tortillas and process until the tortillas are finely chopped. Pour the tortilla-broth mixture back into the pot and stir in the remaining onion, bell peppers, and the meat. Return the mixture to a boil, reduce the heat to medium low to low and simmer, stirring occasionally and skimming the surface as needed, until the chili is thick, about 50 minutes.

5. Stir in the remaining roasted chiles and jalapeños and simmer, stirring occasionally, for 15 minutes. Skim off any oil that rises to the surface. Season to taste with salt and serve. *—Tim Love*

PER SERVING: 500 CALORIES | 30G PROTEIN | 29G CARB | 30G TOTAL FAT | 6G SAT FAT | 13G MONO FAT | 9G POLY FAT | 70MG CHOL | 900MG SODIUM | 4G FIBER

Fish stock
(recipe on p. 225)

homemade stocks & broths

roasted beef broth

MAKES ABOUT 2½ QUARTS

- **5 lb. meaty beef or veal bones, such as shanks, knuckles, and ribs**
- **2 medium carrots, cut into big chunks**
- **2 medium yellow onions, quartered**
- **1 bouquet garni (1 sprig fresh thyme, 1 bay leaf, and 4 parsley stems, tied with twine)**
- **1 Tbs. black peppercorns**
- **1 Tbs. tomato paste**

1. Position a rack in the center of the oven and heat the oven to 450°F.

2. Put the bones on a large rimmed baking sheet and roast until beginning to brown, about 20 minutes. Add the carrots and onion and continue roasting until the bones and vegetables are very brown, 30 to 45 minutes more. With a slotted spoon or tongs, transfer the roasted bones and vegetables to a stockpot, leaving any rendered fat in the pan. Add the bouquet garni, peppercorns, tomato paste, and 5 to 7 quarts cold water (enough to cover the bones and vegetables by a couple of inches) to the pot. Bring to a boil slowly over medium heat, reduce the heat to medium low or low, and simmer, uncovered, skimming the surface occasionally with a slotted spoon until the broth is flavorful and reduced enough to just barely cover the bones and vegetables, 4 to 5 hours.

3. Strain the broth into a large bowl, cover, and chill. Skim off any fat before using. The broth can be refrigerated for up to 3 days or frozen for up to 2 months. —*Anne Willan*

add flavor with a bouquet garni

Bouquets garni (pronounced boo-kay gahr-nee) are little bundles of herbs and spices tied together with twine or wrapped in cheesecloth. These packets can be added to soups, stocks, sauces, braises, or any other dish with a lot of liquid and a long simmer. A bouquet garni keeps all of the herbs together, making them a cinch to remove before serving. Parsley, thyme, and bay leaf are the standard trio—use 4 or 5 parsley stems, a sprig or two of thyme, and a bay leaf.

You can tie a bouquet garni with twine, but if you're using small spices like peppercorns or cloves, or if you're worried about thyme leaves getting into a clear soup, you should bind everything in cheesecloth.

chicken broth

MAKES ABOUT 3 QUARTS

- **1**   **5- to 6-lb. chicken**
- **1**   **lb. yellow onions (2 medium), cut into 2-inch pieces**
- **½**   **lb. carrots (3 medium), cut into 2-inch pieces**
- **¼**   **lb. celery (2 medium ribs), cut into 2-inch pieces**
- **10** **black peppercorns**
- **3**   **large sprigs fresh flat-leaf parsley**
- **2**   **large sprigs fresh thyme**
- **1**   **bay leaf**
- **¼**   **tsp. kosher salt; more to taste**

For the clearest broth, cook at the barest simmer and avoid stirring or agitating as much as possible.

1. If the giblets were included with the chicken, discard the liver and put the rest in a deep, narrow 8-quart stockpot. Remove the breast meat from the chicken and save for another use. Pull off and discard any large pieces of fat from the cavity opening.

2. Rinse the chicken, especially its cavity, and put it in the pot. Add 3 quarts cold water, plus more if necessary to cover the chicken. Bring to a simmer over medium-high heat and then reduce the heat to maintain a bare simmer. Cook for 30 minutes, skimming off any scum with a slotted spoon or skimmer. Add the remaining ingredients, cover, and continue to cook at a bare simmer for 2 hours, adjusting the heat and skimming as necessary.

3. With tongs and a large slotted spoon or skimmer, remove most of the solids, transferring them to a bowl to cool before discarding. Slowly strain the broth through a fine-mesh sieve set over another large pot. If there are cloudy dregs as you near the bottom, stop straining and discard them.

4. Taste the broth; if you'd prefer its flavor to be more concentrated, simmer it until it's as flavorful as you like. Depending on how you'll be using the broth, you may want to season it with more salt at this point. If the broth is very fatty, chill it and then remove the solidified fat with a slotted spoon. Refrigerate for up to 5 days, or freeze for longer storage.   *—Fine Cooking editors*

golden chicken broth

MAKES ABOUT 2 QUARTS
REDUCED BROTH

About 6 lb. chicken parts (1 large older bird or 2 cut-up broilers), excess fat removed, plus extra necks and backs, if possible

2   medium onions, halved

2   to 3 carrots, peeled and coarsely chopped

1   large or 2 small ribs celery, including small, crisp leaves, chopped

1   leek, top and root trimmed, halved lengthwise, chopped into large pieces, and rinsed well (optional)

Bouquet garni of 2 or 3 sprigs fresh thyme, 6 sprigs fresh parsley, and 6 to 8 peppercorns, bruised; add 1 small bay leaf and 2 cloves garlic, if you like

Kosher salt

1. Cut the breast meat from the chicken and refrigerate for another use. Put the rest of the chicken and parts in a large stockpot (at least 10 quarts) and add cold water to cover by 2 inches, at least 5½ quarts. Bring to a boil and then lower the heat to a simmer. Skim the scum from the surface and simmer gently for 30 minutes, skimming as necessary.

2. Add the onion, carrots, celery, leek (if using), and bouquet garni and continue to simmer for another 2 to 3 hours. With a slotted spoon or Chinese skimmer, remove and discard the solids. Set a fine-mesh sieve or a strainer lined with wet cheesecloth over a pot or bowl big enough to hold the broth (you'll have about 4 quarts). Strain the broth through the sieve and chill it uncovered in an ice bath or the refrigerator. When it's cool, cover and refrigerate until the fat congeals on the surface. Scrape off the fat with a spoon or spatula. (Reserve ¼ cup fat for matzo balls, if necessary; otherwise, discard the fat.)

3. To intensify the broth's flavor, bring it to a low boil and reduce, skimming if necessary, until it's as rich and chickeny as you like; it may need to reduce by half. (Since the broth hasn't been seasoned yet, you might want to add salt to the sample that you're tasting for flavor.) Chill the broth as before, waiting until it cools before covering it. Before serving, simmer for at least 10 minutes and season to taste with salt.

—*Joyce Goldstein*

The broth keeps in the refrigerator for 3 days, at which point it must be simmered for 10 minutes to prevent bacterial growth before it can be held for another 3 days, simmered for 10 minutes, ad infinitum. Frozen, it keeps for at least 3 months.

turkey stock

MAKES ABOUT 9 CUPS

- 2 Tbs. vegetable oil
- 1 carcass from a roasted 12- to 16-lb. turkey (plus bones and wings, if saved)
- 1 large onion (unpeeled), halved
- 2 ribs celery, coarsely chopped
- 1 large carrot, coarsely chopped
- ¼ cup brandy
- 1 1-inch chunk fresh ginger, peeled and sliced
- 1 bay leaf
- 1 sprig fresh thyme
- 10 peppercorns

Because the stock is made from a cooked turkey carcass, it has a light flavor. For a richer turkey broth see p. 224

1. Position a rack in the center of the oven and heat the oven to 425°F.

2. Pour the oil into a large flameproof roasting pan. Break or chop the turkey carcass into 3 or 4 pieces and put it in the roasting pan, along with the onion, celery, and carrot. Roast for 30 minutes, stirring two or three times to ensure even browning.

3. Transfer the turkey and vegetables to a large stockpot. Pour off and discard any fat from the roasting pan, set the pan over medium heat, and add the brandy. Stir with a wooden spoon, scraping up all the browned bits. When the mixture is bubbling, pour the drippings into the stockpot. Add the ginger, bay leaf, thyme, and peppercorns to the pot. Add about 12 cups cold water (or enough to almost cover the turkey pieces). Bring to a simmer, skim any foam that rises to the top, and then reduce the heat to a very slow simmer. Simmer for 2 hours (if you used more than 12 cups water, you may need to boil it down a bit further for flavor).

4. Strain through a fine-mesh sieve into a large bowl, let cool, and refrigerate. The next day, skim the fat. —*Jennifer McLagan*

PER 1 CUP: 20 CALORIES | 2G PROTEIN | 1G CARB | 0.5G TOTAL FAT | 0G SAT FAT | 0.5G MONO FAT | 0G POLY FAT | 0MG CHOL | 40MG SODIUM | 0G FIBER

The Difference between Stock and Broth

The art of stock and broth making is one of the first subjects you're taught in culinary school. Bones, you learn, are what make a stock a stock and not a broth. The bones, with little to no meat on them, lend gelatin to the stock, giving it body. Stock may or may not also contain aromatics, like vegetables or herbs. Broth, on the other hand, is made from meat, vegetables, and aromatics. Though it's sometimes made with meat still on the bone (as in broth made from a whole chicken, like the one on p. 221), broth's distinguishing flavor comes from the meat itself. Compared with stock, it has a lighter body and a more distinctly meaty (or vegetal) flavor.

Broth is more or less ready to eat, whereas stock typically needs some enhancement from additional ingredients or further cooking to turn it into something you'd want to eat. So if you're making a quick soup, broth is your best bet, but if it's a long-cooking soup, then either would work. In a reduction sauce, stock may be the better option because it will produce a nice consistency without needing additional thickeners. Reduced broth becomes very flavorful, but it lacks the body of reduced stock, and if the broth was highly seasoned to begin with, reduction may make it overly salty. This is especially true of commercially produced broths, which tend to be much saltier than homemade versions.

turkey broth

MAKES 6 TO 7 CUPS

- **1½ to 2 lb. turkey parts, such as backs, wings, or legs**
- **1 large onion, coarsely chopped**
- **4 large ribs celery, coarsely chopped**
- **2 small carrots, coarsely chopped**
- **2 cups dry white wine**
- **6 cups homemade or lower-salt chicken broth**
- **Half a small bunch fresh flat-leaf parsley (about 1 oz.)**
- **Half a small bunch fresh sage (about ½ oz.)**
- **Half a small bunch fresh thyme (about ⅓ oz.)**
- **3 bay leaves**
- **1 Tbs. whole black peppercorns**

This broth can be refrigerated for up to 4 days or frozen for up to 2 months.

1. Position a rack in the center of the oven and heat the oven to 350°F.

2. Put the turkey parts in a small roasting pan (approximately 9x13 inches) along with the onion, celery, and carrots and roast until the meat is well browned, 1 to 1¼ hours. Transfer the turkey parts and vegetables to a 4-quart saucepan.

3. Add the wine to the roasting pan and scrape any browned bits with a wooden spoon to release them into the wine. Pour the wine into the saucepan and add the chicken broth, herbs, bay leaves, and peppercorns. Bring to a boil over medium-high heat, reduce the heat to medium low or low, and simmer gently until the meat is falling off the bone, 30 to 40 minutes, skimming occasionally to remove the fat and foam that rise to the top.

4. Strain the broth through a fine-mesh sieve, cover, and refrigerate until ready to use. Remove any solidified fat before using.

—Ris Lacoste

fish stock

MAKES ABOUT 3 QUARTS

3   **cups crisp, acidic dry white wine, such as Sauvignon Blanc**

5   **lb. white fish bones, cut into 5-inch pieces (lobster, shrimp, or crab shells may be used, too, but avoid fatty fish like salmon)**

2   **onions, coarsely chopped**

2   **carrots, coarsely chopped**

2   **ribs celery, coarsely chopped**

2   **cloves garlic, peeled**

1   **tsp. black peppercorns**

4   **sprigs fresh thyme (or 1 tsp. dried)**

1   **bay leaf**

Fish stock is one of the fastest stocks to make (under an hour) and adds distinctive flavor to chowders and other fish stews. As with other stocks, the foundation is bones, but you can also eke flavor out of shells from lobster, shrimp, or crab. Be sure the fish bones and shells are clean by rinsing under cold water before starting. And longer simmering doesn't mean more flavor: Overcooked fish stock can taste bitter, so keep an eye on the clock.

1. Combine all the ingredients in a large stockpot and add 3 quarts water. Bring to a boil, lower the heat, and simmer uncovered for 30 minutes, skimming occasionally.

2. Strain through a fine-mesh sieve. Taste and reduce for flavor if necessary. Chill immediately in an ice bath or in the refrigerator. When chilled, skim off the fat. —*Irving Shelby Smith*

PER 1 CUP: 80 CALORIES | 4G PROTEIN | 3G CARB | 1.5G TOTAL FAT | 0G SAT FAT | 0G MONO FAT | 0G POLY FAT | 0MG CHOL | 0MG SODIUM | 0G FIBER

Tips for Making Your Own Stock

Choose the right pot. The right cooking vessel is important. A tall, narrow pot is good because it maintains a nice, slow evaporation, so you don't have to constantly add more water. Too wide, and you'll encourage too much evaporation too soon.

Start with cold water. Start your stock by putting the ingredients in cold water. Plunging vegetables into boiling water causes the surface starch cells to swell. This is good when you want to keep flavor in the vegetables, but with stock, you want to leach out the flavor.

Skim often. Proteins from bones will coagulate in clumps and float to the surface. Skimming these clumps and foam frequently as the stock simmers is the key to preventing cloudy stock. Start skimming once the stock boils, then frequently during the simmer time.

Simmer, don't stir. Once you bring the stock to an initial boil, lower the heat and keep it only at a simmer. Boiling and stirring will cause the fat and water to form an emulsion and will result in a cloudy, greasy stock.

vegetable stock

MAKES ABOUT 1 QUART

1½ Tbs. unsalted butter or olive oil

2 cups large-diced yellow onion

2 cups large-diced outer ribs celery

1 cup large-diced leek tops

1 cup large-diced fennel tops or bulbs

¾ cup large-diced carrot

1 head garlic, halved crosswise

8 fresh parsley stems

2 sprigs fresh thyme

Avoid onion skins and carrot tops, as they'll make the stock bitter; trimming or peeling other vegetables is optional. Scrub or rinse all vegetables well, especially if they're not peeled.

1. Heat the butter or oil over medium-low heat in a large stockpot. Add the onion, celery, leek tops, fennel, carrot, and garlic. Cook uncovered, stirring frequently, until the vegetables have softened and released their juices, about 30 minutes (don't let them brown). Add enough cold water to just cover the vegetables, about 4 cups. Tie the parsley and thyme in a cheesecloth bundle and add it to the stock. Bring to a gentle simmer, cover, and cook without stirring until the stock is flavorful, about 45 minutes (adjust the heat to maintain a gentle simmer).

2. Strain the stock immediately through a fine-mesh sieve, pressing gently on the vegetables. Let cool to room temperature and then refrigerate for up to a week, or freeze for up to 6 months.
—Allison Ehri Kreutler

PER 1 CUP: 50 CALORIES | 2G PROTEIN | 2G CARB | 4.5G TOTAL FAT | 2.5G SAT FAT | 1G MONO FAT | 0G POLY FAT | 10MG CHOL | 0MG SODIUM | 0G FIBER

Make Ahead

Instead of tossing out vegetable trimmings, stash them in the freezer until you have enough to make stock.

customize your vegetable stock

The basic recipe at left makes a nicely balanced vegetable stock that's good for almost any dish, but you can adjust it depending on the trimmings you have or the dish you're using it in. If you're making mushroom soup with marjoram in it, you might add 2 cups mushroom trimmings and a sprig of marjoram to the stock recipe. Here are ideas for other additions. Depending on how dominant a flavor you want, use 1 to 4 cups of these enhancement vegetables.

SUBTLE FLAVORS

Use these vegetables or their trimmings with abandon.

- Celery root
- Corn cobs
- Eggplant
- Mushrooms
- Parsnips
- Tomatoes
- Summer squash
- Swiss chard
- Winter squash (seeds and stringy insides, too)

ASSERTIVE FLAVORS

Use these vegetables or their trimmings judiciously and only when you want to emphasize the vegetable's flavor (for example, using an asparagus-enhanced stock in an asparagus soup).

- Asparagus
- Beets (red ones will turn the stock pink) and beet greens
- Broccoli
- Brussels sprouts
- Cabbage
- Cauliflower
- Potato
- Rutabaga
- Turnips

HERBS

Tender, leafy herbs such as basil, cilantro, and tarragon add a decidedly fresh flavor to a stock. Add 4 to 8 stems to the basic recipe. Tarragon is strong, so use it sparingly. Woody herbs such as marjoram, oregano, rosemary, and sage are more potent and the stems can impart a bitter flavor if left in a stock, so just use a couple of sprigs and strain immediately.

METRIC EQUIVALENTS

LIQUID/DRY MEASURES

U.S.	METRIC
¼ teaspoon	1.25 milliliters
½ teaspoon	2.5 milliliters
1 teaspoon	5 milliliters
1 tablespoon (3 teaspoons)	15 milliliters
1 fluid ounce (2 tablespoons)	30 milliliters
¼ cup	60 milliliters
⅓ cup	80 milliliters
½ cup	120 milliliters
1 cup	240 milliliters
1 pint (2 cups)	480 milliliters
1 quart (4 cups; 32 ounces)	960 milliliters
1 gallon (4 quarts)	3.84 liters
1 ounce (by weight)	28 grams
1 pound	454 grams
2.2 pounds	1 kilogram

OVEN TEMPERATURES

°F	GAS MARK	°C
250	½	120
275	1	140
300	2	150
325	3	165
350	4	180
375	5	190
400	6	200
425	7	220
450	8	230
475	9	240
500	10	260
550	Broil	290

CONTRIBUTORS

Hugh Acheson is the author of the James Beard Foundation Award-winning cookbook *A New Turn in the South* and chef/partner of the Athens, Georgia, restaurants Five and Ten and The National, and the Atlanta restaurant Empire State South. He is a James Beard award winner for Best Chef Southeast and was named a Best Chef by *Food & Wine Magazine*. Hugh competed in Bravo's Top Chef Masters, Season 3, and currently stars as a judge on Top Chef.

Pamela Anderson is a contributing editor to *Fine Cooking* and the author of several books, including *Cook without a Book*. She blogs weekly about food and life with her daughters Maggy and Sharon on their Web site, threemanycooks.com

Jennifer Armentrout is the editor-in-chief of *Fine Cooking*.

John Ash is the founder and chef of John Ash & Co., in Santa Rosa, California. He teaches at the Culinary Institute of America at Greystone and is a cookbook author. His book, *John Ash: Cooking One on One*, won a James Beard award.

Dan Barber is the executive chef and co-owner of Blue Hill at Stone Barns in Pocantico Hills, New York, and the co-owner of Blue Hill in New York City.

Nancy Verde Barr was the executive chef to Julia Child from 1980 to 1998 and the culinary producer for PBS's Baking with Julia and ABC's Good Morning America. She has written for *Gourmet, Food & Wine, Bon Appétit, Parade,* and *Cook's Magazine* and is the author of three award-winning cookbooks.

David Bonom is a food writer in New Jersey.

Julie Grimes Bottcher is a recipe developer and food writer.

Michael Brisson is the chef/owner of l'etoile restaurant on Martha's Vineyard, Massachusetts, is a cooking teacher, and writes for culinary magazines.

Biba Caggiano, the chef/owner of Biba's restaurant in Sacramento, California, is also the author of numerous cookbooks, including *Northern Italian Cooking, Modern Italian Cooking,* and *From Biba's Italian Kitchen.* Her cooking show, "Biba's Kitchen", was seen on the Learning Channel.

Floyd Cardoz is the executive chef/partner of Tabla restaurant in New York City and author of *One Spice, Two Spice: American Food, Indian Flavors.*

Paula Disbrowe was the chef at Hart & Hind Fitness Ranch in Rio Frio, Texas, from January 2002 to December 2005. Prior to that she spent ten years in New York City working as a food and travel writer. Her work has appeared in the *New York Times, T Living, Food & Wine, Spa, Health, Cooking Light,* and *Saveur,* among others.

Abigail Johnson Dodge, a former pastry chef, is a widely published food writer, cooking instructor, and *Fine Cooking* contributing editor. She has also written numerous cookbooks, including her latest *Mini Treats & Hand-Held Sweets.*

Brooke Dojny is the author or co-author of more than a dozen cookbooks, including *Lobster!, Dishing Up Maine,* and *The New England Clam Shack Cookbook,* as well as the *AMA Family Cookbook,* which won a James Beard award in 1997.

Beth Dooley is the restaurant critic for *Minneapolis/St. Paul Magazine,* a columnist for the *Minneapolis Star-Tribune,* and a reporter for the NBC affiliate KARE-11 TV, covering farmers' markets and the local food scene.

Maryellen Driscoll is a *Fine Cooking* contributing editor. She and her husband own Free Bird Farm in upstate New York.

Eve Felder is the managing director of The Culinary Institute of America Singapore.

Suzanne Goin is the chef/owner of Lucques in West Hollywood, California. Her cookbook, *Sunday Suppers at Lucques,* received the James Beard award for Best Cookbook from a Professional Viewpoint in 2006.

Joyce Goldstein is one of the foremost experts on Italian cooking in this country. She is an award-winning chef, prolific cookbook author, and cooking teacher.

Alexandra Guarnaschelli is a Food Network celebrity chef and the world-renowned executive chef at both New York City's Butter restaurant and award-winning The Darby restaurant.

Peter Hoffman is the chef/owner of Back Forty and Back Forty West, both in New York City. He is also a cooking teacher and leader in the culinary community.

Kate Hays is the chef/owner of Dish Catering in Shelburne, Vermont. She is also a recipe tester, recipe developer, and food stylist.

Martha Holmberg is a cookbook author and food writer based in Portland, Oregon. Her latest book is *Fresh Food Nation.*

CONTRIBUTORS (CONTINUED)

Jill Silverman Hough is a cookbook author, food and wine writer, recipe developer, and culinary instructor from Napa, California.

Madeleine Kamman is a James Beard Award–winning cookbook author and a mentor in the culinary arts. In the mid-1980s, she hosted the PBS show Madeleine Cooks, and later founded the School for American Chefs.

Eva Katz has worked as a chef, caterer, teacher, recipe developer and tester, food stylist, and food writer. She is a member of the Program Advisory Committee at the Cambridge School of Culinary Arts in Massachusetts.

Jeanne Kelley, the author of the award-winning cookbook *Blue Eggs and Yellow Tomatoes,* is a food writer, recipe developer, and food stylist.

Allison Ehri Kreitler is a *Fine Cooking* contributing editor. She has also worked as a freelance food stylist, recipe tester, developer, and writer for several national food magazines and the Food Network.

Ris Lacoste has been an award-winning chef for 25 years, including 10 years as the executive chef at 1789 Restaurant in Washington, D.C. She opened her restaurant ris in Washington, D.C., in 2009.

Donald Link is recognized as one of New Orleans' preeminent chefs, opening several award-winning restaurants in New Orleans' Warehouse District. Link's work at his flagship restaurant Herbsaint earned him a James Beard award in 2007 for Best Chef South.

Seen (Christine) Lippert was a chef at Chez Panisse for 11 years. Currently a resident of Connecticut, her focus is on cooking with locally grown foods.

Ruth Lively trained at La Varenne in France and was senior editor at *Kitchen Gardener.*

Lori Longbotham is a recipe developer and cookbook author whose books include *Luscious Coconut Desserts* and *Luscious Creamy Desserts.*

Tim Love is known for his signature urban western cuisine. He is the chef and owner of both The Lonesome Dove Western Bistro and The Love Shack in the historic Fort Worth Stockyards district.

Deborah Madison is a cookbook author, cooking teacher, and consultant. Her most recent book is *Vegetable Literacy.*

Ivy Manning is a cooking teacher, food writer, and cookbook author; her most recent book is *Crackers & Dips.*

Domenica Marchetti is a food writer and cooking instructor whose focus is on contemporary Italian home cooking. She is the author of *The Glorious Soups and Stews of Italy* and *Big Night In.*

Nancie McDermott is a cooking teacher and cookbook author specializing in the cuisines of Southeast Asia.

Jennifer McLagan is a chef, food stylist, and cookbook author; her most recent book, *Fat: An Appreciation of a Misunderstood Ingredient, with Recipes* was named the 2009 James Beard Cookbook of the Year.

Perla Meyers teaches cooking at workshops around the country and has cooked in restaurants throughout Italy, France, and Spain.

Susie Middleton is editor at large for *Fine Cooking* magazine. She is also consulting editor, writer, and photographer for *Edible Vineyard* magazine, as well as a cookbook author.

David Norman is a former *Fine Cooking* contributor.

Nancy Oakes is chef and co-owner of Boulevard and Prospect restaurants in San Francisco. She is the author of *Boulevard: The Cookbook.*

Brian Patterson graduated from L'Academie de Cuisine's Culinary Arts Program in 1987 and taught recreational classes at L'Academie for 17 years. Brian became the Chef Instructor in the Culinary Career Training Program for L'Academie de Cuisine in 2008.

Liz Pearson worked as the kitchen director for *Saveur* magazine before moving back to her native Texas, where she is a freelance food writer and recipe developer.

Melissa Pellegrino, a former assistant food editor at *Fine Cooking,* is the author of *The Italian Farmer's Table* and *The Southern Italian Farmer's Table.*

Mai Pham is the chef/owner of Lemon Grass Restaurant in Sacramento, California. A respected expert on Southeast Asian cuisine, she writes for national publications, conducts cooking classes and seminars, and serves as a consultant to various food organizations throughout the United States.

Randall Price is the resident chef at La Varenne's Chateau du Fey and cooks for private clients in Paris and the Auvergne.

Julissa Roberts is the associate food editor/test kitchen manager at *Fine Cooking.*

Tony Rosenfeld, a *Fine Cooking* contributing editor, is the author of two cookbooks. He's also the co-owner of b.good, a Boston-based healthy fast food chain, and the creator of cookangel.com, a culinary troubleshooting website.

Samantha Seneviratne, *Fine Cooking*'s former associate food editor, is a graduate of the Fresh Culinary Institute as well as an avid baker.

Tania Sigal is a food writer and chef/restaurant owner/caterer in Miami.

Maria Helm Sinskey is a noted chef, cookbook author, and culinary director at her family's winery, Robert Sinskey Vineyards, in Napa Valley, California. She is a frequent contributor to *Food & Wine, Bon Appetit,* and *Fine Cooking* magazines. Her most recent cookbook, *Family Meals; Creating Traditions in the Kitchen* was a 2010 IACP Cookbook Award winner.

Joanne McAllister Smart, co-author of two Italian cookbooks with Scott Conant and *Bistro Cooking at Home* with Gordon Hamersley, is a senior editor at *Fine Cooking*.

Irving Shelby Smith is a contributor to *Fine Cooking*.

Ana Sortun is a restaurateur, chef, and cookbook author whose specialty is eastern Mediterranean food, particularly the cuisine of Turkey—with French influences. She owns Oleana restaurant in Cambridge, Massachusetts, as well as the Sofra Bakery and Café, also in Cambridge.

Molly Stevens is a food writer, cookbook author, editor, and cooking teacher living in northern Vermont. She is a contributing editor to *Fine Cooking*. She won the IACP Cooking Teacher of the Year award in 2006; her book *All About Roasting* won a 2012 James Beard and two IACP awards.

Heidi Johannsen Stewart is one of the founders of Bellocq Tea Atelier in Brooklyn, New York. Her award-winning tea company offers a unique and evocative line of handcrafted artisan blends.

David Tanis is a well-regarded chef and cookbook author. He has been featured in *Saveur, Gourmet,* and *Town and Country*. His writing has appeared in the *Wall Street Journal* and *Fine Cooking*. David currently writes the weekly City Kitchen column for the *New York Times*.

Anna Thomas, a screenwriter and chef, has written many cookbooks, including *Love Soup*. She cooks and entertains in Ojai, California, and teaches a screenwriting workshop in Los Angeles.

Poppy Tooker is a food personality, culinary teacher, author, and host of a weekly radio show, "Louisiana Eats," which airs on NPR's affiliate station in New Orleans.

Lucia Watson blends French and Minnesotan traditions to create the menu at her Lucia's Restaurant and Wine Bar, and Lucia's To Go, the Twin Cities' favorite neighborhood establishments. She has written two books, *Savoring the Seasons of the Northern Heartland* with Beth Dooley and *Cooking Freshwater Fish*.

Annie Wayte is formerly the executive chef of Nicole's and 202 in New York City. Her first cookbook is *Keep It Seasonal: Soups, Salads, and Sandwiches*.

Bruce Weinstein, a one-time advertising creative director and a Johnson & Wales graduate, and **Mark Scarbrough**, a former professor of American literature, write and develop recipes. They have co-written more than 15 cookbooks.

Joanne Weir is a James Beard Award-winning cookbook author, chef, cooking teacher, and television personality. Her latest book is *Joanne Weir's Cooking Confidence,* the companion book to her public television show of the same name. She is also executive chef of Copita restaurant in northern California.

Anne Willan is recognized as one of the world's preeminent authorities on French cooking. She founded École de Cuisine La Varenne in Paris in 1975. She is the author of more than 30 cookbooks and has been awarded the IACP Lifetime Achievement award, James Beard award, and Bon Appétit Teacher of the Year award.

Clifford Wright is a James Beard Award-winning author of 16 cookbooks, and his articles on food and cuisine have appeared in *Gourmet, Bon Appetit, Food & Wine, Saveur,* and *Fine Cooking*. He is also a contributing editor to ZesterDaily.com

Dawn Yanagihara is a cookbook editor, recipe developer, and food writer. Her first book is *Waffles*. Dawn lives in San Francisco.

INDEX

Numbers in **bold** indicate pages with photographs